WARTIME WOMEN

Dorothy Sheridan has been at the Mass-Observation
since 1974. She lives in Sussex

Also by Dorothy Sheridan

Speak For Yourself:
A Mass-Observation Anthology
(with Angus Calder)

Among You Taking Notes:
The Wartime Diary of Naomi Mitchison (ed.)
(Phoenix Press)

Mass-Observation at the Movies
(with Jeffrey Richards)

WARTIME WOMEN

A Mass-Observation Anthology
1937–45

Edited by
Dorothy Sheridan

PHOENIX
PRESS

5 UPPER SAINT MARTIN'S LANE
LONDON
WC2H 9EA

A PHOENIX PRESS PAPERBACK

First published in Great Britain
by William Heinemann Ltd in 1990
This paperback edition published in 2000
by Phoenix Press,
a division of The Orion Publishing Group Ltd,
Orion House, 5 Upper St Martin's Lane,
London WC2H 9EA

A CIP catalogue record for this book is available
from the British Library.

Printed and bound in Great Britain by
Clays Ltd, St Ives plc

ISBN 1 84212 213 4

CONTENTS

PART FIVE: Towards a New World for Women?

Epilogue

PREFACE

The work of putting this anthology together mostly took place in 1989, fifty years after Britain went to war with Germany. That year was marked by a spate of commemorative publications and events – special '1939' or 'World War Two' issues of magazines and serials, museum exhibitions and school projects, books of reminiscences as well as films and radio and television programmes. The Second World War continues to hold us in its thrall. The fiftieth anniversary was simply another excellent opportunity to indulge in our national preoccupation with that moment in our past. With the faithful recreation of the moods and atmospheres of the forties – clothes, street scenes, the interiors of homes and shops, the sound of the air raid siren followed by the 'all clear' and the strains of Vera Lynn singing 'We'll meet again' – even those of us born after 1945 think we can imagine what it must have been like then. What may have been for some a time of deprivation, uncertainty and loss is today symbolic of intensity of feeling, of community spirit and national cohesion, and of heroic sacrifice.

Fantasies of adventure, courage and militarism associated with warfare have usually been seen as a male preserve. Women were not expected to share in this sense of adventure. Since the emergence of a new wave of feminism in the seventies and eighties, however, there has been renewed interest in the more active role played by women in the Second World War. A current debate focuses on the degree to which the economic demands of war, by forcing social changes, enabled women to break out of strictly gender-defined roles. The enthusiasm for reclaiming women's lost or 'hidden' history has led us to look to the war period for images with which to identify. We can be Rosie the Riveter with our spanner, turban and dungarees. We can be in the

Resistance, cycling round France in our summer frocks with our clandestine wireless sets strapped inside our rucksacks. We can defy social taboos by dancing the jitterbug with GIs in provincial dance halls. Or maybe we see ourselves as heroic mothers and housewives, keeping the home fires burning, tending the hearth, whipping up tasty meals from snoek and dried eggs . . .

These are not new images born solely out of the wistfulness of looking back; they were active and compelling at the time and they have been worked and reworked in the intervening fifty years not only in film and fiction and 'propaganda' of all kinds, but also in the imaginations of women who lived through the war as well as in those of younger women. Tantalisingly, they combine aspects of radicalism, liberation and challenge with conservatism, oppression and containment.

By putting this anthology together, I want to offer more than yet another pot-pourri of wartime anecdotes. I hope it will suggest other, more radical, interpretations of women's experience. But it will still be familiar ground. Stereotypes may indeed be confirmed, and in the end it may become impossible to declare that 'myths' can so easily be disentangled from 'what it was really like'!

All the same, I want to emphasise that this is an unusual book for two reasons. One reason is that it contains writing done at the time. I do not claim that this makes the stories more real, more truthful or more honest than stories which are remembered many years later. I claim simply that these are different and allow us to reflect on the meaning that people (and in this book, it is women) gave to their lives on a day-to-day basis without the benefit of hindsight.

The other reason is that this isn't exactly a book about the Second World War at all, or it isn't *only* a book about the Second World War. It's the story of the war as told at the time by a small group of people in the hope that it would be of interest and value to people in the future. This enterprise was initiated and co-ordinated by an organisation calling itself 'Mass-Observation'. I have a special interest in Mass-Observation (having been its archivist for the past fifteen years) and wanted to produce a book which not only covers the war but also gives a flavour of the organisation itself. Inevitably the war figures heavily in these pages, but it is filtered through the lens of Mass-Observation.

This book is therefore also about Mass-Observation and about a very particular group of women who, in responding to its appeal, took on the task of writing about their lives.

University of Sussex
September 1989

ACKNOWLEDGEMENTS

Literally hundreds of people have been important in putting this anthology together. I mean, of course, the original volunteer Mass-Observers who contributed so much of themselves, often under very difficult conditions and without any expectation of immediate reward. I hope that some of them will see this book and enjoy reading their writing.

I also want to thank Viki Junor who works with me in the Mass-Observation Archive. She has been responsible for typing most of the extracts, a task which involved much more than straightforward copy typing since much of the material was difficult to read. I am grateful to her for bringing to bear her interpretative skills in the typing process. I am also grateful to my colleagues in the University of Sussex Library for their interest and to my other co-workers in the Archive, Joy Eldridge, Judy Pickering and Ann Page, partly for their encouragement but mostly for sharing my enthusiasm for Mass-Observation and all its oddities!

In making this particular selection, I was informed by discussions held with various people, in particular Stephen Yeo, who supervised my MA dissertation on women and wartime. Ideas about war and memories of war, as well as ways of thinking and writing about history, have been the themes of the discussion group to which I belong. I therefore want to give special thanks to fellow members of the group, Graham Dawson and Alistair Thomson, for their advice, criticism and friendship.

I would probably not have decided to make an anthology of women's writing if I had not been a feminist; I therefore owe a debt to my education through feminism and through discussions with other women, above all, my friends Kate Page and Julia South.

This is my fourth 'M-O' book: it hasn't been easy to live with and nor have I. Love and thanks for putting up with me to my friend Barry Stierer and my son Luke Wainwright.

Finally I would like to thank my colleague, Professor David Pocock, and the other Trustees of the Mass-Observation Archive for giving me permission to reproduce extracts.

ABBREVIATIONS AND GLOSSARY

Ack ack	Anti-aircraft (usually referring to gunfire)
AFS	Auxiliary Fire Service
AMP	Demolition workers
ARP	Air Raid Precautions
ATC	Air Training Corps
ATS	Auxiliary Territorial Service (women's section of the army)
B[U]F	British Union of Fascists
CB	Confined to Barracks
CO	Commanding Officer
ENSA	Entertainments National Services Association
M-O	Mass-Observation
MOH	Medical Officer of Health
MT	Motor Transport
NAAFI	Navy, Army and Air Force Institutes (who run canteens and shops for Forces personnel)
NCO	Non Commissioned Officer
NFS	National Fire Service
OCTU	Officer Corps Training Unit
OR	Operations Room
PBI	'Poor Bloody Infantry'
POW	Prisoner of War
RAF	Royal Air Force
RAMC	Royal Army Medical Corps
RTO	Railway Transportation Officer
S.Ad.O.	Squadron Administrative Office
SHAEF	Supreme Headquarters Allied Expeditionary Force
SHQ	Squadron Headquarters
Snoek	A type of mackerel sold in wartime (generally not very popular)
WAAF	Women's Auxiliary Air Force (or a member of it)
Waafery	Recreation room for WAAFs
WVS	Women's Voluntary Service

INTRODUCTION

Four days after Britain declared war on Germany, Miss K., a young Jewish woman earning her living as a journalist in London, wrote in her diary: 'My horror of all this war business is qualified by an eagerness to be a unit of it. I feel as if I have been waiting for this all my life and I have just realised it.'

Her sentiment expresses exactly the dilemma of war: the arming of a nation for battle unleashes certain possibilities for the individual – escape, adventure, the testing of loyalty, courage and endurance, and the extension of personal horizons beyond what is possible within the unfractured patterns of peacetime life. But all this has a terrible cost. It can only be realised through involvement with the machinery of destruction, with the devastation of cities and countryside and with the terrible, unconscionable acts of genocide. Men as soldiers have always been actors on the cutting edge of this dilemma. Women have come to it more recently.

Twentieth-century warfare has seen a shift of women out of the wings and if not into the centre stage (which in military terms would be active combat), then at least onto the stage itself. I do not suggest that women have not been touched by war in previous centuries, only that their role was usually seen as passive. It was only the extraordinary woman who could transcend the prescriptions of her gender to become an active participant. These women recognised something which has now gained wider currency: that *active* participation in war might be advantageous for women, even, in a limited way, emancipatory. The incorporation of women is partly the result of the development of military technology. Total warfare and the capacity for aerial bombardment have put whole populations at risk on a scale previously unseen. Women at home and women in non-military jobs are almost as likely as soldiers in uniform to be killed (certainly during the blitzkrieg of European cities in the Second World War). Total warfare also requires the fullest possible mobilisation of labour resources for military production. The recruitment of British women into munitions production in the First World War was repeated on an even more massive scale in the Second World War.

There is another crucial dimension to this incorporation: women themselves have struggled to take part. Despite the association between feminism and pacifism that has existed since before 1914, another strand of feminism has sought active participation, seeing the right to fight for one's country (or one's cause) as an extension of civil rights generally. The right to belong to an official paramilitary organisation was won in Britain in 1917 with the formation of the Women's Army Auxiliary Corps. Full military status was granted in 1941 to two of the three women's services.

This anthology tells the stories of women who were mostly still in traditional 'women's jobs'. They were either at home taking care of their families or in different forms of employment: nursing, shop or factory work, clerical work, teaching and so on. But even traditional jobs took place in an entirely new context. Britain was the only country involved in the Second World War to conscript women into the war effort. It wasn't necessary to be a member of the armed forces to be caught up in the contradictions that war work could raise. In fact, only a very small proportion of all women mobilised into the labour force belonged to the military and those who did left far fewer records of their experience. It is unlikely that their conditions of work (or living generally) were conducive to regular diary-keeping. This is not to suggest that the writers of the accounts in this anthology were less busy. They probably had more control over how their hours were spent and they also may have had more privacy. Some of the writers often found themselves alone (may even have been lonely) and discovered that diary-writing met a certain need for reflection. One writer described her wartime diary as 'an invisible shoulder'. Recording the day's events could impart a sense of order and control when daily life was disrupted, uncertain, sometimes exciting, often demanding. Most women had to work hard, combining domestic responsibilities with some form of war work either voluntary or paid. The exigencies of wartime made even routine chores more onerous. Shopping involved working out rations and queuing; cooking meant doing your best with scarce ingredients; dressing yourself and the family meant dealing with more ration books and 'making do and mend'. Public services were unreliable, childcare provision inadequate and transport unpredictable.

And yet we find women like Miss K. who welcomed the arrival of war, women who even deep into the war years commented on the degree of personal fulfilment they have enjoyed as a result of changes wrought by war. It is very clear too from the accounts of VE Day that many women, especially the younger ones, were ambivalent when war ended. War spreads its losses and gains unevenly. The debate about its emancipatory impact for women continues. Most feminist historians, myself included, agree that progress was limited. Challenges to women's subordination were contained within an overarching nationalist rhetoric which positioned woman at the heart of the family in her idealised role as wife and mother. But it is vital that in coming to this conclusion we do not depict wartime women as passive victims, flotsam on a tide which washes women in and out of the labour market according to the dictates of the economy. Our lives are always shaped by the structures of our time, material as well as cultural. What is interesting once we have defined those structures is how we manage to live our lives within and beyond them and how we struggle for change. Wartime women made certain choices and felt in certain ways about war and about how they should live. That is why looking at contemporary women's writing is so important if we are to understand the choices through their eyes.

In this anthology it is not the horrors of war which strike you immediately. Muriel Green's mother may imagine the tramp of Nazi jackboots on the lanes of her Norfolk village but images of death and destruction are mostly absent. For many women the tragedies of war were distant. Muriel and her friends could afford the luxury of wondering whether tennis would be allowed to go on under Hitler because, unlike the people of most of the rest of Europe, the British were spared that last unspeakable catastrophe, the invasion. For those whose lives were shattered by bombing and for those who lost loved ones, the suffering was enough. For the rest it was a mixture of the familiar and the strange and the coping with injustices inflicted on them by their own society. And even the strangeness had become ordinary by 1945. It was peacetime which posed all the frightening uncertainties.

We have to thank Mass-Observation for affording us this opportunity. No similar enterprise, bringing so much women's writing together and ensuring its survival, exists – so far as I know – in any other part of the world or for any other era. Founded in 1937 by a group of young, upper-class, male intellectuals, it set out to create what it called 'an anthropology of ourselves'. It challenged the claim of the press to represent the views of ordinary people and, by its unique blend of anthropology, American-influenced sociology and psychoanalysis, endeavoured to tap a deeper level of human consciousness in the British social character. The key figures were Tom Harrisson, a self-trained anthropologist and adventurer, Charles Madge, poet and journalist, who later became a professor of sociology, and Humphrey Jennings, painter, poet, writer and film-maker.

The central tenet of their approach was to 'observe': to watch and to record people's behaviour and conversations. Harrisson was the keenest on this form of work and with a team of investigators, subjected the town of Bolton in Lancashire to his 'scientific' scrutiny for the two years before war was declared (the Worktown Study). Later, during the war, much fascinating material was gathered by investigators based in London using similar techniques but employing sample surveys and interviews as well. The observation of behaviour by trained investigators was only part of the work, however. Madge and Jennings initiated another project which involved persuading people to observe themselves. They set about recruiting volunteer writers through newspapers and books. M-O quickly became well-known, and by 1945 at least 3,000 people had been on their mailing list at some time, mostly as respondents to the monthly open-ended 'directive' or thematic questionnaire. About 300 of them kept full personal diaries throughout the war. The achievement was extraordinary because the millions of words produced by these volunteers might never have been set to paper and certainly may never have survived to form an archive, if it had not been for the impetus of Mass-Observation.

The autobiographical writings formed a pool of information from which the M-O staff drew conclusions – with greater or lesser success, for the material was dense and difficult to use – on the state of the nation. By 1940, as a result of Tom Harrisson's machinations, M-O was feeding reports on morale to the Ministry of Information, a practice which continued for about a year. Jennings had by then disentangled himself from the movement and was fully occupied making documentary films for the government with the Crown Film Unit. Madge left in 1940 to pursue his separate interests and because he felt uncomfortable with what he called 'home front espionage'. Harrisson became the figurehead until he too decided to seek more exacting adventures and left the country with the Special Operations Executive to be parachuted into Japanese-occupied Borneo.

By then the volunteer writers had the habit. Although the discontinuities of wartime life led to some stopping and starting, a substantial number of diarists formed a loyal core, submitting lengthy instalments to Mass-Observation every month. When the war ended, most of them felt it was time to give up but a few continued even though the feedback from M-O was getting less regular and less encouraging. The postwar boom in commodity production fostered an interest in consumer behaviour and this in turn led to the growth of market research organisations. After registering as a limited company in 1949, Mass-Observation moved more fully into this kind of work. It is operating to this day (with entirely different personnel) from its London offices as Mass-Observation (UK) Ltd with no formal connection to the present-day Archive at Sussex. Since the end of the nineteen-sixties, an interest in autobiographical writing and 'people's history' has emerged, significantly aided by the influence of feminism, and the merits of such qualitative, subjective material can be placed back on the agenda of social research.

The selection of extracts in this anthology has been a very idiosyncratic process; someone else with the same remit would almost certainly have chosen quite different pieces. Serendipity has played a major part. For every piece I have included there are thousands of others, some still unread, in the Archive. This selection, then, cannot be taken to represent the whole Archive, or even the best of it. I have tried to draw on different forms of material in order to indicate the different kinds of writing which can be found. Autobiographical writing appealed most to me and is one of the features of Mass-Observation which differentiates it from the results of other research operations so I have deliberately given more space to diary extracts, long questionnaire replies and letters than to the drier 'objective' style of the Reports. At the same time, Mass-Observation's research on women and women's organisations (which is summarised in these Reports) was substantial and deserved to have some space. It is also true that working-class women's voices in the Archive are more often represented by the professional Mass-Observers (as in the reports on the Aston canteen and factory workers) and to omit these reports would be to lose that presence. It will soon become apparent that I have some favourites: Mrs Last has already had her own publication (as *Nella Last's War*) and yet she appears here twice with pieces of writing not already in print. I admit to having had great difficulty in cutting down the diaries of Muriel Green (who perhaps deserves a book all of her own) and of Amy Briggs whose frustration with life calls out for sympathy and release. Many of the diaries quoted are enormous and cover several years. Mrs Last wrote for thirty years; both Mrs Trowbridge and Mrs Crawford produced at least five or six thousand words *every month* for a span of years. Extracting a short part is necessarily an arbitrary act. In almost any month they might be writing something of equal or even greater interest.

If the anthology only bears a loose relationship to the Archive as a whole, it bears an even looser relationship to the totality of women's experience of wartime – however that might be defined. I tried to include women of different ages, classes and geographical origins; there are married, single and widowed women, women with and without children, women doing different kinds of war work and women with different political perspectives. The writing styles vary and represent the relative ease or difficulty with which contributors reproduced their thoughts on paper (which has almost nothing to do with the intrinsic interest of what they wrote). But I was necessarily constrained by the Archive itself and by the nature of the Mass-Observation enterprise: some important subjects were not covered in any depth, mental illness and physical disability for example. Some gaps are surprising, given the enormous range of subjects which *were* covered; others can be related to contemporary priorities and the desire of Mass-Observation to balance its reputation for being provocative and 'advanced' with its desire to earn a living and attract friends in high places. Hence its wary treatment of sexuality.

Just as there are gaps in the subject matter, there are absences among the people. Few working-class people became diarists; even fewer working-class women. Mass-Observation has sometimes been scorned for its middle-class bias but at least in relation to the panel of volunteers, this isn't entirely fair. A project which depends upon the willingness of people to take part does not operate in a cultural vacuum. Whether people see themselves as having something to offer is dependent on the cultural notion of what it means to be 'a writer' so it is not surprising that M-O appealed to students, librarians, clerical workers, teachers and journalists, people from the middle and lower middle classes, and working-class people involved in politics and adult education. M-O's radical stance, its determination, certainly in its first years, to be seen as independent, anti-establishment and democratic (in that it championed the value of people writing their own history or creating their own social science), drew volunteers from the left, from the same social networks as the WEA, the New Left Book Club, the left of the Labour Party and sections of the Communist Party.

It is often claimed, I think rightly, that most diaries, even the most personal and private, are written with a sense of audience. People who wrote diaries for Mass-Observation were aware of a very specific audience; either it was Charles Madge in 1937–8, or, later in wartime, first Tom Harrisson and then Bob Willcock. Sometimes it was seen as a group of people, usually thought of as young men, who staffed the London office where diaries and replies to directives were sent. The volunteer writers rarely met any of the key figures in M-O. Attempts to catch Harrisson in his office by diarists visiting London were usually foiled by Harrisson's rapid retreat, saying that he was too busy (or too important?) for a meeting. Disappointed visitors who may have received letters from Harrisson couched in the most encouraging terms, were fobbed off on the (usually female) office staff. There are occasional references to hearing Madge or Harrisson speak at a public meeting, or more often, in Harrisson's case, on a radio programme. Muriel Green reports hearing his voice on the radio and thinking it sounded 'quite normal and cultured'.

Apart from that, there were always the books and the steady stream of articles in the press on which to build a picture of what the founding Mass-Observers were like. Some writers express a profound admiration and respect. Mrs Grant talks of 'clever young men who do things' although she is just as likely (elsewhere) to talk of men generally in disparaging tones! The degree to which some women feel discounted as public beings makes them grateful to be able to write for M-O and to have their ideas taken seriously (and identifies one of M-O's attractions for women especially). Mrs Arnold writes: 'I am only a little old woman . . .' Mrs Grant speaks deprecatingly of 'scribbling mothers' like herself. This contrasts with the confidence of a younger woman, Muriel Green, who embraces M-O as her own. She and her sister Jenny (also a diarist) march round local bookshops and libraries checking that M-O books are in stock. 'We feel a proprietary interest in the publication [*War Begins at Home* which came out in 1940] and feel that everybody ought to sell it and read it.' They comb through the pages of *War Begins at Home* looking for quotations from their own contributions and competing with one another over the amounts quoted. Muriel's easy identification, her sense of belonging to a movement, allowed her to tease Harrisson: 'We have always wondered why the cannibals did not eat Mr Harrisson,' she wrote. This flirting with the 'clever young men' was not uncommon among the younger women and no doubt spiced up a drab or routine day. The Leeds nurse, Amy Briggs, frequently addresses M-O directly; on one occasion asking them to send her mince pies to eat on night shift. It is not always clear whether her questions are rhetorical or whether she expected (or indeed received) a reply. Like several other writers, she developed a trusting relationship with the Mass-Observers which enabled her to reveal that she had a secret admirer, someone she met briefly once or twice a week.

Amy uses her diary as a kind of confessional, a place where she can write out her frustration and rage and play out her fantasies. Mrs Grant uses her diary to confide her anxiety about her daughter who suffers from epilepsy. Mrs Arnold says: 'These are thoughts I may only express in my M-O report.' The London Mass-Observers are imagined as kindly, educated, progressive, tolerant and, above all, interested and therefore validating. This version of the audience, explicit in some diaries, inexplicit in others, sustains an enormous variety of styles and approaches. It was sufficiently nebulous to permit the diarists to construct their own models for what a Mass-Observation diary should be. Amy Briggs says in passing that she hopes her first instalment is 'up to standard' but this feels like a gesture. She has already decided how she is going to use her diary and the pattern hardly changes. She simply becomes more trusting and therefore more candid. Muriel Green's diary displays a common pattern. At first she concentrates on the impact of the arrival of evacuees in her village. This is 'objective reporting' and presumably how she first thought an M-O diary should be. How different is her 1945 writing where she ponders her future and the possibility that she may be suffering from 'sex starvation'.

The concept of 'proper Mass-Observing' hovers uncertainly in most writers' minds: Mrs Last apologises in 1938 for having so 'few contacts'. Miss French worries that she is unrepresentative and that her social circle is limited: 'If only my M-Os could extend to the East End [of Glasgow],' she writes in 1938 but her reservations do not prevent her from keeping a lengthy and detailed diary throughout the war years without any noticeable extension of her social circle. It is interesting that several people use the excuse of Mass-Observing to get into conversations. There are fuller reflections on what it means to be a Mass-Observer (and what M-O itself means to the first batch of volunteers) in extract 1. So for each writer, the task became a compromise between what they thought they should be writing about (i.e. the war) – partly based on their perceptions of Mass-Observation itself and its presentation through publications – and what they themselves enjoyed doing. Not all the extracts in this anthology are taken from the diaries but it is in the diaries that there is the clearest expression of the relationship between M-O and its correspondents. It was a relationship which at one and the same time facilitated writing and yet imposed upon it a specific context.

It was understood between Mass-Observation and the volunteer writers (diarists and directive respondents) that extracts from their contributions would be freely used in reports and in printed books. The only qualification was that real names would not appear and that people should not be identifiable from the quotations. I have honoured this arrangement but not without some regret. It would be fitting, I think, for the people who wrote for Mass-Observation to get some credit today for their time, commitment and talent. Unfortunately, it would be almost impossible to trace the writers whose works I have included in order to get permission to use their real names. The publicity which the Archive has received in recent years has resulted in a few former contributors getting in touch with us again but they represent only a tiny proportion of the whole group. Many writers will not now be alive of course. So the names used here are all fictitious except for Nella Last (whose wartime diary has already been published under her real name) and the full-time paid Mass-Observers. It is still possible that people would prefer to remain anonymous and until I hear otherwise, I am bound to respect the original understanding. It may be that someone reading this book may suddenly recognise themselves. I hope if they do that they will get in touch with me.

The anonymity of the writers has its advantages. I was not inclined to purge the extracts of offensive or uncomfortable passages even though today the writers might regret a certain expression of feeling or turn of phrase. Valuing women's writing should not mean romanticising women and it is important to acknowledge the sometimes virulent prejudices which prevailed during this period. Particularly noticeable is the level of anti-Semitism especially before and during the early months of the war. Mrs Crawford talks of 'Jewboys' in 1940 and Miss Pringle describes, without comment, people's concern in 1938 that gas masks should be disinfected after Jewish people had tried them on. Mrs Grant, apparently progressive in other respects, is explicitly anti-Semitic but favours a solution 'without bloodshed'. Throughout the description of the Irish factory workers in Birmingham there is a strong sense that the Irish are inferior. This is also evident in one of the other pieces from Birmingham describing a street fight and in one of the accounts of the VE Day celebrations when the British finally oust the (American) singer of Irish songs from the stage in order to burst into a rendition of 'There'll always be an England'. Class snobbery is even more prevalent than racism. It is most striking in the Reports prepared by full-time Mass-Observers, which is ironic in view of their intentions to be more objective than their volunteer counterparts. In her report on wartime women's organisations in 1940, Stella Schofield refers to the 'lowest social class of women' with palpable disdain. By 1944 the M-O investigators were more sensitive but there is still, in Celia Fremlin's account of her interviews with four sisters in Kent, the whiff of the social worker as she looks round poor Freda's recently bombed out home to assess her house-keeping capacities. The superior tones of Mrs Hamilton in contemplating the prospect of evacuees invading her home go a long way to explaining why women like Agnes decide to leave their billets: 'We were treated like bits of dirt by the locals.' To be fair, not all of these prejudices and petty snobberies are expressed by the writers themselves. Often they are reported, but it is the very matter-of-factness that can be shocking.

I have given considerable thought to the process of editing and have concluded that almost any changes to the original text (even transferring it to a printed form) can be construed as a form of violence to the author's intentions. But once having taken the decision to publish, any editor has to work out what makes a book readable (and of course sellable) and from that follows inevitable interference with the raw material. In any case I think it is possible that by being too purist in these matters, a disservice is done to the writers: most of the M-O material was written in quite difficult conditions, often in haste and without the opportunity to go over the text and correct mistakes. With this in mind, I have corrected spelling and 'improved' some punctuation although the use of extra punctuation for emphasis has been retained. Some repetition and extraneous (to the main theme of the extract) references have been omitted and cuts are indicated by three dots. Grammar remains the same. Square brackets are used for editorial comments – for unclear or missing words or for brief explanations. Footnotes have not been used because this is not intended as an academic book (although I hope it will have academic uses). Some long passages have been broken into shorter paragraphs. Otherwise, I have been at pains to reproduce as far as possible the original sense of the pieces. I console myself with the thought that the whole, unedited archive remains for anyone who wishes to examine the original texts and who has the time and material resources for such an enormous task!

I did not set out to write a history of women in wartime and I have therefore kept background information to a minimum.

Readers who want to have more factual information will find it useful (and enjoyable) to read this anthology in tandem with *Out of the Cage: Women's Experience in Two World Wars* by Gail Braybon and Penny Summerfield (Pandora). For further reading on the war generally, Angus Calder's *The People's War* (Panther) is still the best account of life on the home front between 1938 and 1945 and is especially good for reference. For more on Mass-Observation itself, there is an earlier anthology, *Speak for Yourself: A Mass-Observation Anthology 1937–49* edited by Angus Calder and Dorothy Sheridan (OUP) and a one-theme anthology, *Mass-Observation at the Movies*, edited by Jeffrey Richards and Dorothy Sheridan (Routledge). A number of early M-O books have been republished recently including *War Factory* (Cresset Library, Century Hutchinson) which describes life in a radar equipment factory where women comprised the majority of the workforce and which was first published in 1943; *Britain by Mass-Observation* and *The Pub and the People* (both also Cresset) and *May 12th* (Faber). Two whole (albeit radically edited!) M-O diaries have been published: *Nella Last's War* (Sphere) and *Among You Taking Notes: The Wartime Diary of Naomi Mitchison* (OUP). A selection of photographs taken by Humphrey Spender as part of the 'Worktown Study' of Bolton has been published as *Worktown People: Photographs from Northern England 1937–8* (Falling Wall Press).

ONE

WRITING
FOR MASS-OBSERVATION

_____

Why I joined Mass-Observation

Towards the end of 1937, when it had only been active for
about a year, Mass-Observation sent a questionnaire to all
its volunteer contributors asking them about their reasons
for becoming Observers. Over 200 people replied, of whom
about half were women. Seven of these replies are
reproduced below. The questions were:
1) Why did you join M-O?
2) What do you think it is for?
3) What did you yourself hope to gain from it?
4) What suggestions have you for work it should
   undertake?

Mrs Grant
Mrs Grant was a housewife from Gateshead. When she
first began writing for M-O in 1937 she was in her early
fifties. She corresponded with the staff of M-O for eight
years mostly in the form of monthly diary instalments.
She was married to a clerk and had two teenage
daughters, one of whom suffered from a form of epilepsy.
In 1937 epilepsy was poorly understood by the medical
profession; much of the early research associated the
condition with antisocial and even criminal behaviour.
People who experienced epileptic fits were often
stigmatised. Mrs Grant's concern about her daughter and
about coping with her daughter's illness is frequently
reflected in her writing for M-O.

Dear Sir,
Have just read M-O Sept 12th. Notice the observer quoted
writes simply and concisely. Now I have a lot of soliloquising and
in fact seem to empty my poor brain of its contents on you. I study
M-O. Do tell me if my stuff should be sorted out more if for
instance you are interested in epilepsy.

PS I have had great trouble in putting the above into words. I merely do not wish to give such very busy people trouble in sorting out stuff if they have no use for it. Have written to [local] librarian asking to have M-O [publications] put on their list.

Why I Joined M-O
1) Interested in article by Madge and Harrisson in about May – something fresh – different from usual article – *human*.
2) I could carry on at home.
3) If I understand aright, it's the very thing I'm unconsciously always doing, so should be easy to me.
4) Lastly, the *un*selfish wish to help clever young men who *do* things.

What I Think It Is For
To learn a bit of everything human and natural in life – the M-O tells me – to help doctors and scientists and all sorts of compilers of things natural and human. That's why I mention *epilepsy*. (Psychology I study continuously without knowing a single fancy name.)

Hope To Gain
1) Education.
2) Joy in scribbling about the very things I'm always studying in life – I've done it unconsciously for ages. *Why?* Has always interested me; even the *why* of certain illnesses.
3) If it comes to anything and I can help in any way at long last, I *may* have some paying job (this latter is at the back of my mind but it's there), or, at the psychological moment (in which I firmly believe) some idea for writing articles or a book along the lines of *Annals of a Little Shop* (Ann Heppel) might occur to me. If it doesn't, I shan't worry. But I do admire people who work and think, and will always do anything to help and be proud if I can.
4) Suggestions? After reading M-O how could I offer suggestions? Yet can it be used in the study of epilepsy and heredity? I do hope so.

Miss Fisher
Miss Fisher corresponded with M-O only until war was declared in 1939. She was a single woman, living in London (aged 44) and was employed as a clerk and proofreader.

Continuing the controversy raging on what Mass-Observation can and cannot be expected to do . . .

Personally, I think the idea of giving it an 'ideal' most dangerous. After all, people do not study the life history of earthworms to prove that Fascism is right and Communism is wrong. The moment you want to prove something to your own satisfaction, you will cease to observe anything – you will be continually falsifying all your observations to make them square with the point you want to prove. That is the outcome of the phrase 'that in itself will give you a lead as to what kind of facts are needed', as quoted from a sentence in your last Bulletin. You cannot leave out, no one can ever know just what little bit of information may be wanted at any time. I should not be surprised if, when the last observation came to be written, it would not have done more good to the observers – by making them observe – than it had done to the world at large by any collation and digest of the facts brought to light.

I hope you will go on for some time just grubbing up facts of everyday life. It is really early days even now to attempt to estimate what will be the ultimate direction in which these will lead. Patience, patience! Why are we all in such a blinking hurry to see results? Answer adjudged correct – because life is so abominably short, and long before we have begun to think properly or had time to organise our lives so as to get even the little best out of it that is there to be got, we are dead.

One last complaint – can people be prevented from alluding to it as M-O? It sounds so like the more repulsive advertisements: SHE NEVER KNEW WHY HE SHUNNED HER – *M-O*.

Miss Atkinson
Miss Atkinson was a filing clerk from Tonbridge in Kent. She wrote for M-O only during 1937 and no more details about her have survived.

1) I joined Mass-Observation because of an article in the *Daily Herald* which I read and I thought it seemed interesting. I thought I should like to take part in what I thought was a scientific investigation into people's lives and habits.

2) I do not feel that it has yet been decided what exactly it is for, but I can see various uses to which it could be put. I feel that an investigator looking at people from the outside, or cross-examining them, would never get such a complete picture of them and their habits and thoughts as if they write about themselves and their observations. The studies of daily lives with every little detail should be very interesting to posterity in the way the Samuel Pepys diary is. To contemporary people it should be useful: e.g. a housewife's activities might be useful to an architect planning a house. Comments on Sunday might aid the Churches to know where the Church fails to attract. Descriptions of people's meals might give nutrition experts useful knowledge. Many things might help social workers wishing to improve the condition of the workers. I feel all knowledge is useful when it has been classified.

3) I do not hope to gain anything from it personally, though I am interested to read the bulletins and hope to read the books produced later.

4) It would be interesting to find out what people think about broadcast programmes especially talks such as *Plain Thinking* and *House Design*. Also what is the real opinion on the Americanisation of our ideas via the films, music and newspaper methods. I am very interested as to how much people are affected by propaganda, both obvious and subtle. I should like to know how people on very small incomes live, such as old age pensioners. Also how spinsters without any family ties fill their lives. Also an enquiry into hobbies would be interesting – are hobbies most constructive when people have a mechanical job?

I am doubtful if the people who do Mass-Observation are representative of the population as a whole in spite of their different classes and jobs, because it isn't everybody who would take the trouble to write their impressions, even though they may be good at observing. They must all be people willing to work for a cause.

Miss Chapman

Miss Chapman wrote to M-O from Scarborough. She was 15 years old in 1937 and spent her day taking care of the family home while her father was at work. She refers to the 12th day of the month because that was when she kept an account of her activities for M-O.

1) I read in the *News Chronicle* articles about the work, and especially the account by an ordinary housewife of her day. Mass-Observation, it was something new, something to talk about, the things I do in the house are monotonous but on the 12th day are different somehow, letting the dog out, getting up, making the dinner, it makes them important when they have to be remembered and recorded. It is in the nature of scientific work, but not necessarily by experts, and I am interested in science. It also widens my horizon. I had never really wondered what people had on their mantelpieces, and maybe these reasons are vague but I like the work, it gives me a sense of importance, whether justified or not I don't know.

2) I think ultimately it will be for the good of mankind. It puts people through the Bulletins in touch with other people of differing habits and ways of living. First there is the unit one person, then the family, and then the social intercourse with people. The more that is known about people and their habits, a sense of unity is formed which is surely progressive, and also social improvements can be made with added knowledge.

3) I hope to gain a finer perception for noticing things with practice, a sense of expectation when the postman calls, which I think is stimulating, and some knowledge of the vast undercurrents of modern life which I hold will be of immense interest to Sociologists of the future who will write of the twentieth century. Then there is an added interest, and anything that makes life fuller makes it happier, also a sense of usefulness to the community other than just looking after a house and my family, a sense that is wider I think.

Miss Earnshaw

Miss Earnshaw was a copy typist in London when she first began writing for M-O. By 1940 she had become a key member of the full-time staff of investigators employed mostly on studies of blitzed towns. After leaving M-O, she joined the staff of a new research organisation to continue her career as a professional social scientist.

Like a good many other people I look upon the mess that the world is in at the present time as a sort of mass neurosis. By 'mess' I mean mostly widespread poverty, danger of war, drug entertainments, the ugly and unplanned side of industrialism, advertisements, lack of education and independent thinking, and so on.

People of the left wing in politics are attacking the problems of civilisation in one way. The political approach is probably the most urgent and important at the present time, but it seems to me that another line of approach is also necessary.

Although psychology has advanced so much in recent years the great mass of people have not benefited at all as a result of its work. It has been used more by interested people against them rather than by anyone for them. A psychological approach to the neurosis of civilisation is needed, and this is the line that Mass-Observation is taking, and this is what I think it is for.

Mass-Observation (like Matilda's Aunt) has a strict regard for truth. I believe that it is only by carefully observing, probing, and finding out the truth that anything useful (i.e. therapeutic) can be done. Having found out so much, M-O presents the result of its work to the public and the public is at length forced to recognise the truth and eventually to do something about it.

I am a creature of few hobbies. I cannot play the piano or paint, I know nothing about wild flowers, birds or butterflies, fossils, stamp-collecting etc.; my work is inexpressibly boring; and yet I like to have something to do that is slightly more definite than reading and talking to my friends. Mass-Observation fills the gap. Political activity is a possibility, but although I am quite definite in my political views (left wing Marxist), I am worried by the constant call to propagand. I admire immensely the people – communists mostly – who spend nearly all their spare time, and more energy than one can imagine anybody having, doing something practical to forward the cause they believe in. I cannot do this. It may be simply that I'm too lazy or it may be that one needs, as well as conviction, the propaganding temperament. I haven't got this and I am not sufficiently moved emotionally by things not immediately present (i.e. to me), and I find – not without pangs of conscience sometimes – that local politics and political activities in local detail bore me. Mass-Observation is a thing I can be interested in and do without having to attend meetings at awkward places and times. I tend rather to look on people as specimens and to take a rather armchair and academic view. This is very likely a bad thing – but it is true – however though it is of no use in politics I might turn it to some use in Mass-Observation thus salving my occasionally troublesome conscience.

In short what I, personally, hope to gain from Mass-Observation is something amusing to do with a clear conscience and the idea that I am not wasting time.

Mrs Grimshaw
Mrs Grimshaw was a housewife in her late forties living in Essex.

After reading the article on Mass-Observation in the *Daily Herald*, and later in the *Daily Mirror*, I thought that it was a good idea. I hesitated to join it thinking that I was not a good enough reporter, and that in my uneventful and humdrum life there would be nothing worth reporting. Then a friend who knows me well assured me that I was capable of reporting, and forthwith I joined up – with gladness, because I love reporting the truth, and writing or typing is to me a *recreation*. I like it because it demands TRUTH, and because there is no pay to it I can trust that observers stick to the truth, and do it for the love of the thing. If it were in any way a paid job, I should lose interest knowing that every lurid liar capable of putting pen to paper would rush in and spoil everything.

I have read what it is for. It is to investigate and take note of the apparently trivial things that people do, have, think, and say. It finds out FACTS of everyday life untinged by the bias or emotional toning that press reports are guilty of. These facts will be used to advantage later on.

I only hope to gain from it the recreation of writing, and the pleasure of knowing (and hoping) that I am doing something definitely USEFUL for the future of society.

Re suggestions for work to be done by M-O I leave that to Mr Madge and Mr Harrisson. Anything I might suggest might sound revolutionary, or be impracticable. One thing I will suggest is: 'What newspaper do you take?' 'Why do you take it?' as the subject of a questionnaire. After all newspapers play an enormous part in our lives – too great a part I sometimes think. Also a questionnaire on 'Why did you have your children?' 'Would you have them if you had your time over again, and why?' And later on ask all Mass-Observers: 'Would you have your life over again exactly as you have already lived it – all the time being quite unable to remember your first life?' THIS WOULD BE A *REVELATION* OF THE *SORROWS* OF LIFE.

Mrs Aldington
Mrs Aldington, a housewife from Burnley in Lancashire in her late forties, kept a diary for M-O until the end of 1944 and answered the regular 'directives' or questionnaires sent to her by M-O from 1937 until 1945.

I joined Mass-Observation as a result of reading an article in the newspaper asking for observers. I had for some time been convinced that many of those who supply the people's needs (either in newspapers, on the wireless, in Parliament and in other ways) are often a long way out of touch with what people really desire and need. They supply what people are *popularly supposed* to require, and by a long process of trial and error they at length arrive at something nearer the mark. Mass-Observation appeals to me because I hope it has no 'axe to grind'. As soon as I sense anything of that sort, I shall cease to worry about it. If you want a slogan, I would suggest 'The Truth and no Propaganda'. In other spheres everything is controlled by money – big money. If people do not require a thing, they are first *made* to want it – then it is supplied. All this is so opposed to truth and freedom that my sympathies are with Mass-Observation in studying people's habits more truthfully and accurately. Here at any rate is a store of information which can be made use of if need be.

I myself most hope to gain from Mass-Observation a power of detachment and an impersonal and accurate way of observing life. I have already gained a good deal of amusement and interest from the bulletins. I wish they were longer and in case they are in future, would be glad to pay say 6*d* each, if of any use, but as soon as money is mentioned no doubt many observers would feel disillusioned and lose interest.

I cannot suggest much that Mass-Observation should undertake, but care should be taken to keep it free from any suspicion of being 'sold' to any interested powers, either the Press, the brewers, the film magnates, and so on. Observers can become very 'observant' and would soon 'guess', or should I say 'deduce'. Not that the *results* should not be sold, but the 'guidance' of the movement is what I mean. One problem which appears is that as most of your observers who *continue* to write in will probably be thoughtful kind of people, how are you to estimate the habits and opinions of those who are 'thoughtless' (shall we say) and ready to be moved by anybody who cares? How great may be their numbers might make all the difference in a time of emergency. They buy and sell, work and play, they also vote or abstain. Do they sway the balance at elections or is it the thoughtful ones who do that? You may be sure the thoughtless will not write in to your Mass-Observation.

TWO

IF HITLER COMES . . .

By the time war was actually declared in September 1939, people had already been forced – a year earlier during the Munich crisis – to confront their worst nightmares of what war would mean. This section covers both the period in 1938 when Britain reached the brink of war, and 1939 when war finally became a certainty.

The news about the attacks on Spanish cities in the Spanish Civil War had shown the horrific effects of aerial bombardment. It was assumed that Hitler would begin bombing Britain immediately war was declared. Estimates of casualty rates were high. The first official circular on air raid precautions was issued to local authorities by the government in 1935. In April 1937 the Air Raid Warden service was introduced and by mid-1938 200,000 ARP personnel had been recruited. Anti-gas attack measures received high priority.

Mass-Observation did not ask for full daily diaries until August 1939, just before war was declared. During 1938 the panel of volunteer writers was still responding to specific prompts: one-day diaries and questions. As tensions heightened, however, they were asked to start keeping a continuous record of events and to describe their own feelings and opinions. Hitler had already been in power in Germany since 1933, and even after he had occupied the Rhineland, Britain and France pursued a policy of non-intervention. Neville Chamberlain, the British Prime Minister, favoured a policy of appeasement. In the spring of 1938 Hitler annexed Austria; by early September he was threatening Czechoslovakia. There followed a series of negotiations in an attempt to dissuade Hitler from seizing the German-speaking areas (Sudetenland) of Czechoslovakia. On 25 September, all ARP services were mobilised and on Tuesday 27 September Chamberlain urged the country to prepare –

everyone expected war by the weekend. Two million people were evacuated from London. The distribution of gas masks was mobilised and a state of emergency was declared. By 30 September it was all over. Chamberlain returned from Munich on 1 October in triumph; it was, he said, 'peace for our time'. As the extracts show, the relief was immense although many people believed that it had been a grand betrayal. Despite the agreements, Hitler occupied Czechoslovakia in March 1939.

The 'peace' could not last. The British government was compelled to honour its promise to stand by Poland and when news came that German troops had marched into Poland on 1 September 1939, people realised that war had become inevitable. On Sunday 3 September war was declared. Chamberlain's speech on the radio at 11 a.m. was swiftly followed in most areas by the eery sound of the air raid siren. But no bombs. The period of 'Phoney War' had begun on the home front.

The Munich Crisis, 1938

Miss French
Miss French, aged 36, a single, middle-class woman,
worked in the offices of a shipping company in Glasgow.
She lived in a well-to-do part of Glasgow, Kelvinside, with
her elderly mother.

24/25 September 1938
As a Mass-Observer perhaps I should be writing daily reports
detailing the crisis in Glasgow and the views of those with whom I
live and work. That is beyond me. The situation distresses me
intensely, and I find it difficult to express my thoughts on paper.
The following notes are set down without any particular plan
behind them, and represent those aspects of the crisis that have
more or less thrust themselves upon me.

Whence comes my knowledge of the crisis? Not from the newspapers so much, as might be thought. On Sundays I carefully
study the *Observer* and the *Sunday Times*, but on weekdays I do
not do that, even avoiding the illustrations. I am afraid to touch
anything that might break the calm bearing that I am forcing
myself to assume. My knowledge of the crisis comes from the
wireless, for I never miss any news bulletins that I can possibly
have. I also see hundreds of newsbills, from the bus going to and
from work through three miles of Glasgow thoroughfares. I hear
conversations also. I avoid discussing the situation for this
heightens my distress, and as far as possible leave the room when
I think someone is going to speak of it. Avoiding conversations is
not difficult for many of my associates seem to be bent on doing
likewise. In some cases I suspect they desire to spare my feelings;
in one or two instances I know the silence is due to indifference: in
most cases I think it is due to a realisation of the gravity of the

situation. As an instance of the reticence I record that never once have I overheard reference to the crisis from a bus passenger during my four journeys a day. This is just the reverse of the previous crisis, viz. the abdication of Edward VIII . . .

During the first ten days of September I went about fairly normally, for while I had never any doubts about Hitler's designs on Czecho-Slovakia, I believed that he had qualms about risking a war as yet. The thought of the Nuremberg Conference speech to come lay in my mind like, say, a splinter in the finger – a source of irritation rather than a pain.

On Saturday 10th September I visited the Peace Pavilion at the Exhibition. Up till the present I have never heard anyone say a good word for it, some people assessing it as 'very dull', others complaining about 'the horrible pictures on the walls – Guernica and things like that'. This Saturday the building was crammed with visitors; a crowd three or four deep continuously surrounded the Peace Cairn, and the air of solemnity was marked. A book is provided for those who wish to sign their names as associating themselves with the Peace Movement and glancing through it I found only half a dozen people a day were signing.

. . . Our firm does business with several German importers and from business correspondence you would not think there was any crisis. An account for £1,200 fell due on the day of the Nuremberg Speech, and despite our worries the money came through. On behalf of an English firm we shipped a large cargo of coal to Germany only three days ago. The Dresden firm to which Herr H.J. [business contact] belongs (chemical dealers) have not imported much during the past two years for they could not get import licences. These seem to be becoming available and we are getting enquiries. On Saturday 24th September I wrote two letters, one to Dresden offering 10,000 tons of a certain by-product, 'if we are allowed to ship', and the other to the Admiralty offering our services for the bunkering of mine-sweepers.

. . . From time to time I take lessons from Herr T.D., a Swiss tutor of German in Glasgow and early in August I enrolled for a class 'limited to 8', starting on 1st September. Only one other pupil has come forward (Miss B). I should be congratulating myself on getting so much more attention than I had paid for, but I am not, for I don't want to be reminded of Germany just now and each Thursday I am torn by a conflict, on the one hand I want to skip the class and on the other I don't think that is fair to Herr T.D. Last Thursday, Herr T.D. told us that he is down by 3/350 [one-third] pupils on last year (September of course being the month when practically everyone starts their studies). The following is the gist of his remarks: Herr T.D.: 'The German geography books include Switzerland in "Greater Germany". The Swiss say: we are not with you yet. Every road from Germany to Switzerland is mined so that Switzerland can be cut off at a moment's notice.' Miss B: 'When he gets Sudetenland, that might satisfy him.' Herr T.D.: 'No, that will make him more drunk for power. We have two hopes. One is that the Russians will break through. Hitler won't get his way then. The other is that the undercurrent of discontent in Germany will rise.' Self: 'My German friends don't seem to like Hitler.' Herr T.D.: 'Look what they have to put up with.' Miss B: 'What of Italy?' Herr T.D.: 'Oh, Italy does not go into a war until she has time to see which side will win. You'll find her ending up on the British side.' Self: 'The Anglo-French attitude seems to have lowered our prestige.' Herr T.D.: 'The Americans cannot afford to say anything against you. It will be time enough when they express themselves willing to defend democracy.' Herr T.D. continued that Hitler would not get Czecho-Slovakia as easily as Austria. The Czech Army is bigger than the British Army and they mean to fight. Nothing can stop the war from breaking out.

On leaving Herr T.D.'s house, I crossed Kelvingrove Park. The dearest little twelve-months old boy came up to me and his mother. The five minutes that I spent with them, however, filled me with compassion for all the child victims of war. I thought with sorrow of Herr H.J.'s little girl of eighteen months away in Dresden.

The crisis has made me grave, and yet there are those whom it has not yet touched. For instance, there are A.M. (36) bookkeeper, B.C. (29) typist and M.C. (29) typist, all on our office staff, peace-lovers who have always prided themselves on being above politics. About ten days ago, A.M. was most indignant with me for assuming that Mr Chamberlain's visit to Berchtesgaden could possibly be of interest to her. Just now she is looking forward with pleasure to the ARP Review at Hampden Park on 9th October at which the Air Force are staging a mock air attack, and which she thinks will be similar to the festivities at the Coronation. As for the two others, the following dialogue on Thursday, 22nd inst., speaks for itself. A pot of tea is made each morning and we go through to the cloakroom in relays for a cup. I: Do you think I could 'steal' a little more tea? B.C. and M.C.: Why? I: The political situation upset me so much yesterday that I could not eat or drink, and I feel thirsty now. – Had I announced the end of the world I could not have caused greater surprise. – B.C. (with incredulity): You don't say Hitler annoys you? (sic) – On my side I was bereft of speech. – M.C.: It will be time enough to think of politics when the air raids start. B.C.: You're like my mother. She's actually taken to reading the newspapers. Stupid I call it.

16th October 1938

The Munich conference will, I imagine, enter into office conversation for months to come, but whether any remarkable individual contribution will emerge remains to be seen . . . whereas the peace has been a matter of joy and thanksgiving to me, it has received a hostile reception from my fellow workers.

I move in a narrow commercial circle, in constant touch with a score of individuals, and having little serious intercourse beyond them. I often wonder how far my associates are typical Glasgow people, of whom of course, I see thousands on the bus, the streets, the Exhibition, night classes, church, etc. Probably they are fairly representative of that larger section engaged in the city. There is a deep gulf, however, I should say, between black-coated workers and the 'working classes', and if my mass-observations could extend to the East End (Mr Maxton's and Mr McGovern's constituencies), probably I should find quite different reactions.

In any case politics have never appealed much to the majority of Glasgow's businessmen, and most people are clearly uninformed upon foreign policy. My brother who pays a monthly visit to London tells me that in the Clubs there politics are being thrashed out all the time, whereas here it is always business.

When will war break out? My views have not substantially changed since the day in August when your questionnaire on the chances of war was sent. I think the Great Powers will continue to postpone the evil day. In August I fixed the date as thirty years hence, and when one wants to indicate a long time ahead, that is as good a date as any other.

As already mentioned, if war comes during my working life I

shall probably be engaged on clerical work in connection with the bunkering of minesweepers. When do other people expect war to break out? A fortnight ago none of my associates believed that peace had come – it was simply a lull. That view still prevails, though the anticipated duration of the lull is extending; from a few days it became a few weeks, then a few months. And now certain optimists think even a few years.

My home does not occur often in these M-O reports, partly because it is too private, partly because little has been said, the crisis in regard to the home being a subject we all find too deep for words. On Friday I asked Mother if she meant to get a gas mask, and she said that Mrs S. (40, wife of wholesale butcher, an intelligent and well-informed neighbour) had warned her against the queue. Mother thinks that if anyone wants her to have a gas mask they will have to bring it to her. Mrs S. regards the distribution as a farce because (1) many of the masks are defective, (2) no instructions are given as to their preservation, (3) no wrappings are supplied in which to take them home, and as we have been having heavy rain all week many masks must have been ruined in the weather long before the recipient reached home.

I mentioned to Mother C.'s views on the unhygienic conditions and M.'s view that there was a danger of spreading lice. Mother has read criticisms of this nature in the Press. On Saturday 15th October, the newspapers stated that Glasgow ARP wardens will call at our homes to fit elderly people next week. Mother does not intend to be fitted unless she is satisfied on the score of cleanliness. Mother wonders what our neighbour Mrs F. will do if anyone comes to fit a gas mask, as the crisis has distressed her so much that she has been ill in bed for a fortnight. My brother does not intend to get a gas mask yet.

Mrs Arnold
Mrs Arnold from Ilford, Essex, aged 80, described herself as engaged on 'own home duties'.

28th September 1938
It is difficult to get any definite or any coherent answer from the class of people I get in touch with. I am just one of a group fitting in

a word here and there. All are very excited, seem to think war might break out any minute. The men look very serious but I am only a little old woman, have no commanding presence and never try to approach them.

My landlord, an upholsterer, about fifty years of age, served in the last war from beginning to end but thinks he may be called again. Landlady, somewhere near forty years of age, before marriage worked at same trade as husband. Now attends only to home duties. They have two children, girls, 15 and 8 years of age. They have friends in Devon who will have the children. The mother can't make up her mind.

30th September

Had a little chat with a hairdresser today, a woman about 38 or 39. The first optimist I have met. She thinks war will come but not yet. I asked her what she would do if war broke out. She has no husband, has a boy of 9 years old. He is going into the country with the school. 'About yourself?' I said. She said, 'I have no idea – can only wait.' That is very much how I feel. The more one thinks about it the less you feel you know. I have spoken to some mothers who are glad that the children can go with the schools but don't seem to care what happens to themselves. I feel something like that but if I had children I should wonder what would happen to them if I were killed. Have offered myself for ARP and have been accepted. I know I can be of *some* use.

Saturday 1st October

I'm a mystery to myself. Ilford has seemed to me such a 'dead-and-alive' sort of place that I felt as if I was the only one who felt really alive. Today *everyone* is *crazy* with delight – and it all makes me quiet.

I'm thankful, truly, deeply thankful that the cloud of horror has lifted. Not so much for myself – my race is nearly run – but for the millions who would have suffered such agonies to no good purpose. Further my poor old heart can feel the 'Tramp, Tramp, Tramp of soldiers' into Czechoslovakia, and though thankful, I cannot rejoice. These are the thoughts I may only express in a Mass-Observation report.

Miss Pringle
Miss Pringle, aged 24, a teacher from Liverpool. Teachers
were expected to take part in the work of gas mask fitting
as well as organising the evacuation of the children in
their care. Miss P. helped out with the clerical work
involved in issuing gas masks to the local people around
the school where she works.

Up to Sept 26th I treated ARP as rather an unnecessary thing.
Gas masks came to school, a distribution centre, last Saturday.
We enrolled for anti-gas instruction last week. We had two staff
meetings on the matter. This is exceptional as a staff meeting in
our school is a rare occurrence.

Sept 27th
A.M. Third staff meeting called to arrange about the day's work.
In the morning we fitted the children. This was strenuous work,
undertaken by the older members of the staff while the younger
ones looked after the classes.

In a school of 440 boys, we had two cases of fright – in a
backward class of seven-year-olds. Most of the others treated it as
a huge picnic. We carefully avoided all reference to the matter in
our classrooms but we did not keep to our ordinary timetable
because the children were too excited to work properly.

In the girls' department there were more cases of fright but the
staff in both departments said how well-behaved and plucky the
children had been. They also said how difficult it was to keep
saying the same cheerful inanities and yet be fitting the children
with equipment such as that. Some children thought that the gas
was in the defence valve and said they could smell it. Actually it
was the Izal used for disinfectant.

P.M. Children sent home until Thursday 9 a.m. Lunch in the
staffroom after clearing up all classrooms in readiness for adult
gas mask fitting. Some furious telephoning on congested lines to
alter appointments and mealtimes because I had to be in the gas
mask depot as a clerk. At 2 p.m. we began our testing. At first
there were crowds and many willing helpers. The comments were
interesting. Why, these won't be much good. They won't send gas
here, it will be high explosive. What about my baby? Do you think
I can wear a gas mask while she is undefended? As clerks and

fitters and stewards the ARP wardens and the school staff worked furiously. The women were at first loath to touch the heads of people who, from experience, were known to be verminous, e.g. parents of dirty children but this was restrained and forgotten in the rush. The clerks commented on the number of illegitimate children under 5 enrolled for babies' precautions.

We had offers of help from big boys who knew the way of the school and they worked as hard as any seniors at disinfecting trial masks etc. The police were in and out all day directing the operations but our own headmaster was a marvellous leader. One war cripple wore his stripes and told all the young men they would be wanted as soldiers. They looked at him in mild but tolerant amusement. 'OK, dad, we know,' they said. There was little or no waiting and no panic or fright.

At 6.30 I had a meal and heard about other centres. Mrs F. had one and a half hours to wait before she was fitted. The people around her commented on the Jews in the crowd. She hoped the masks were disinfected.

The station where I worked seemed efficient compared with the one used by her. Mrs B. said the gas mask felt suffocating. Her mother, a nervous case recovering from an operation, lost all appetite and said the business made her realise how near was war.

September 28th
Duty began in gas mask fitting station at 2 p.m. and was somewhat lackadaisical for a while. At 3 p.m. business became more brisk as the public houses closed. Cheerfulness was an effort and work was dull and monotonous – name, address, invalids, children under 5. Tea reliefs were brought and some men from the railway came in to be fitted. They were full of sarcasm. Various rumours were current but none were believed. At tea men from the City Treasurer's department left us to report for all night duty at mask fitting and assembly station. Returning to duty to console elderly and very frightened old ladies did not appeal in the slightest. Everyone complained of headaches and was short-tempered. The Izal fumes filled the room which was cold yet stuffy. There was no repartee among a usually jovial clerical staff, all good friends even away from work.

5.30 approx. Sergeant returned from his local police station wreathed in smiles. The glad news of the 4 Power conference had come on the station wireless.

The place almost went mad. It was a slack period in fitting and to celebrate the occasion we clerks released our overwrought nerves by having a paperball fight with the spoilt forms. We sang, we whistled, we made jokes. The caretaker of the school went and bought a late *Echo* and we read the stop press news. The atmosphere changed miraculously from deep despair to exuberant hope. The last few people to come in gazed at our mad antics as though in pity. Then we told them the news and the weight of sadness lifted before hope on their faces.

We had expected a rush period from 6 p.m. to 8 p.m. and had prepared to remain fitting until the bitter end if need be. But there were dozens instead of hundreds and by 8 p.m. only single citizens at long intervals. We waited until 8.30 p.m. and packed up joyfully – headaches dispersed, hope alive again – a sentence of almost certain death removed at any rate for a while and possibly for good.

Miss Bromley
Miss Bromley, accounting machine operator and typist employed by the London County Council at County Hall. Aged 18.

1) When is there going to be a war?
I haven't a full answer here. I frankly hadn't the heart or the nerve to go round asking this. But from what people said I gathered that nearly every one thought, at the beginning of the crisis week, that war, if it came, would start on October 1st, though we might not be involved immediately. Directly the news of the Munich conference came, people thought there would be no war.

2) What will you do?
In my family, myself, my sister (22) a shorthand typist, and my brother (25) a clerk, are pacifists, and intended doing nothing that would in any way further the war. He would be a conscientious objector, and I think we all realised he'd be in trouble soon, though no one said anything about it. My sister is an active worker for pacifism (I won't say peace, because 'peace' workers

have been demanding war with Hitler). I think she intended agitating against war, if it came. Myself, I decided I wasn't going to join anything, as that might further war, but I couldn't think what to do to further peace, not having much faith in propaganda at this hour of the day. Mother, who I think secretly agrees with us, was very worried and flustered. I don't think she would have done anything, but just carried on. Father isn't a pacifist. He announced he was going to join up. But he's 56, and has a 'heart', so we weren't worrying about that. Of my friends at work (County Hall), most hadn't decided to do anything. But Kathleen (19) said on the 28th that she would like to join the Women's Auxiliary Territorials. She didn't do anything, though.

3) ARP

The LCC arranged 3 or 4 months ago to give a day's instruction on ARP to all the staff. Most of us were to get it at a school erected in Battersea Park, in relays of about 40 to 50 a day. No compulsion was used to force anyone to go.

I went in June. I consulted my conscience and other pacifists, and decided it wouldn't do anyone any good if I stayed away, but it might help me if I went. If they had said we must go, I and others might have refused, and made a fuss, and brought our point of view forward.

Everyone treated the 'day in the country' very gaily. I went with a girl I knew, but knew no one else. The lecturer was really very pleasant, friendly, and a most amusing talker. There were 2 dummies used for demonstrating, named Kenneth and George, and altogether a very pleasant time was had by all. We learnt about different types of gases, how to combat and treat them, first aid, gas-proofing a room, etc. The special treat was 5 minutes in the gas chamber, followed by tea and biscuits.

When I thought about it, it made me feel sick and ashamed, and contemptuous of the high spirits of the others, but I stopped thinking, and joined in the fun, and laughed with the rest. Perhaps they all felt the same.

It is significant, I think, that explosive and incendiary bombing were not so much as mentioned.

For conscientious reasons I have had nothing to do with any recent ARP work. But work has gone apace at County Hall. They first decided that in the event of a raid, the staff if present should repair to chosen 'cover' points, deemed safest. Orders were issued by the Clerks Dept. The Architects, planning section, surveyed the building, and chose the cover points. These were corridors on the 4th and 5th floors, protected by double walls. We've only 7 floors, and I think most of us would have preferred the sub basement. But they told us that even that wouldn't be deep enough to shield us against a direct hit. The Architects, mapping and drawing section, then produced lots of notices.

Each section had its own spot to make for. There was a rehearsal of the exodus to cover points on a day when I was on holiday. It was quite successful, but everyone said the corridors became unbearably warm and stuffy.

Next the Engineers got to work. They stuck up the notices, then sandwiched all corridor windows between cellophane, producing a sort of rain at sea effect. After a few days of this they stuck brown paper on top. This is still there, as I fancy no one has the courage to order its removal. So to see our way, either the windows are opened wide, or the lights switched on. As winter is approaching, I fear the Council's light bill will soar.

County Hall unofficially treats the whole cover point idea as an immense joke. A typical comment, which appeared in our staff magazine, *London Town*, I attach – we all think it rather good, but then the perpetrator, an 'Architect', David Langdon, draws for *Punch* and *Lilliput*.

However, we weren't going to stay at County Hall in wartime. A skeleton staff (the Suicide Squad) were to carry on. This was mostly women over 25, and men over military age. The rest of us were to stay at home, till we could be scattered over London. For instance part of the Education department was to be housed in Furzedown College. Some of my department comptrollers were apparently to go to South East London Tech., which I believe is fairly near such military objectives as the Arsenal, Deptford power station and various gas works, not to mention M-O headquarters.

So you see the LCC, besides arranging for the evacuation of school children, and eventually such civilians as wished it, had made plans, not perhaps fully appreciated, for the safety of the staff. But I think we were more amused than annoyed.

All our important records, by the way, were to be sent to safe homes in the country.

Mrs Last

Mrs Last, a middle-aged housewife from
Barrow-in-Furness whose wartime diary was published in
1981, began writing for Mass-Observation in 1937 and
continued for thirty years. The extract below is typical of
her early contributions, not full diary instalments but
diary-style recording of how she responded to the crisis.

Thursday Sept 30th

Last night we learned that Mr Chamberlain was going to see
Hitler again and today seems to balloon out of the week like a
weak place in a hot water bottle. I cannot settle to my work and
after getting a ginger cake in the oven and finding I have put no
lard in it, and breaking a cup of a tea set and cutting my hand with
a blunt vegetable knife – I feel I must just go out. I wandered idly
out, and passed my grocers. He was at the door and beckoned me.
Told me to send my order in. I get my 'big' order monthly – dry
goods – and order weekly the perishable things. Point out that it
is not convenient but he says he will send in account at month
end. Everybody getting orders and if things don't alter will be
glad if I order a few days in advance. Wonder what to do with
myself. Not used to aimless wandering. Go for gas mask. Try it on.
Come out. Never realised how sweet ordinary air was. Still only
two o'clock. Wonder what Chamberlain is doing and think I'll go
out again.

   Later . . . Passing a church I went in – wished I hadn't. Clergy-
man a man who I remembered as a 'buckteethed' boy who was
always afraid of dogs and the dark. At fifty he has cold damp
hands and has hair in his ears. I knelt opposite a brass plate
'Sacred to the memory of the two sons of James Butler'. I knew
them both – such 'devils' of boys and always 'up to tricks'. One was
killed at 20 and the other at 22. They said at the time the latter
lingered for two days with the lower half of his face shot off. His
mother crossed to France and sat by his bed till he died. He had
such a big wide mouth when he smiled – like my Cliff who will be
20 this Xmas. I think of my Cliff's teeth biting into new crusty
bread on baking day and my head starts ticking and I come home
again.

   When I get in I find that Murphy, my cat, has killed a robin. It
died quickly for its feathers are unruffled; and it's my fault, for I

forgot to throw Murphy's ball till he was tired and went to sleep till my dear wild birds fed off their table. He was such a nice robin and liked me from the start, when I came here three years ago. He pecked at the window for a crust dipped in warm tea – and now he is dead. In a day of stress and emotion I feel it's Hitler's fault and I cry and cry till I am spent. It has taken the 'ticking' out of my head and I remember I have only had two aspirins all day. Have a cup of tea and wash my face – never do to worry my husband and boy when they come in. Feel very sick.

Friday October 1st
The paper came early and it is Peace. The sun is shining today and its warmth has brought two late rosebuds out. So glowing red and warm. Feel very bewildered when my next-door neighbour shakes his head over joyful news – he talks about 'betrayal and weakness'. My schoolmaster neighbour across the street who 'reads the stars' is very triumphant, with an 'I told you so' manner. Ask him when he thinks we will have war and he says – in another year.

Quite like these Mass-Observation questions. Have few 'contacts' and it gives me an excuse for speaking to people. Find people fall roughly into two classes – the 'mind your own damned business' class, and the ones who like to talk and give their opinions.

Later . . . I've asked so many people [M-O] questions that I have lost count of individual answers. Quite half seem to think we are 'putting off war' till we are in a stronger position. In a town like Barrow where the shipyard dominates the town, bits of gossip leak out – of big orders for small arms and shells going to America – out of date anti-aircraft guns that are erected on our Town Hall – of the dates on other guns and boxes of ammunition, and of 'shortages'.

There was not the joyful feeling abroad I had expected. It was there certainly but the prevailing spirit was of wariness if not doubt. And resentment that we had to 'give in' to Hitler . . . Learn we have to take care of our gas masks, and the big trench in the Public Parks is to be finished. Wish I knew a clever man who would tell me his views. Clever women would be no use. Women's views limited to welfare of loved men – whether grown up or tiny. My Cliff still talks about the rival attraction of the Navy and Air

Force. I bought four papers and read them, and going by the editorials the rest of Britain is as muddled in their opinion as we are here in Barrow-in-Furness. I remember my Quaker Gran's serene blue eyes and her unfailing slogan in any kind of trouble: 'We must do the best we can my child and remember we are all in God's pocket.' Her world had few problems – wonder what she would have thought of world today.

Shopkeepers complain of bad trade. In the few days' crisis, trade was at a standstill except in [grocers] who did a brisk trade in sugar and tinned goods. Picture houses were badly patronised too. Felt myself that I could not be far from wireless – hurried in to listen to news bulletins at 10.30, and 1 o'clock. Wished I knew German when I heard foreign talk.

Will send in another report later unless I hear they are cancelled.

Mrs Hamilton
Mrs Hamilton, housewife aged 40 living with her husband and young daughter (Margery) in Marlow, Buckinghamshire.

Not having been able to leave the house during the last week, the first part of this report will be concerned with the happenings at home during the crisis.

There has been an eager waiting for news on the radio, and listening intently when it was broadcast. In spite of everything my husband and myself think there will be no war as far as England is concerned, although hubby thinks we should help Czechoslovakia because if we do not do so the annexing of this country by Germany will give Hitler a greater power in Europe than he already has, and will only postpone war.

Hubby and I have been talking about what will happen if war does break out. He says he might join the ASC. As a skilled man (he is an engineer) he would get about 6/- per day.

On Sunday 25th a man called from the ARP with gas masks. Margery opened the door to him. She went quite white when he told her what he had called about. I asked him in, and asked Margery to try on a gas mask but she wouldn't, so I tried one on first and was able to persuade her to do so. Hubby was not at home so the man put down on his list one a size larger for him. The man said Marlow was considered by the government to be a safe area and some of the children would be sent here when evacuated from London, and the people here would have to take them in. I told hubby about the man calling and he asked if we had tried on the masks.

End of report written from memory. No notes made.

Sept 27. From notes
Newspaper eagerly awaited in the morning and hubby and I both disappointed that there was no further news in it. During the morning hubby talks about what he might do, and says he will write to his captain (of the last war) and ask him what he intends doing. I say I will go to Pontings on Thursday to do some shopping, because if there should be a war, things will get very expensive.

I go to Maidenhead in the early evening and I hear no comments passed by the passengers. The driver and conductor both together in the front (it is an old-fashioned bus) are talking earnestly all the way but I cannot hear what they are saying. In Maidenhead we pass two private cars labelled ARP and notice there are gas masks on the seat, otherwise I notice nothing in the town to indicate there is anything unusual going on. The same driver and conductor are on the bus coming back to Marlow and still talking together all the way. Two lady passengers on the seat at the side of me are talking about the crisis. They both have newspapers on their laps. One says, 'Not a very good day to launch the *Queen Elizabeth*. Did you hear it on the wireless. The Queen has a beautiful voice.' Then I could only hear snips of conversation such as 'very serious', 'I wonder what will happen', 'The London schoolchildren are coming here', 'Poor little things', 'Yes Chamberlain must be worn out, almost on the point of collapse I should imagine', 'Speaks on the wireless at 8 o'clock'. Just before I get to my house I see a neighbour painting her gate and stop and ask her what she thinks of things. She says her husband is at the moment cementing cracks under the window preparatory to making a downstairs room gas proof. I suggest that an upstairs room would be better because my hubby says gas lies low. I tell her that we have a large piece of lino ready, to cover the whole of the window of one room. The idea is to place it in position in an emergency and seal the edges. She says that Marlow is considered a safe area, and we have the added advantage of living on the outskirts of the town, on the edge of open country . . .

30 September

By the first post on 29th I receive a letter from a sister in Croydon saying that one of the children is to be evacuated to Wiltshire, and the headmaster has advised all adults who could to get out of Croydon. She asks if she and the remainder of the family (4 altogether) could come here and could I let her know by return – I had expected this letter – I do not want them here. They are a family we do not get on very well with for more than a few hours. I show the letter to hubby and he says, 'If the house is going to be full of quarrelling relations I'm getting a tent and clearing out.' I say, 'I'd come with you,' but it doesn't help to solve the problem of how to answer the letter. However I make an attempt and tell her I sympathise with her having to part with D (the youngest child) and explain that the people of Marlow have been informed that they will have to take in refugees, and that if war does break out and the people of Croydon are not evacuated, and they find themselves in imminent danger, they could come here and we would put them up somehow until they could make other arrangements – I wrote another letter to my mother in London, telling her that we were expecting the London schoolchildren here at any time, and everyone was preparing for them, and that in the event of her being evacuated and her sending me the address of her billet I would endeavour to go and visit her – this was a much more difficult letter to write because I felt she should come here and I would have welcomed her but I know she wouldn't leave my father, and I wouldn't have that damned swine staying here.

Going down the road to catch a bus to Wycombe I meet a neighbour. She is a carpenter's wife but you wouldn't think so to look at her. They live in an ornate detached house in this road. I ask if she is taking some children. She says, 'No I wouldn't be bothered with children.' I say, 'We may be compelled to take them,' and she replies she has told the man her house will be full of her own people and adds that she has nobody coming really. I tell her I can't stop as I have a bus to catch, and I can't help thinking how selfish some people are.

When I return from Wycombe (about 6.30 p.m.) I find 3 people (with a car) distributing gas masks. My next-door neighbour asks me if I have seen the man who is calling at the houses about the refugees. I reply that I have just returned from Wycombe. She says, 'He called a little while ago and I would not open the door to him. We don't want children. They are a tie, and require a lot of looking after. Although if we don't have children we might have adults dumped on us. Which would be worse for you have got some sort of control over children.' She dodges in when she hears a car coming up the road thinking the man is returning. I go to the gate to see how far away the gas mask people are, and a woman who has three children stops me and asks me if I have been called upon regarding the refugees. I tell her 'No' and she says she will have 3. She would feel grateful if she lived in London to people who took her children, and feels she is only doing her duty. She asks if I will have any. I reply that I have only a single bed available and would take one or possibly two. She says she doesn't know what to do about the young children because gas masks have not been issued to them, and thinks in a gas attack the best place would be the cupboard under the stairs. I received 3 gas masks the next day (30th) at about 3.30 p.m. There is a knock at the door and I open it to a good-looking young man who tells me (in an Oxford accent) that he has called to see how many refugees I can take in. He asks how many rooms there are and how many people living here. I tell him 5 rooms and 3 people and he informs me that I can take two. I explain that I can't have young children because my husband comes home from work sometimes at 1 a.m. and has to sleep during the morning. He says I'll put you down for 1 woman and child and the mother will keep the child quiet. (Man-like he thought keeping a child quiet a simple matter.) He asks me to allow the woman facilities for cooking. He bids me 'Good afternoon' and departs.

I have spoken to four people representing 4 different households and the impression I have is one of mild resentment at having thrown open their houses to strangers. Then there are my own reactions. At first I felt I would take in refugees but did not want them. Analysing this I came to the conclusion that I would welcome them if they were *of my own choosing*. I mean if I could pick them out of a crowd.

War is declared, September 1939

The two extracts below are taken from the diaries of two women who went on to write extensively for Mass-Observation throughout the war years. The first diarist is a single woman in her thirties who works in a fish and chip shop run by her family in Birmingham. She submitted regular diary instalments throughout the war.

Friday 1 September, 12.20 p.m.
Started day as usual except that we were anxious as to whether our fish supply would arrive from Aberdeen. It did but the fish was very dear. About 5 to 11 my mother said [on hearing a man selling newspapers in the street], 'I think he's shouting "special".' I went out to buy one and met the window cleaner crossing the road. He made a gesture (putting his hand under his armpit) signifying 'under the arm' (no good) and I said, 'What do you mean, the "Special's" no good?' (We have been caught with specials just having a little item of news and not really anything fresh.) He said, 'No, it's war,' but I could already see people running out of their houses to get a copy of the paper which included news of the Polish invasion. We gathered in little groups, all the faces being white and anxious-looking. A few of the expressions which I put down almost immediately were: 'We've got to stop him now', 'Bloody well stop him'. My mother and another woman said together, 'Put him on an island like the Kaiser,' but my mother said, 'Give him a villa like the Kaiser.' 'He's started it then', 'Blooming devil, we can't let him do that, can we?', 'Just heard it on the wireless.' All working class people, mostly women, I think, in the proportion of 4 or 5 to 1 man. I was surprised at how upset my mother [was]. I thought she would be a lot less anxious but she was properly upset and has been all day. Myself I am surprised at how calm I have felt which I attribute to

reading so many books on the war the last 2 years and as I have always said and prepared for it I was not so worried. I have in reading the war books endeavoured to find out what spirit makes the nations win the war and think it is remaining calm and doing your best, so I am deliberately forcing myself to be calm. Every now and then I have an anxious moment but on the whole I have been too busy to worry very much. (This sounds a bit priggish but I don't know how to express it better.)

Of course there has been nothing else talked about with the exception of a fight which took place between two men at about 2.10 this afternoon. There are a lot of Irish men working on the shelters at the flats opposite and one of these got into an argument with two other men and they really *did* have a running fight. What was said I don't know but at the end when the other two were going for a policeman and two or three were holding the navvy, he shouted, 'We're British, we are not bloody communists. We'll fight, we'll fight.' He had had something to drink and really was fighting mad. Among the crowd that collected there was expressions as follows, 'I don't know, as if there isn't enough trouble', 'Fancy fighting among themselves', 'It's this war, it's getting on the chaps' nerves', 'They ought to send all the lot back to Ireland'.

I bought quarter lb Bournville Cocoa 6d, 1 tin of chicken and ham roll 6d, quarter of tea 9d, 2 lbs sugar 5d for the store cupboard today.

Gwen, Ron, May and Colin came down tonight. Ron loosened the cellar grating which was cemented down. Colin bet me 3 to 1 there would be no war but it was just bravado and I wouldn't argue with him as I felt nice towards him as I know really he is worried about going.

May said Colin told her he would have cried when he saw Bobby off this morning in the evacuation but Bobby went off happily enough. I went to the school as instructed this afternoon to help with the children but found they had plenty of help so didn't stay. All the children looked cheerful except one little boy who was crying because he had to have a strap or something about his waist. Doreen's friend, a Mr Wainwright, came to say goodbye and bring some bandages etc. which he obtained for us through the firm, Southall Bros & Barclays, where he is, or was, in the dispensing line. He had been called up to join his regiment,

RAMC I think. Doreen's girlfriend, Agnes, is staying the night as her brother with whom she lives has been called up and she didn't want to stay in the house alone.

Put all the blackout curtains up tonight. Everybody seems tired. Some young men, about 4 or 5 of them, stood singing songs on the corner for about half an hour, 10–10.30. Balloon barrage caused excitement at 6.30 tonight, everyone running out to see but as I was in the shop I couldn't hear comments. (People do not seem to understand the purpose of the barrage, one or two thinking they had men in them to spot the enemy.) The people were very excited and stood about looking at them for a good while . . .

Saturday 2 September, 12.15

The first of the mothers and children under school age went this morning at about 8 a.m. The streets seemed like Sunday and holiday Saturday combined with all the people standing about and there being such a lot of people with luggage. Everybody was quite cheerful and we laughed and joked on the corner with 3 families who were going away. Another woman joined us who said she had already heard from her children who went yesterday and they were alright.

About 10.30 one of the women who helped the neighbours with luggage came back and said, 'There are thousands on the station. I wished I could have gone.' 'Couldn't you?' 'No I haven't got one young enough to go with them.' Listened to the *News from the Children* broadcast and thought it an exceedingly good idea. It will help comfort people a lot when they get used to the hour and wait for the news. I went to Woolworths for some phosphorous paint which I couldn't get and the only counters which had crowds round them were those selling coloured electric globes, small flash lamps and batteries etc., and of course ARP paper.

There are still a few people who do not realise what the blackout means, contenting themselves with red or green that shows up. They will have to be strict with them. Several people have complained in the shop tonight about neighbours showing lights realising that it affects them too. We had a bad thunderstorm about 10.30 and it was terrible with the blackout as well. My sister and friend came home soaked up to their knees through treading in flooded horseroads and puddles they couldn't see.

Have listened to most of the wireless news throughout the day, read the *Birmingham Mail*. My sister who came this morning said that they were singing at nearly all the publics last night when they went home. Heard about three different people give versions for how long we have given Hitler, two said until 12 tonight and one till 6 tomorrow.

Sunday 3 September

My sister Doreen woke us with a cup of tea this morning saying that they had just asked everybody to stand by for an announcement at 10 a.m. We discussed what would be said and Doreen said, 'If Hitler comes I shall kill myself, I wouldn't live under him.' Me: 'Oh he won't invade England, he would just take all that makes England. It would not be the England we know if he beats us.' My mother: 'Oh, he won't beat us, he might cripple us for life, but he won't beat us.' Me: 'No, I don't think he will.'

We listened at 10 a.m. to the announcement that the time limit was at 11 o'clock, then Agnes, a friend who is staying with us said, 'Well, we have another 25 mins of peace, come on, let's enjoy it,' and we did a dance round the room. We went on working until the Prime Minister's speech, which we all thought very restrained, my mother remarking, 'I feel sorry for him,' also 'Fancy, it's the same time Armistice was declared. Fancy declaring war on Sunday.'

I looked out of the window while listening to the speech and there were a good many people in the street acting as usual, I said, 'There's a good many not listening in.' I put it down to the fact that people rise late on Sundays and missed the announcement of it. There was no excitement at all, just a few groups talking. I think people have regarded us as at war since Friday morning, and regarded today's announcement just as confirmation.

People have been going up and down all morning to the Hope St school centre where the children's gas masks are being given out. One said she had been down twice and had got to go down again after dinner. Another young married woman was looking out for her husband who had been on AFS service all night and was due home at 8 a.m. but hadn't come then (11.30). She said she had eaten nothing since Thursday night and felt proper bad and worried. She had cooked his breakfast twice, but couldn't eat anything herself.

Doreen and Agnes have been clearing out the cellar ready to be used as an air raid shelter. Tried on my Air Raid Warden's suit and etc's this afternoon, much to my own and everybody's amusement. I must say I think I look comical. The suit is the same size as a man's and I am rather slender so there was plenty of room. After listening to the King's speech I sat looking out of the window, and in the half an hour I sat there not a single person passed carrying his or her gas mask. My sister and friend refused to take theirs with them to Chapel, saying they felt silly carrying them and there wouldn't be an air raid tonight . . .

> The second extract is from the diary of a 17-year-old
> schoolgirl acting as a pupil teacher in her own school.
> She lives with her parents, two sisters and her brother
> in Romford. Although she began working for
> Mass-Observation as a volunteer diary-writer, she soon
> became one of the full-time Observers and later, after
> joining the WAAF, sent in reports on Forces life.

Friday 1 September 1939
When I arrived at the Senior Girls' School where I am pupil teaching the staff were deep in conversation about the international situation. The general feeling was optimistic. There was a murmur of assent all round when the history mistress affirmed that 'this evacuation business was a brilliant propaganda stroke on the part of Mr Chamberlain. He only did it to fool Hitler into submission. No possibility of war now.'

Yesterday (Thursday) we installed a wireless set in the staffroom, and our headmistress decreed that someone was to be in the room all the time, in readiness for any special radio message. At eleven this morning, as I was only observing a lesson, I decided to go to the staffroom to see if there was anyone there. There were three others there and together we listened to the announcement that 'serious developments in the international situation' had occurred. As the details of the Poland air raids were unfolded, one of the staff, an intending missionary, kept muttering to herself and clicking her tongue. This caused great amusement between the other two who began to giggle a little hysterically. All four of us knew it was virtually war.

At break everyone was asking everyone else, 'Have you heard

the news?' or 'Has there been any more news?' At the dinner table, anecdotes of ARP, evacuation and the last war were exchanged, and now and again someone would say, 'I can't believe it's here.' Everyone looked wise; they had anticipated it from the first, they said. The history mistress declared that even though the evacuation of schools *had* been labelled a 'precautionary measure', she had realised as soon as they put the date forward, that war was at hand.

Every now and then above the burble of conversation, a deep 'boom boom', followed by a metallic clang could be heard and was obviously distressing some of the staff. Talk faded and gradually it became evident that many of them were anticipating the bangs. At last one woman asked, with self-conscious casualness, 'What was that?' 'Only the tables being set up and laid next door,' laughed Miss J., and the chorus of relieved laughter that greeted this explanation proved that more than one woman had been worrying.

After dinner, we listened to another news bulletin. Our headmistress, and the headmaster of the joint boys' school were present – no man had ever before been in our staffroom. Everyone was terribly grave and most eyes were on the ceiling. When a child knocked on the door, we switched off the radio because we did not want the pupils to learn the news just yet.

A few of the bigger girls did get to know, however. One class (13–14) was particularly ill-behaved. Afterwards I asked them why they were so naughty, contrary to normal circumstances. 'Well, miss,' was the reply, 'you see, we might not be here next week.'

At afternoon break, we gave a pathetic little leaving party to Miss F. who had joined the staff of an evacuating school. The Head made a speech of tribute, regretting the unpleasant circumstances that accompanied so great a turn in Miss F.'s career, and hoping all would be well soon, etc., etc. The staff presented her with a book voucher ('Better spend it tonight before it's too late') and her special friend gave her a sponge bag for evacuation purposes. Then tea and cakes all round and nobody very happy.

At 4.15 we all said prolonged goodbyes 'in case we're not here next week'. That sentiment had affected the routine of the lazier teachers; one of them threw aside the time-table she was printing for the year's work and many of us decided not to prepare

Monday's lessons. Actually I think I was the least upset but I was the only one who had not experienced the last war.

After tea, a friend called at our house for me to go to supper with her. I was about to go when my mother arrived and unconditionally refused to let me go. 'You are not to go away from home,' she declared dramatically. 'If we die, we all die together.' So I spent the evening at home, reading. The conditions were not exactly pleasant. My sister is 'somewhere in Europe', we don't know where. My mother is worried out of her life about her and about my 18-year-old brother. My father insists upon listening to every news bulletin. And our makeshift blackout arrangements involve the use of a light so small that it strains the eyes.

It's only ten but I'm going to bed.

Saturday 2 September

After I'd gone to bed last night, a telegram came from my sister and early this morning, she arrived herself. She had been obliged to return early from Denmark because her companion, a school mistress, had been recalled. She described the attitude of the Danes as: 'We do feel sorry for you English people.' I didn't go out until four o'clock. Then a telegram arrived with arrangements for my sister's evacuation so I had to go out and find her. When I returned a boyfriend was waiting for me and he suggested a visit to the cinema 'to get away from all this'. After tea, we went to my father's shop where it took me ten minutes to persuade my mother that I would be safe and even then I had to promise to be in by ten.

The cinema was almost full and the audience very worked up. It cheered and booed wildly in the appropriate places, and roared with laughter at the topical allusions in the film which were often painfully ironical in the circumstances.

They were more subdued while the newsreel was showing. It was a little out of date which made it sound childish but Chamberlain earned a hearty cheer and Mussolini was in for some heated hissing. We had to leave early to satisfy my waiting mother. The blackout was much more successful than yesterday (yesterday several houses on our street ignored the blackout). We could see nothing at all, except the buses which were half-lighted. I couldn't even see my companion. There were a good few people about – we heard them.

Thought for the day: what an anticlimax it would be if there were no war!

Sunday 3 September

What a storm it was last night! I lay awake, wondering whether the flashes were of lightning or gunfire, until well into the morning. My small sister kept calling out, 'Are they here?' and my mother was awake.

In the morning, however, the weather was good. My mother considered the news much more cheerful. She didn't think a war would be needed at all.

At eleven-fifteen, I was playing the piano in the front room, when suddenly my mother burst in, shouting, 'Stop that noise!', and then flung open the window, letting in the scream of the air raid siren, and the scuffling noise of neighbours in a hurry. Immediately, my father assumed the role of the administrative head-of-the-house, issuing commands and advice: 'All get into your gas masks! Steady, no panicking! Every man for himself! Keep in the passage!' My small sister (11) began to sob; 'Will it be alright?' she kept querying. My mother was frightened, but was trying to take control of herself. My heart beat hard for the first few seconds, and then calmed down. I think my brother and elder sister felt much the same as I did. We gathered in the passage (we have no shelter) and sat on the stairs. After a few minutes, we decided that it was either a false alarm or a trial, so we went to the front gate (all except my mother and small sister, who kept calling to us to come back) and remained there until the 'All Clear' was given. Most people were clustered in groups at the front gates. A few babies were crying, and air raid wardens, with gas masks and crash helmets, were running up and down. After the 'All Clear' we learnt for the first time about the declaration of a state of war. Most people were glad. 'High time someone showed Hitler he wasn't such a god as he made out,' was a typical comment.

I soothed my small sister by explaining in even tones, with great scientific and statistical detail, how very small the danger from air raids was. She soon calmed down, but was very subdued all day, and often burst into tears.

After dinner, we made more lasting blackout arrangements, and gathered into one place all 'Wartime Accessories', such as torches, fire pails and black paper, that we could lay our hands on. At teatime, oh, a boyfriend came to see me. He is a refugee, and was very worried as to his position as an alien. He expressed willingness to enter National Service, or the Army, or whatever they asked of him. He was, I think, sincerely grateful to England for its protection, and wanted to prove it actively. After tea, other refugees arrived. They wanted to know different details of wartime banking and postage. They were all terribly upset.

When they had gone, P. and I decided we could not stop indoors; the blackout curtains made the rooms stuffy, and the light bad. We went into the town 'to see what was going on', because my mother would not let me go far. Evidently, others had come out for similar reasons, so every street corner was ornamented with little groups of people; almost everyone carried a gas mask. One in six of the men was not in civilian clothes.

Before we went to bed, we put warm coats where they could easily be found, in case of emergency.

War comes to a Norfolk village: the diary of Muriel Green, 1939

Muriel and Jenny Green
Muriel and Jenny Green began keeping diaries for
Mass-Observation in August 1939 and wrote regular
instalments until the end of the war. Although they
seemed to have intended writing a joint diary, they soon
turned to separate accounts. Muriel, the younger sister,
wrote the most regularly and the extracts below are taken
from her diary for the last four months of 1939. The sisters
lived with their mother and worked in the family
business, a small village garage and sweet shop.

This is the diary (generally muddled and badly spelled) of Muriel
and Jenny Green, garage assistants, aged 18 and 25, single . . .
    We are sorry we have missed out several days mainly through
laziness and disinclination to make a start to write, but we will
try in future to keep a diary of everyday occurrences throughout
the war.

Aug 30th
Life as usual. Excitement, annoyance and worry in village owing
to expected evacuated children tomorrow. We are not having any
if possible.

Sept 1st
Business as usual. Children do not arrive. First night of blackout
with air raid wardens on duty. A local farmer stands on the corner
with a six-foot stick and runs after the cars with too much light.
Eccentric Jewess arrives at her country house from London.
Neighbours begin to build elaborate splinter-proof air raid shelter between our house and theirs. Our butcher who is on the

supplementary reserve is called up, he brings our meat in an almost tearful condition.

Sept 3rd Sunday
Customer tells us of declaration of war. Feeling of hopelessness followed by annoyance at same. Think through friends who will eventually be called up. Decide to think of them as killed off and then it will not be such a blow if they are, and will be a great joy if at the end they are not. Spend the afternoon preparing for blackout. Stick brown paper over back door glass panel etc. Bring out Public Information leaflets and ARP book and read through the lot. Decide bathroom to be the refuge room in air raids because it is downstairs and has only one small 18″ sq window, and has outside walls 18″ thick. It already has most things in ARP book, washing things, disinfectant, bandages etc. We take in a tin of Smiths potato crisps, 3 bottles lemonade, several packets of chocolate from business stock, and some old magazines to read.

During the afternoon a friend from next village comes to see us. Says he has volunteered for the Navy for the duration, as he is 21 and says he would far sooner drown than sit in a trench for days on end. Evacuated mothers and children arrive in village from Shoreditch and Hoxton. Wrong trainload arrive – only children expected. Organisers have great difficulty in getting people to take them in. Three families taken to country mansion buried in trees. Two families refuse to get out of car because of weird atmosphere of place.

6th
Wakened by neighbour calling outside house that there was an air raid warning. Dash out of bed and sally downstairs putting on dressing gown at the same time. J. (sister) and Mother stop to dress. Mother goes and stands outside back door and keeps saying she can't hear anything. All neighbours are seen standing outside looking up and down. Then ARP warden is seen cycling furiously down the road ringing a loud handbell. We don't know meaning of this and get out ARP book and it says handbells indicate that poison gas has been cleared away! We decide it can't be that as no sign of p. gas or people in gas masks, not even a sign of an aeroplane. Nothing happens. I stand in back garden and watch, and see people going to work, so decide it must be all over, then

small boy goes by and tells me the bell was the all clear sign. The warning previously was PC blowing whistle. Nobody was woken up by same but a few people had seen him and warned others. All day general indignation in village over the air raid warning. The handbell was loud enough to hear which was not so important.

Oct 7th

Morning spent in blackberry and apple jam making. We don't usually make jam but this year as we have an excess of apples and blackberries we thought we had better as there is a war. I have slept in room with Mother since Father died and Mother has been threatening to move me into spare bedroom all summer owing to face powder being spilt on the carpet. Today she moved me because she said if a bomb hit her end of the house, I might be saved up the other end. She says if we are spread out there might be one survivor to have the money left behind. Mother sent the Peace Pledge Union 5/- . . .

23rd

Today fetched gas mask for self and Mother and J. from ARP warden. Have not had one until now, surprised to find not too unpleasant to wear as everyone else had said they could not breathe. Have practised wearing it in private and think I could keep it on any length of time if necessary.

Yesterday heard a mine had washed up on our beach, but today I went to look at it and it has washed away again before naval authorities could come and explode it.

29th

Nothing worth reporting to M-O seems to happen in the country. We receive no air raid warnings and would not know a war was on apart from radio, newspapers and people's conversations, and continuous filling of ration coupons for petrol . . .

In the large houses the evacuees found the servants treated them badly. One said, 'The parlour maid giggles all the time, and the whole lot laughed when we asked how to light a fire with sticks.' [In] another house the servants would not let them have any water as they went home late, and told their mistress it was because they had come home drunk. Another woman said, 'I'm not saying anything against Miss—, she is a lady, but them

servants . . .' Three women said they were starving themselves in
order to pay the fare home. Many evacuees returned to London
because on the night of Sept 3rd and the morning of 6th there was
an air raid warning. They said they thought they had been sent to
safety areas but they decided they were no safer on the East coast
than in London especially as they have air raid shelters in their
gardens and in the parks. There are none here. One woman said,
'In our own blocks of flats we have had ARP practices and know
just what to do, but here there are no shelters and we seem to be in
as much danger of passing raiders.' The first bomb in England fell
in this village in the last war . . .

Other women said that they found such difficulty in the country
shops. Food was much dearer at the village grocer's. Nothing can
be bought ready cooked and they did not understand the coal
cooking ranges of the country. They all grumbled at the inconveniences of travel, now only one bus each way every two hours,
and about 3 trains a day. They were not used to living three miles
from a station and bus stop. Some said there was no cinema and
one wanted to know where she could get her hair permed . . . They
found the country very quiet and lacked amusement. One woman
said, 'I'd rather be bombed on me own door step than stay here and
die of depression.'

Difficulties for the hosts were the inconvenience of having
other people in your house. Many grumbled at the dirtiness of the
evacuees, and their bad language. I have never seen such dirty
women with children. One woman who came to our shop smelt
positively filthy and her clothes were disgusting. Most of the
children had impetigo and red flea bites all over their bodies. One
village woman rushed round to the organiser of the scheme and
vowed she would not go home until he had fetched out the family
he had taken into her nice home. I heard many instances of the
evacuees not being 'house trained' and many carpets were ruined.

The village people objected to the evacuees chiefly because of
dirtiness of their habits and clothes. Also because of their reputed
drinking and bad language. It is exceptional to hear women swear
in this village or for them to enter a public house. The villagers
used to watch them come out of the pubs with horror . . .

Nov 6th
In discussion with our mechanic on a possible invasion of England

from the Norfolk coast we were saying the enemy would loot our petrol, he amused us by saying, 'If they came for it, I should have let them have it. I haven't got nothing to defend myself with. I'd tell them we'd make it right with the coupons afterwards.'

Nov 8th

In the afternoon about 3, I was sitting knitting in the garage talking to an elderly retired man. Suddenly there was a terrific noise just as though something very large had fallen on the garage roof. The floor seemed to bounce up and down again. For a second I was deafened. I knew it was really nothing falling on the roof as nothing could fall with such force without coming through. It was far louder than if the house had fallen down beside the garage. I instantly thought it was an air raid and a heavy explosive bomb had fallen in the neighbourhood. The elderly man said, 'Blast, what's that?' I did not know whether to rush outside and see what had happened or stay in case a second bomb fell. I found I had bit my tongue in the excitement. We waited a minute in frozen horror and then ran outside. Everything was whole. I looked to see if all the houses still stood. Our mechanic was filling up the car of a retired army general. Afterwards he told me he said, 'What's that, what's that?' The mechanic: 'I think a bomb has fallen.' 'Hell of a noise, hell of a noise.' He got out of his car and we all stood for some minutes wondering what to do. The grocer's assistants from across the road and all the inhabitants of the houses, including the policeman, had come out and were looking around. Nothing further seemed to happen so we came in. Other people were going back in their houses. I thought about my mother and sister who were at Beach House and wondered if they were alright. We heard aeroplanes very high in the sky and went out but could not see them. I returned to my knitting and in the meantime my sister returned on a bicycle. She said she had been cycling along when she had suddenly heard this thundering noise, and seen black smoke issuing from about a mile along the beach. She did not think it was a bomb as she could see no planes and knew it had been in the direction that a mine had been washed up.

About 20 minutes after the first noise we heard a second minor explosion and later still a third but as they decreased in loudness we thought it was other bombs being dropped further away.

About 3.40 the police patrol car came for petrol and we were told that the noise was mines being exploded about 4 miles away. As our mechanic said afterwards, 'I really did think that old Nasti had come this time.'

Dec 25th

Morning received a pair of gloves from a lady friend also a box of Black Magic from another. Jenny bought me a Penguin book and bar of chocolate, could not afford any more. We had a good laugh because I received a letter from a girl whose father has an antique business in which trade has flopped. The mother has got a job in a petrol rationing department and the father is in a pantomime as the front legs of a horse. Jenny had a letter from a lady in Surrey who said she has one girl evacuee. She had three, but she sent one girl away as she broke out with impetigo and one little boy nearly frightened her to death, as he strayed down to the station (half mile away) and watched a porter cross the line and followed him and fell over the live rail and was nearly electrocuted. The station master brought him [home] burnt on the legs and arms. So he had to go as well.

Christmas Day tea we all went to a lady friend's and stayed to supper (turkey). The party consisted of seven women.

At night felt quite sick through eating continuously all day.

Dec 26th

Afternoon Mr and Mrs F. turned up and stayed to tea. At noon Fred, just conscripted to Navy, came to see us. He has grown about 2 inches in 4 weeks and attributes it to drilling. Says they have good food, finds the discipline very strict and the camp very damp. He had a bad cold. He looks very smart in naval uniform. In the evening M. and Mrs F. went with us to whist drive and dance organised by Boy Scouts for parcels for ex-boy scouts in the forces and funds. Mother played and got 2nd prize (a shaving set) and Mrs F. got 1st lady 10/6 and miniature (box of chocolates). At beginning of whist a boy sat at my table. I got into conversation with him and found out he used to go to the grammar school when I was at the high school and he knew all the boys and girls I knew when at school. He took school cert. when I took it and has since been working in police office in London. I spoke to him lots of times during whist and at the end he came and sat with us. I spent evening with him. He bought me refreshments and I danced with him all evening. He was a rotten dancer, but exceed'ly nice to talk to and quite handsome. Mother for a wonder was not annoyed at him picking me up. He lives at next village and I remember was very brilliant at school and at sports, so she made no objection to him. I hope I shall see him again, but he does not come home very often. There was only 4 soldiers in uniform and 1 RAF man at the dance. Out of 200 people. More girls than men. They had 'Lambeth Walk' (still very popular) and 'Boomps-a-Daisy'. Popular tunes included 'Washing on Siegfried Line', 'Kiss Me Goodnight, Sergeant Major', 'Wish Me Luck' and 'Beer Barrel Polka'.

We had expected Don and his mother to lunch. (Don is Jenny's young man's brother who sent us a box of chocolates for Xmas) but I was glad they did not come as he would have been here when Fred came to see me. Fred is my ex young man, also Don.

Dec 27th
We (Jenny and I) were cooking mince pies when we heard a very loud aeroplane and saw through the window a very peculiar looking plane. We both said at once, 'I am sure that's a Nasty.' But we both stood and watched making no attempt to take any precautions. About 5 mins later we heard more aeroplanes and Jenny rushed out and said she saw 3 Spitfires chasing over after the other aeroplane going very fast. A few minutes later the 1st plane went dashing back and the three others went over again, and Mother and Jenny rushed out in the garden and then rushed back declaring they could hear gunfire. The dog barked and jumped about and I was still eating my dinner and refused to get up and Mother announced that if there was anything to be seen she wasn't going to miss it. She said we might as well be killed while we were excited as anytime. Several times during the afternoon we heard the roar again of aeroplanes and Mother and Jenny dashed in the garden but saw nothing unusual. I felt so tired from the dance last night I could not be bothered to go and look. I remembered you should keep under cover but could not be bothered to go in the bathroom as arranged or get my gas mask from upstairs. I looked out of the window every time although I knew you should not. I did not feel in the least afraid but rather excited to think I had seen a Nasty. Mother who wanted to move

from East Coast was enjoying it ever so and was quite annoyed because she never saw it and since then has rushed in the garden to look every time she hears an aeroplane. She has decided they are much nicer than Zeppelins as they go so quick. She did not seem a bit frightened. I feel worn out from the dance and have lounged about eating chocolates all day. Arthur J. (a boy we know) called in to see us, limping with a stick and a plaster on his head. He said he was a victim of the blackout. In the fog on Sat night he wrung his ankle on the pavement and fell hitting his head on the wall. He has cut his head and sprained his ankle.

Dec 28th
Learnt today with horror that the new M-O news sheet costs £1 per year. Neither Jenny or I could possibly afford all that now the war is on. We are genuinely hard up. Everyone in the motor business is. We cannot afford a copy between us either. I feel disappointed but I hope someone will take pity on us and send us an occasional free copy . . .

Evacuation

The official evacuation schemes made arrangements for
schoolchildren to be evacuated with their teachers.
Destinations were not known in advance and parents
usually had to wait until their children had arrived before
they heard where they had gone. The scheme was
voluntary but parents in the large cities were strongly
advised to take advantage of it for their children's safety.
Arrangements were also made for the evacuation of
expectant mothers and mothers with children under five.
One and a half million people were evacuated to reception
areas in the first week of the war. People offering homes
(billets) to the evacuees were paid a weekly allowance:
10s. 6d. for a single child or child over 16, 8s. 6d. for each
extra child and mother. Many hosts felt it wasn't enough.
Prices varied a good deal in wartime but in 1941, for
example, the following prices would have been typical: a
2 lb loaf of bread cost 4d., a pint of milk 4½d., butter was
1s. 7d. per lb, cheese 1s. 1d. per lb.

There were considerable problems of adjustment
between the evacuees and the hosts, mostly related to
different class backgrounds and differences between
urban and rural life. For a long time after war was
declared there was no bombing and people felt it was not
worth putting up with either the separation of family
members or, in the case of adults, the inconvenience and
distress of living in someone else's home. By spring 1940 a
million evacuees were back home.

The next two items present very different versions of
the evacuation: the first, written by a friend to a
Mass-Observer, describes quite briefly one woman's
dissatisfaction with the experience; the second, by a young
woman teacher evacuated from Walthamstow to St
Albans with her school, is considerably more positive,
seeing the evacuation of children as a wonderful

opportunity for them to enjoy the countryside and a more privileged way of life.

> Greenford
> Middlesex

Dear Mrs Street,

I am writing to let you know that I have left Dunstable and am at my sister's. I couldn't stick it any longer. We were treated like bits of dirt by the locals as though it wasn't bad enough going through what we did to get there. We started at 11 o'clock and did not get to Dunstable until 5 – after five changes by train and bus and standing on the curb in Luton for an hour and twenty minutes. We arrived at a skating rink and then were picked out so you can guess what some poor devils were like who had four or five children. They were still there on the Sunday afternoon and then eight families were put in an empty house and different people gave them bits of furniture. I admit some of them were a bit too much with their hair in curlers and overalls but we are not all the same.

I was lucky I was in a very nice house and spotlessly clean. It was a Warden's Post but I felt in the way as they were so busy and if I had stayed there I could only see my husband about every four weeks but down here I can see him two or three times a week (I hope).

Well, I hope you and Mr Street are keeping well. Robert is in his glory here and looks as though he has had a month's holiday and I feel much happier here.

Best love, Agnes.

Putting up with 'Eva', December 1939

On Friday September 1st our school assembled at 8 a.m. and we kept the children happily occupied until lunchtime. After this picnic meal the children were got ready for the journey to an unknown destination. We assembled in the playground at 2 p.m. with our little infants heading the army of evacuees. Some of them had packs almost as big as themselves but a helping hand was always forthcoming. The marshalling along the roads to the station and all the transport was excellent. The children were very excited on the railway journey and the barley sugars which we teachers had found room for in our ruc-sacs were a great boon. Never again can I look a barley sugar in the face without thinking of 'Eva' – might as well be friendly as we don't know how long we may have to put up with her. At the end of the train journey, we assembled at the station 'somewhere in Hertfordshire' and were then told to wait. As our children are only babies – 5–7 years old, we told them to sit on their ruc-sacs on the platform. This had just been tarred and we discovered the ruc-sacs were agreeably patterned when we got up for our next marching orders. We then got on buses and were taken to a school which became the distributing depot. At 4.30 p.m. with two billeting officers we set forth with 30 of our kiddies for the job of billeting. We were dumped at the end of a road where several inhabitants came out of their houses and 'picked what they liked'. Little did they know that a leopard cannot be judged by his spots – although he may only be a five-year-old. Thereupon the billeting officer requested me to inspect the bedrooms which the children were to occupy. Never before had this unusual inspection been my lot and I regret to say that the hasty observation was not as thorough as I would have liked, but, as time proved, the truth will out and so will many other things.

May I say how exceedingly kind were these people. Just a little example of this was shown when a lady, outside whose house we had been dumped, furnished all the kiddies with slices of bread and jam! It was at 9.45 p.m. when we managed to get the last child of our batch settled for the night and he, poor chappie, was in a state of collapse. During those memorable five hours the weather clerk had decided that a little rain would perhaps afford a little light relief. Needless to say we had no time to consider whether it damped our feelings or not. I was fortunate in securing a billet that night with people who, having passed us in their car when we were leaving the distributing depot, had relieved the kiddies of their ruc-sacs and ration-bags (these consisted of 1 tin Ideal Milk, 1 tin bully beef, 1 packet biscuits, 1 bar of chocolate). These kind people followed us around in their car and relieved the kiddies of their belongings whilst waiting to be fixed up with a billet. It seemed incredible to me that no arrangements had been made for teachers and we had to depend on people's kindness of heart to supply us with accommodation for the night. Ah well, our quest was ended at 10 p.m. and when I arrived at my billet I set to and wrote off new addresses to the Walthamstow parents. The day had been a memorable one indeed. We can just hope and pray that it may never be necessary to have a repetition of the experiences.

The next and following days proved to be full of district-visiting, interviewing foster-parents, explaining the whys and wherefores of difficult children – various purchases (chiefly mackintosh sheets!) – correspondence with Walthamstow parents. We gathered the children together at least once a day and took them for walks. They just revelled in the glorious sunshine – what a Godsend it was during those difficult days. Since that first week we have taken the children out for rambles in the country and their knowledge of Nature is unlimited. All the nature lessons we had endeavoured to take in the classroom had suddenly become real. The kiddies are fascinated by all the beauty of nature and their keen observation and interest astonishes us daily. Never before have they had the opportunities that this life has given them of admiring beauty and wonder of God's Handwork.

After the first month when we had no school assemblies we were able to share a school with the local people and have had alternate weeks on morning and afternoon shifts. When we are not in school pegging away at the 3 Rs, we become the Evacuee Hikers. This exercise in the beautiful fresh air has made a difference to the health and well-being of these children. It has been of great interest and disappointment to record daily the absence of children who evacuated with us. May I say that most of the children have returned to the vulnerable areas not because they wanted to but because the parents so desired. Those who are with us now are staunch supporters in their little way of 'Eva' and will, we hope, support her for as long as it becomes necessary. During the day many tasks have been the teacher's lot. We, as a school party, did not take any helpers with us so we have had such duties as: taking children (and sitting for 2 hours) to the clinic, being very tactful and tolerant with foster-parents, washing children who come to school a little the worse for wear, and attending to their education. In spite of this, some of us found time to do a little voluntary clerical work at the local Food Control Office so 'Life has been full of a number of things, that I'm sure we have [all] been as happy as Kings'.

Before we evacuated, we teachers became absolutely tired of the very mention of the word 'evacuation'. There was nothing that had been overlooked with regard to reorganisation and administration in order that this big undertaking should be carried out smoothly and effectively. It was not until we came in contact with the rural councils that we congratulated ourselves on the magnificent efficiency and administration of Walthamstow's Education committee. We had had so much, but not too much, organisation and preparation that we were rather taken aback at the apparent lack of it in the reception area. It has taken 3 months to negotiate proceedings which will furnish us with a hall which is to be our school as soon as possible. As yet, this hall is not habitable, but when it is we shall be very grateful to have our own roof, which incidentally we shall share with another evacuated infant school. We have great plans with this 'Hall of Education'. We are thinking of asking Mr Chambers to advise us about the small patch of garden at the rear. This leads me to my next point of discussion regarding deficiencies that might have been remedied. I think they might have been overcome if the evacuated staffs would have got in touch with the reception areas *before* evacuation took place – more preparation for evacuees could have been made. It would have been better, too, if more definite instructions could have been given regarding the governing body from whom evacuated staffs could take orders. The difficulties arise probably because we are employed by one council and are working in the town of another. I think that if the home council of all evacuated schools had set up an office and medical staff in each reception area so that we had our own officers to represent us, the organisation might have been considerably simplified. We have with us *one* of Walthamstow's nurses who has the colossal job of visiting all the schools evacuated in this area.

For the children who have been billeted in better houses than their own, I can see that a probable result of evacuation, on their return, will be severe dissatisfaction. They will be very critical of all their mother does – will demand better clothes, more attention and maybe more expensive food. They will return home, having enjoyed the freedom and beauty of the countryside, to the drab London streets. Having tasted of the fruits of such a good life, they will be very loath to settle down again to their own routine of home. The foster-parents may have spoilt them and lavished far more love and attention than was their wont. For many of the children this evacuation has put them on their feet and has developed that magnificent independent spirit which will greatly help them to make a success of life in later years. It has revealed to them (those kind people who have taken them into their homes) that life does not serve us all alike with the luxuries money can buy. They have been astounded at the poor clothes these evacuees brought away with them. They have expressed surprise at their habits and environment. Perhaps evacuation has done good in that it has revealed these conditions under which many of our children have been reared. May great improvements be the outcome of these revelations. We London teachers have also discovered that rural schools have not got the facilities for modern education which we value and enjoy so much at home.

The children's education is allowed to go on and a normal disciplined life is possible. For the non-evacuated children they tell their own tale. There are far fewer disturbing elements of warfare in a reception area and the child is not continually reminded of the unnatural life which has suddenly been thrust upon us. Quite a new and different education has become the child's gift which has taken the form of appreciation in a real way of the beauty and lessons of nature. The child's mentality is not warped in any way and no severe effects will show themselves in later life. As yet, not having experienced any air raids we cannot vouchsafe that the reception area will be exempt from such disturbing influences but we can take a sporting chance. Should a family be divided up during these times? I say 'No!' but civilis-ation must go on and it is better to preserve the buds of our manhood and womanhood than have a nation of people whose mental and physical suffering might never be eradicated.

Let us build up an A1 nation, not to be fodder for the battlefield but to be representatives at the discussion table of the modern Utopian Europe!

THREE

WAR BECOMES
A WAY OF LIFE

The early part of 1940 must have been a strange time to live through. Many of the children and mothers who had been evacuated in the first panic returned home. Although the pain of war would have seemed very remote from most people's lives, there were small everyday reminders that the situation was abnormal – the blackout, for example, and then the introduction of food rationing in January 1940. During these early months, Mass-Observation spent most of its time studying the impact of various forms of propaganda and government information, particularly public response to films and the news. They were also especially interested in women's response to the war and argued cogently that the government had to take account of women's needs separately from those of men in order to mobilise them fully behind the war effort. A grant from Mrs Sieff (of Marks & Spencer) enabled them to start studying women's views, particularly those of the woman at home. The two reports in this section, the first on women's organisations and the second on women's morale generally, resulted from this attention.

The mobilisation of the labour force had a curious effect on women workers. The transition to war production had resulted in some groups of women who had been employed in light or 'inessential' industry, losing their jobs. Ironically, unemployment among women rose during the early part of the war. Women who wanted to join the various organisations (for example, the Women's Land Army) found that their services could not be used because the organisations were not geared up for the numbers applying. The women's section of the Army, the Auxiliary Territorial Service, was forced to expand rapidly to cope with volunteers. This caused all sorts of hiccoughs in the process (no uniforms ready, inadequate accommodation, administrative chaos and poorly trained officers). In general the country was not at all prepared to utilise women's energies effectively.

Any complacency which may have been engendered by the Phoney War period gave way when Hitler invaded Belgium, Luxemburg and Holland in May 1940. The historic evacuation of British and Allied troops from Dunkirk took place shortly after Belgium had surrendered at the end of May. On 14 June the Germans entered Paris. A full-scale air attack on south-east England (the Battle of Britain) in August was the prelude to the blitz. By the end of August, German bombs were being dropped on British targets.

6

M-O Report No. 26: Women in wartime, January 1940

This report was written by a member of M-O's full-time staff, Stella Schofield, who had joined the organisation in 1939. Her conclusions are based on interviews she carried out with the officials of the women's organisations late in 1939 on the impact of war on their membership.

This war has presented women immediately – and much earlier than in the 1914–18 struggle – with acute, far-reaching problems. Now it is not only their men who 'go' or who are liable to 'go'. Too often their children have already gone, or other people's children have been admitted under difficult circumstances into their homes. Evacuation and Reception have set up dislocations in family life which are psychic as well as physical, and the woman in the street is beginning to think there is a lot to be said for 'sticking together the same as we did last time'. Yet she accepts the war as an inevitable event: we saved 'peace' by a miracle at Munich, Hitler obviously let us down since then, and in September 1939 we had no alternative but to stand up to him. Underlying, deepsearching effects can be judged by the remarks of a working class woman who said: 'I used to believe in God, but now I don't know I'm sure. Look at a man like Hitler. It does seem we've got to have a war.' This is the type of woman, unattached to any organisation, at the mercy of rising prices and the hazards of employment – there has been a severe increase in unemployment amongst wage-earning and salaried women since August – who is bearing the brunt of this home-front war, and this largely is the fatalistic spirit in which she bears it. In addition our investigations have shown that the blackout causes her special uneasiness and must be reckoned as an important factor increasing nervous tension and lending an almost nightmare atmosphere to the prospect of future winters of war.

Inside their organisations women are more consciously critical, more questioningly aware of the war processes. They find themselves once more precipitated into world war by a man-monopolised society. It would be idle to speculate whether or not the present situation could have been avoided had women held executive government positions – there are, of course, women who believe this – but it is very much to the point to realise that, however unorganised the mass of women may be today, they were far less organised in the last war. And all the evidence goes to show they are hanging on like death to their voluntary organisations. That they are conscious of not being used as they might be used to advantage by the authorities is indicated in the statement of the December bulletin of the Women's Freedom League, the surviving militant arm of the suffrage movement. 'Women as responsible citizens,' they write, 'are taking a big share in the work of civil defence, but it cannot be claimed that the Government is making anything like a full use of the Woman Power of the country – in the Departments, on Committees, in posts or in general works, where the knowledge, aptitude and experience of women would be most valuable.' The 10,156 professional women registered as unemployed with their Employment Exchanges would seem to support this claim.

In reviewing women's organisations and their wartime reactions one realises how widespread are the informed interests which women have developed during their short period of emancipation since the last war, and how important a factor for the formulation of public opinion and the creation of civilian morale they have become. Let us consider some of those which, if not actually formed since 1918, have grown to maturity since that date.

The National Council of Women with its membership of 13,101 drawn largely from the middle and upper middle classes and therefore representing an educated type, its branches in 83 towns and its 138 affiliated societies, dates back to philanthropic efforts begun in 1876, but was only constituted in its present form in 1920.

The National Federation of Women's Institutes, representing 338,000 country women – a more naive, less academic type, came into being in 1915 as a direct result of the wartime need for women in country districts to combine in the production and preservation of food. The parallel organisation for townswomen, the National Union of Townswomen's Guilds, which flourishes particularly well in the heterogeneous soil of new housing estates, did not materialise until 1933 although it claims descent from the women's suffrage societies of the last century. It now comprises over 544 branches with an average membership of between 10 and 20 per branch. Each of these organisations noted a feeling of paralysis amongst their members at the outbreak of war. Branch secretaries left to do war work; local halls were commandeered by the military, by ARP authorities, by evacuated children. Office staffs were reduced, premises cut down, publications appeared drastically diminished in size. The National Council of Women considered the question of cancelling their annual conference due in October but this was held, although on a much shortened programme, and the effect was to rally the branches. The President made it clear in her address that as an organisation they should, whilst occupying themselves with war work, not lose sight of their peacetime ideals. By the end of November they were as busy as ever, holding as many as nine sectional committees in London in one week.

In the September paralysis many Women's Institutes considered closing down but like the branches of the NCW they too rallied into renewed activity. Indeed they had little choice. Armies of evacuees were let loose from the towns and the broadside brunt of their approach monopolised WI members for many days. Nor has their work ceased after the first settling in, for much reshuffling had to be done, then parents began to visit their children and different kinds of provision had to be made. Many Institutes now have their regular 'evening' for entertaining evacuated mothers, regular Sunday 'teas' for visiting parents. To read the Institute magazine for this period is to review a positive saga of the evacuation – or rather of the reception, for it is the country folk who are in the position to tell the other side of the story. This impact of town on country has made a permanent impression on the country woman's mind. The particular form it has taken – the showing up of certain deficiencies in town life and also in government administration – has gone a long way towards banishing her sense of inferiority. She finds that things are not necessarily done better in the towns, and the town mother can be shown a thing or two by her country sister. The practical motherliness of the country woman may, and certainly has, prompted her to enormous sacrifice on behalf of evacuated children, but as one of them rather succinctly remarked, the evacuation scheme had obviously been organised by men. That she can accept the blackout's nuisances with good humour is shown in the light articles they inspired in their magazine. But the breaking up of families is for her a matter for acute uneasiness. The secretary regrets that the problems of receptionists have not received anything like the press publicity given to the smooth running of the actual evacuation. It is interesting to note that the problems of evacuation and questions of the effect of the war on children seriously occupy the Townswomen's Guilds and are the type of matter suggested for discussion 'as we sew and knit' at branch meetings. The war has given these two organisations a dramatic common interest.

We meet again the educated type of woman in the Soroptimist Clubs comprising 3,500 professional women. They guard the professional status of women, and carry on many forms of social service through their 70 branches. They find that the war has increased the need for such work. The Sheffield branch, for instance, has recently opened a home for old women. Social work has also occupied the 6,000 Toc H League of Women Helpers more busily than ever since September.

The lowest social class of women I have found organised in the 600 Women's Mutual Service Clubs, average membership per club – 20. These were begun by local Social Service Councils a few years ago to help the wives of the unemployed. The women pool the experiences of their poverty-ridden lives to mutual advantage. Here again the war has intensified rather than diminished the desire and determination to keep together for such benefits.

There are also organisations with a specific educational appeal like the Women's Electrical Association sprung up since the last war. This organisation has 85 branches spread throughout the country and a membership of close on 10,000. Interest has been so stimulated since the war that membership is actually on the increase.

Foremost amongst women's organisations which have sprung up during, or in anticipation of, the present war, is the Women's Voluntary Services for Civil Defence co-ordinating, under the chairmanship of the Marchioness of Reading, 59 voluntary organisations and meeting for the first time as long ago as May 1938. They have enlisted the following number of women in the different services: ARP 186,000; transport 37,000; nursing auxiliaries 63,000; hospital services 86,000; evacuation 148,000; canteens 8,000; Auxiliary Fire Service 5,000. The number of women enlisted in the military services runs into some thousands, but the authorities do not favour the publication of such information.

The Women's Land Army is the only women's civilian service under direct government control. Under the honorary directorship of Lady Denman, 30 civil servants drawn from the Ministry of Agriculture and Fisheries conduct its business from the sanctuary of her home at Balcombe Place in Sussex. This department has come in for some criticism which Lady Denman is well able to meet. Figures show that 30,000 girls enrolled enthusiastically in the Land Army at the outbreak of war. Of these 4,000 have been trained and 2,000 are in regular employment. According to the figures issued at the end of November enrolments numbered 18,650 and the total number in training in colleges or at Farm Institutes was 1,100. Lady Denman explains the discrepancy between the first enrolments and the present 'live' register by admitting that 'no one foresaw that the blackout and the shortage of petrol would throw out of work men like mechanical garage hands who found employment on the land as tractor drivers'. Hence an inevitable unemployment. Lady Denman considers the 'wastage' of those who have dropped off immediately after or during their training, is partly psychological: in the last war, if a woman began work on the land and discovered she didn't like it, she carried on because the incentive of her country's need kept her going. She felt that she was trying to win the war. Today that need hasn't yet become so obvious and if a woman disliked land work she didn't stick to it but sought more congenial employment elsewhere.

The Women's Group on Problems Arising from Evacuation is the immediate outcome of the war situations on the civilian front and is therefore an important indication of women's spontaneous realisation of the need for measures to supplement government policies and of their prompt determination to supply that need. With the Rt Hon. Margaret Bondfield as chairman, it comprises 20 voluntary organisations – industrial, social, religious and educational, a large proportion of which represent women's bodies: Women's Section of the British Legion, Women's Mutual Service Clubs, National Council of Women, National Union of Townswomen's Guilds, National Women's Citizens Association, National Federation of Soroptimist Clubs, National Federation of Women's Institutes, Standing Joint Committees of Women's Industrial Organisations, Toc H League of Women Helpers, The Church groups, Women's Christian Association, and the Women Public Health Officers' Association. The four sub-committees under which their advisory work is being carried out deal with such problems as clothing, education, publicity and personal hygiene.

A further interesting outlet which women have found in this war is in the Citizens' Advice Bureaux where they supply between 60 and 70 per cent of the personnel. Here they deal first-hand with intricate human problems: old women left alone through the evacuation of neighbours, suffering from fear and loneliness, children evacuated to unsuitable places, young girls wanting 'soldier sweethearts', rent problems and problems arising out of new legislation. Noticeable too is the fact that women for the most part bring forward the problems.

It is clear, I think, that women organised into units consciously participating in public affairs, suffering as individuals and as members of their various organisations the immensely diverse and widespread repercussions of the present situation, represent, or should represent, a force to be seriously reckoned with in the war. Their detestation of war and their desire for improved conditions of life are fully exemplified in the objects of their societies, and these they are determined to preserve in the face of tremendous odds. The breaking up of families, the new mingling of population, while temporarily dislocating individual branches will undoubtedly produce a compensation of new life and new functions.

7

Muriel Green's diary for 1940

Muriel and her sister Jenny were still working at the
family garage in 1940. The 1939–40 winter was harsh and
exacerbated the shortages of certain goods – fuel and meat
especially. Their closeness to the Norfolk coast made them
feel especially vulnerable to invasion but the main
evidence of warfare was the sound of (British) guns and
the crash landings of (British) planes in their locality. The
following are extracts from her diary between January
and May, and from her instalment for December 1940. The
original diary is continuous.

Jan 20th
Spent morning cooking. We always make Yorkshire tea-cakes
with yeast now because they have no butter in them like other
cakes. A man who lives on the beach told us we must go and look
at the sea, as it is frozen, so in the afternoon Jenny and I walked
down. We walked along the beach. It is a most extraordinary
sight. Just like an Arctic scene. For about 10 yds along the edge
the sea is frozen to a white hard snow in the waves. We talked to
lots of people and no one has ever known in memory it to have
been like that before. We walked back by the marsh and watched
the skaters on a sheet of ice. I wish exceedingly that I could
borrow some skates and try. Mrs A. told me she thought Mrs W.
who broke her wrist skating last week would lend me hers . . .

Jan 22nd
. . . In the evening Jenny and I went to a committee meeting of the
WEA at old Mr L.'s house to discuss our next course of lectures.
We also discussed everything else under the sun: the war, apples,
psychology, jam-making, pacifism, H. G. Wells' newest book, local
government, and newspapers to give only a few topics of the

discussion. We stayed 2 hrs and the vicar's son and the shoemaker brought us home . . .

Jan 31st
We have run out of coal. We have no garage fire and are burning wood in the house. We have had no meat this week, as the butcher has not come. He had hardly any last week. A customer brought us 2 rabbits on Monday, so we are not starving, but lots of people, my great aunt among them, have had no meat. Ever so many have had no coal all the week. Arnold shot us 2 pigeons in the wood opposite.

Feb 3rd
. . . This morning I went with Arnold [the mechanic employed at the garage] to Lynn with the car, an Oldsmobile, to take some things to a storage warehouse at which the man told Arnold that the ARP had sent for the boss as they had received warning of raiders 30 miles away. We went round with the car shopping and forgot all about the warning. I saw a lot of girls who I went to school with and hoped that seeing me with A. (he's very fat) and the Oldsmobile they would not think I'd married a war profiteer!

Feb 6th
. . . We yesterday received the first *US* [a printed news sheet produced by M-O]. I like it but hope it will grow bigger. We decided today to stretch a point and have ordered *War Begins at Home* [M-O publication] from the newsagent's. I had given up buying any books except the sixpenny lines but we decided to pay half each. Also sent subscription for *US* . . .

Feb 9th
Much wailing and sobbing because Mother had our cat Henry Hall shot. He has never been a successful cat and had worms and diarrhoea very badly and an insatiable appetite, so Mother said we weren't to cure him again as perhaps we should not have enough food for him soon. Perhaps she is right but it seems a shame – he was so sweet sometimes.

Feb 10th
Mon anniversaire et j'ai dix-neuf ans! I received *War Begins at*

Home. We are very pleased with it and are especially gratified because we have four observations printed in it. I have one on evacuation and Jenny two, and one we both claim because we both put it. The only snag about it is we daren't lend the book to anybody in the village now because we are afraid it would 'get round' whom we had written about and it is not very complimentary to village behaviour . . .

Mother said she would have had Happy the old cat shot as well only the man with the gun could not find him. Happy had 2 abscesses on his head from fighting but as I have cured others before now he is to remain as he does not eat hardly anything . . .

Feb 18th
This morning we were laying in bed and Mother called out what's that noise. I listened and heard machine-gun fire, lay in bed and listened and heard burst after burst of guns. This was about eight o'clock. Mother called out, 'Do you think they are landing on the beach?' She then said, 'If they come I shall get under the bed and lie low.' Jenny said, 'I think I shall be more of a success with them if I stay in bed!' We all laughed and after a time it stopped and I went to sleep again. Lots of times during the morning we heard it again, and lots of aeroplanes went over, Spitfires included . . .

Feb 27th
Arnold announced he was going to join the ARP as he has been asked to. He says, 'Other people have got free water-boots, tin hat and lovely gas mask and I don't see why I should not join if there's something to be got out of it.'

We have not had any bacon for about 3 weeks as the last we bought was so salty and objectionable as well as so dear (2/2 per lb). Mother said she would not buy any more. We are not being very skimping with our sugar. As Jenny and I don't take it in tea the ration just about allows for the rest and then we have the hoard. Mother makes Arnold bring his sugar in a tin for his afternoon cup of tea, as he usually has 3 spoonfuls in his big cup. As for butter, we know some cows . . . !

Feb 28th
Afternoon went for a walk in the rain to look for parish magazine

in next village church, but could not find any inside the church door as advised by H. Willcock for M-O. We decided as we walked there is so many mucky smells in our village, you never would smell a gas attack from some of the other odours in the country. (There's no drainage or sewage here) . . .

Sat 2nd March
We (J and I) got up early and caught the 9 train to Cambridge [to attend a WEA meeting]. Arrived 11 and until 1 walked round the shops and some of the colleges. We always go and look at King's Chapel, but now is not so nice as the glass has been removed from the best windows. Cambridge was packed, we could not get near any coffee in the 'Dorothy' cafe, the atmosphere of which was simply stifling and bang full of undergrads. We looked in every bookshop window we ran into to see if *War Begins at Home* was there, but regret we did not see it at all. Bought a copy of *Peace News* off an undergrad in the street, who was delighted to sell one. At one o'clock we went along to our friends to lunch. Very nice although the lady explained it was only a wartime diet with margarine in everything. The man who is very humorous, and always dresses eccentrically was wearing a checked breeches suit with yellow striped waistcoat, a navy blue fisherman necked jumper and is growing a beard. His joke is he is not yet quite sure whether he is going to do agricultural work, or go on a mine-sweeper, but is getting ready for either. At half past two we went to the Art School to where the meeting was. At 4.15 we all trooped out and walked down the street to the 'Dorothy' and had tea on big tables in the Oak Room there. We went back to the Art School at five and looked to see what books were being sold in front. They included mostly Penguin books including *The Press*, Wickham Steed, *You and The Refugee*, Norman Angel & Buxton, *Finland* by J. Hampden Jackson and *Britain* by M-O. We spoke to the county organiser during the interval and he told us to go and sit by his case in the back row when the meeting rebegan so as we could arrange about our next lectures. The rest of the meeting I haven't the faintest idea about what was said as he talked and wrote notes and fidgeted so as we could not attend, being at the back. The meeting finished at 6.45 and we went to the station. We had about 10 mins to wait and so we walked around and studied the Hitler secrecy posters . . .

Wed 6th

At 8.30 Jenny called up the staircase, 'Did you hear a noise last night?' 'No.' 'An aeroplane crashed and burnt out on the common.' 'No.' 'Yes, Mr K. just told me, he was coming home from the parochial meeting and they all saw it fall, and followed to see. Burnt right out. About 8.30 p.m.' He told her how they had dashed to the place, and all stood round and watched it burn. Then someone stirred the fire and the guns began to go off. All the crowd ran away as fast as they could, while the bullets whizzed by them. I wonder some of them did not get shot. When I went in the shop at 11, A. said, 'Fancy, them silly rotters on them searchlights never put them up to show that there poor devil where he were. He threw out a flare and they never answered' . . .

Thur 7th

Morning I went to Hunstanton and took the money to the bank . . . I saw a sale of furniture was about to happen in the town hall, and I saw a lady I knew going in, so I went with her. I saw about the first 20 lots sold. Auctions fascinate me. The auctioneer announced before he began to sell, that the air raid siren was to be sounded for practice at 12. Just as I got outside it went off, I had never heard one before. It is a very weird wail and sounds like an ill animal. After lunch Fred turned up. He has had tonsillitis and had a week's leave since last Wed. He suggested we should go for a cycle ride, so we decided to go and look for the smashed aeroplane. We did and found it in a field. There was only burnt twisted metal-work and bits of it were all over the field. I picked up a bolt and put it in my pocket. Lots more people were looking. All of a sudden 2 aircraftsmen ran along. They said they weren't supposed to let anyone come close, and if their corporal came back he would be furious. They imparted to F. that under a parachute laying there was the pilot's foot they had just found. They said they had run away to watch another plane which had just landed about a mile away, but as there are so many dykes on the marsh they could not get over to it, and they seemed to have landed safely so they thought they had better continue to guard the old wreck. We could see the other plane in the distance and they asked if we knew the best way to get to it. Then the corporal was seen running down the field, and one RAF chap said, 'Here comes the boss, now there'll be a row.' Corporal: 'What's all that crowd?'

'How could I keep all these women back, sir?' 'I understand, I've tried myself.' Women and RAFs all laugh. 'You aren't taking any bits away with you, I hope.' 'No.' The crowd start dispersing. Fred starts going into details with the corp. and 2 airmen about the engine, plane, etc. The corp said, 'There wouldn't be a piece left at all if this was a jerry, they would have taken it all for souvenirs.' I thought F. would talk all day about how the poor fellows died, details of the crash and the works of the plane. F. picked up a live bullet and put it in his pocket much to my annoyance. I am terrified of cartridges and guns and always suspect they will explode, and he always has the gun and shooting mania.

At last we got away and cycled down the lane to the nearest point to the other plane, and walked ever so far across marshland and it still seemed in the distance. An army officer and a private were following behind, and caught us up and asked if they were going the right way to the aeroplane. We said we thought so and walked the rest of the way across planks over creeks and bogs to the plane. 2 airmen were sitting on the wings and 2 women were just arriving with a pot of tea, cups and saucers, a tin of milk, sandwiches and cakes and giving them to the airmen. About 6 soldiers came and saluted the officer and talked with them and they went off back again. 5 grammar school boys and about 7 other small boys and girls were rushing round the plane and climbing on the wings and peeping inside. 2 young men stood watching and a girl (16) wearing trousers was trying to attract the attention of some, who were talking to the airmen.

We all stood and watched them eat and drink the tea the women had set out for them. The propeller of the plane was smashed and a pool of oil was running out of the body somewhere. The children were swarming all over it and running round and saying what certain parts of it were. The 2 women kept telling the 2 airmen, who were not hurt but rather shaken, about the poor young pilot killed the night before last and telling them how lucky they were to be all right. One of them says, 'We should never have landed her in the dark, as it was we only just missed that ditch.' One woman starts to go home and they thank her for the food and she invites them to come and see her if ever they come to her village. She asks them where they live and one says Yarmouth and one Yorkshire. F. and the other young men look all around plane. One of the airmen told me the pilot had gone to the village to phone, and tells me which aerodrome they have come from. More and more children keep arriving and are climbing all over the plane's 'back'. One of the airmen asks them to get off with no effect and so the other orders them to, and runs after some of them. Then they begin to ask questions *re* the way it works and how they drive it and what it feels like to ride in it. He shows them inside, points out various things and makes a hooting noise with something which he tells is the warning noise for landing, and asks the woman if she heard them do that as they landed. She says she did not, but tells exactly what she did hear and see. Also just what she saw when the first plane came down, and how she thought it was an air raid and then realised that a plane had crashed, and felt she should go as she knew it was near, but her little boy (6) was so frightened she dare not leave him. She then goes on to tell me how the other woman dashed and told her about this one and they ran to the plane and were the first there. She saw the boy with red hair and thought about her son as he has red hair and asked them if they would like some food and drink which they jumped at, so she and the other woman went and fetched some. The girl in trousers I saw was chasing around one of the grammar school boys and she lands in the arms of one of the other young men who seats her on the wing of the plane. The grammar school boy says, '2 plane crashes in 2 days, if there's 2 there's bound to be 3 (a superstition), it would have been safer if you had evacuated to London. You see we see life in here.' This all to the girl. 'Yes, I wish we had, we thought it would be so nice and safe in a quiet little place near the sea.' The grammar school boy brings out a bolt and a piece of metal from his pocket. 'This is a souvenir of the first aeroplane, and this is a bit off this one. I was the first person to get here when this one crashed . . .'

Fri 8th

. . . At dinnertime we had the midday music on the radio in the Oldsmobile in the garage. When at 2 the schools programme was announced Jenny went to switch it off and she gave a wild whoop of delight and yelled, 'Listen! Tom Harrisson.' I rushed to listen. We always have been very curious about why the cannibals did not eat Mr Harrisson when he lived with them, so were very interested in the talk and intend to listen again next week. We also were curious *re* voice of above, and what on earth sort of a person would go and live with cannibals, so part of the mystery surrounding same was solved as he sounds quite normal and cultured!

Tues 12th

. . . Afternoon some customers whose car A. drives asked me to go for a drive with them. We first went to Hunstanton and back round by Segeford, Houghton, Harpley and then A. triumphantly drew the car up at Raynham aerodrome and thought he done us a good turn and given us a treat. I am not a bit interested in aerodromes, they all look alike to me, but A. has the mania. He pointed out with great pride all the guns, petrol dumps, wireless station etc. and we were made to know exactly which sort of plane every one was. He parked the car, and said in his holidays he spent hours up there. I thought we should be arrested under the Official Secrets Act soon if he insisted on stopping. At last we got him away. It seems so awful to think that all that development and building can be done so quickly for destruction and wars, yet if any social developments and improvements are to be done it takes years and no end of talk first . . .

Mon 18th

. . . Spring cleaning pantry all afternoon. Very grieved to find Alec (tortoise) is dead. We had had him 3 years and seemed a permanent institution and he did not eat anything anyone else could have eaten. The cold this winter must have got him down, unless he had just heard about the war and the shock killed him!

Sun 7th

. . . Afternoon – B.R. a boy who used to live here and went to school with Jenny came with a friend of his whom he introduced us to last summer. They wanted to take us out to tea and a ride in his friend's car, but we could not leave the shop and so we invited them to stop and talk to us instead which they did. At teatime Mother asked them to tea and Mike F. and Jenny had tea in the house with Mother and Mr and Mrs F. who had turned up, and B.R. and I had tea in the office. During tea B.R. and I had a very deep conversation on religion. He is religious, but v. genuine about it and I admired what he said, and he persuaded me to consider lots of things which I had never really faced up to before.

I like him very much, it is unusual to get any young person to seriously discuss religious questions. They usually fight shy of discussing it. He registered yesterday but so far is in reserved occ. His friend is very jolly, amusing, and Jenny said he agreed with her in matters both political and religious. Mother liked them both and consented to us going with them out in the evening after we shut the garage. We went to Hunstanton and walked along the prom and cliff about a mile. We tried to get some coffee, but nowhere in Hunstanton is open for non-alcoholic drinks. I observed that one of the young men's gas masks was in the car.

Tues 9th

I was astounded to hear via Jenny and A. of the invasion of Norway this morning. I see now why we laid the mines. It seemed such an extraordinary thing for Hitler to do. I suppose he had to do something quick, but I didn't realise he was getting so desperate. It worries me as to what he will do next. He seems to get nearer. Jenny thought of packing a bag, also A., but he can't see why it would be any safer the other side of England. Mr M. came in the afternoon. He says he thinks they will pack their 'go-cart'. He said he would have to take that to put the dog on, I said why not let her go on a lead, but he said she is such a bad walker she would want to come back by the time they got to the next village. Jenny went to see his wife, and she had hung out an old thick coat to air on the line. She said she had brought it out to flee with if necessary, as she says you want to look scruffy so that if a fund for refugees is raised you will be more pitied. We decided it would be better to wear your best clothes though.

Wed 17th

. . . Morning – overheard a conversation of Mr M. and A. Mr M. said that all Germans were dirty swines and the whole lot ought to be exterminated. I have argued with him about that sort of imbecile talk before and I have the idea he was only saying it so as I heard to annoy [me] as he knows it makes me wild. A. came in the office after he had gone and said, 'Mr M. is feeling very drastic today. Such silly talk about all Germans ought to be killed. I bet you could kill off a dozen and get rid of all the trouble.' I did not ask him which dozen he would have killed. Later in the morning a traveller came. He said trade was picking up now, and they thought the repair business would increase because of fewer new cars. He went on to the war and said there was no doubt that Germany would have to pay for this afterwards. I was just about to deliver him a lecture on the impossibilities of indemnities and reparations and how I considered them partly to blame for the rise of Nazism when Mother sailed in and interrupted and changed the conversation. I felt pretty hopeless (after these 2 men's opinions) about there ever being any lasting peace. Both wanted another 'worser' Versailles treaty, and neither have apparently seen the follies of that sort of peace. Evening went to last WEA class of this winter. I am sorry they are over. This was so interesting and I thoroughly enjoyed all the course.

Fri 19th

Afternoon – Jenny and I went to Lynn. Did some shopping and walked round all Lynn, and picked up some leaflets for M-O. In one shop I saw a leaflet pinned up for a lecture which was over and so I pulled it down and put it in my bag much to amazement and curiosity of 2 shop girls. We went to W. H. Smith's and Sons best and biggest bookshop in Lynn, to buy a Penguin book, and asked if they had got *War Begins at Home* just to see if they had. I did not expect they had as I have never seen it there, and if the girl had produced it I was preparing to say it was too expensive. Anyway she had not got it. Nor *Britain*. I felt insulted and offended with the shop. She did not even seem to have heard of them either which was all the more annoying. I also asked for Oxford pamphlet by a WEA tutor we had. This they hadn't got either. Nor any of his other books . . .

Before we caught the bus home we went in the town library to ask if they had got 'our' book. (We always call it 'ours', hope M-O doesn't mind, but you see we've never had anything we've written in print before and claiming 14 lines and J. 25 lines we feel a proprietary interest in the publication, and that everybody ought to sell and read it.) Were delighted to see that the paper cover was pinned up inside the main entrance with other new books they had bought this month for the library.

Tues 23rd

. . . I had a letter today from Jacques, the new French correspondent. Mother annoyed because I have got a man (bank clerk, 22) and says she knows all Frenchmen are immoral. I said he is likely to be kept a safe distance away. Today lady asked if Jenny and I were twins. Jenny was feeling particularly bumptious only yesterday when she got *US* as she has something in describing herself as 'a young woman' and I have 'garage girl'. She said, 'At last someone realises I'm grown up and not the same age as you. Good old M-O.' I said it was only because they hadn't seen us. People are always asking if we are twins, and we are not a bit alike really, only the same size, and the same coloured hair (hers is naturally curly and mine looks as if it is) and the same figure and both blue eyes. Our complexions are different but J.'s is made up to look pink and mine is pink, but we aren't a bit alike apart from that. She's got big eyes, and I've got a big nose, and she's like Mother and I'm like Father, and we never dress alike. It's so silly of people to think we are the same, when there's 7 yrs between us, especially when they think we are both children about 16. This lady even thought I'm the eldest. It always annoys Jenny when boys of about 16 try and 'get off' with her, and older men and men her age think they are having a lark with her, and being fatherly. Perhaps she'll be glad when she's 40. She'll look about 25 then at the present rate.

Thurs 25th
Went this morning to buy a pair of Lisle stockings in the village. One shop no Lisle and only very few silk and them over 2/11 only. 'It's a job to get any more now. We have only a few.' Went to the other shop in the village. 'We haven't got any nice Lisle only these and they are v. clumsy. They can't make them properly in this country. Those you usually buy are made in Germany, so there won't be any more. Silk stockings we are rationed with, and now there'll be less still.' I came home and took off my stockings altogether 'in the National Interest to save shipping and imports' and also because my legs were too hot anyway. I am quite willing to have bare legs all the summer 'in the National Interest' and I've been doing it for years in my own interests, and other people call it being mean or showing off my legs . . .

Fri 26th
Jenny and I have decided to go for a week each July 27–Aug 10th to the WEA summer school to be held at King's College,

Cambridge. It is only 2 gns a week, so this year it seems a neck to go and stay with friends (even if they ask you) and an ordinary holiday costs a lot more than 2 gns because you would spend more on hotels and amusements, and if you are learning something you will not be extravagantly squandering money, it seems a fairly satisfactory idea, as well as a grand opportunity to stay in college. It sounds so awfully posh. We have always wanted to go, but usually August is too busy for us to be away, but this year we are not expecting such a rush, although the holiday camp proprietor is booked up for August.

It is extraordinarily warm. We have brought out summer frocks [and] discarded stockings again. I never felt so conspicuous in my life as I did when I walked up the village this afternoon in a silk frock and toeless sandals. Every single other person I saw still wore their winter coats and hats although they had their coats undone and looked perspiringly cooking. I caused no end of a sensation looking so summery. When I got home I realised that May was *not* out and therefore no one in the country raises any clout, however hot it is! They bake first. They never wear summer frocks here before July except us. Everyone else stifles in jumpers and skirts or else trousers. No wonder they all suffer from BO . . .

Mon 6th May
. . . Tonight I felt anyhow. Perhaps it is because I am tired. I have the sort of 'don't care if we win or lose' feeling, and is it any good fighting? Is it any good living at all? The sooner we're dead the better feeling. I suppose I shall get over it tomorrow and if the sun shines I shall just forget about the old war and be happy. I can't feel happy when I am thinking about it. The whole show is disheartening. You just have to forget it and be happy doing and talking about other things. Thank God the summer is here!

Tues 14th
Woke up at five. Laid in bed and heard the men go to work at the shingle quarry. I was not listening but overheard the word 'parachutes' by 2 workmen. The next 2 a few minutes later were also talking of invasion of England. Everybody round here has it in their minds about what we shall do if invaded. Most people seem to expect it. Most have v. wild ideas about what we ought to do. Why have we not had instructions? Why not a Public Informa-

tion Leaflet on the subject along with other wartime instructions we have had. After all we had plenty of pre-war instructions on ARP and ever since the war not a word to the civil population on what to do on enemy invasion. I wonder if the government has any plans. Everyone here is wondering if we stay put or hop it if they land. Some think both ways. We keep debating the subject of fleeing or remaining, and do not know whether to pack a case as some people have or not. We have had our handbags ready with bankbooks in since the day war was declared.

Wed 15th
The Germans get nearer. I should not be at all surprised to hear they have attempted to land any day . . . A. says he is going to join the parachute catchers tonight.

Thurs 23rd
Evening played tennis with schoolmaster (26) and grocer's roundsman (29). We had started when the grocers r. came. He said, 'The news is bad tonight, have you heard it?' We said, 'No,' and he told of latest advances then added, 'I think they're going to beat us, don't you?' 'Yes,' said the s.m. We said no more and after a few seconds they said, 'We may as well play tennis while we can.' The g.r. said he was 29 and the s.m. said he was just reserved. One said the Nazis were v. keen on sports, so he expected we'd still be able to play tennis if they did win. The g.r. said he expected general mobilisation for all after this, and the s.m. said he expected an invasion here soon. J. said Mr M. was saying he should paint a swastika under the door knocker ready. We all agreed we shouldn't know what to do if they invade. After that we played tennis, very hard exciting play for 2 hrs and forgot all about the war . . .

> The diary continues as full as ever as the Phoney War period gives way to the Battle of Britain, the evacuation from Dunkirk and the fall of France and on the start of the blitz. At the end of 1940 Muriel wrote the following in her diary:

Tues 31st December
. . . The end of 1940. Who is sorry to see the last of this grim and anxious year? We have certainly lived history this year. How we

have wondered and puzzled what the news in the next week would bring. I'll admit I thought the war was practically done, with us the vanquished when France went under. For a little while I even felt glad that the war was going to be over sooner than we hoped. It was the feeling as on Munich night at which the folly and reality of the situation came back next day. How glad I am now that as the last hours of the old year are fading that nothing of the sort happened and I really feel that we have turned the corner and can really win but we must not be impatient. We have got used to being at war now, and the inconveniences of the petty annoyances such as the blackout and rations have become a habit. We don't stir at night when we hear the guns and Nasties now, we have got used to them.

I would not have believed that a day would come when the petrol pumps would lay empty, J. and I would actually have summer Sundays off from work and most marvellous of all a *week's holiday together* in *August*. The latter was full compensation for the war's dullness. No not really, I will disown that statement. I would rather have had the pleasant conversations and jolly times of the summer business in pre-war days. We have not seen a quarter of our summer acquaintances. Some we shall never see again . . . But it is cheering to think the war must be one year shorter. We shall get over it, and must try to make the world a far pleasanter place afterwards so that the present sufferings will be worth it.

New Year's resolutions. To get up 10 mins after alarum clock goes instead of going to sleep again. Not to lose my temper and snap or cry. To be kind and to think about people less fortunate than myself. To learn all I can. Not to overspend. To take more pains with the housework. Not to overeat. What rubbish! As though I did not resolve to do these things every other week of the year! With success nil. It's a comfort anyway to think that I mean to improve even if I never do. My chief fault is selfishness but I fear it is difficult to improve. I try.

8

Changing routines, October 1940

The following short piece was written by one of M-O's
regular correspondents, Alice Bridges, in reply to a
question about the impact of war on everyday life. This
question was one of M-O's favourites, sometimes taking
the form: 'What are the six main inconveniences of
wartime?' The blackout always featured strongly in
women's replies, followed by the difficulties of shopping
and cooking. As this answer shows, all domestic tasks
were affected by the nightly descent to the shelter. For
those fortunate enough to have their own Anderson
shelter in the garden, it was rather less inconvenient than
going some distance to a public one. The Bridges family
lived in a working-class district of Birmingham. This was
written shortly after the heaviest raids on Birmingham
when 170 people died.

The one outstanding change in my homelife since the war (air
raid sirens etc.) is earlier hours at night.

My husband has always kept terribly late hours – thinks sleep
is a waste of time – that has meant my keeping late hours. I used
to sit up till midnight regularly sewing, doing odd jobs to keep my
husband company but since the actual air raids and the fact that
the shelter is fixed as a bedroom we have had much more sleep.

Everyone I have met since our three night bombardment all
had the same expression on their lips, namely, 'Wasn't it awful?'
A strained looking-ahead expression as much as to say, 'Will it be
my turn next?' A certain type of person, in fact I think the larger
percentage of people now, shrug their shoulders, mentally and
physically and say, 'If there is a bomb with your name on it, it will
get you, shelter or no shelter.'

For myself I find the intensified bombing gradually coming
closer intensifies one's feelings. As the planes drone nearer, the

bombs drop nearer, the ack-ack start up, the shelter quiet, my husband and child asleep, everything seems clear before my eyes. My thoughts turn with gratitude to the goodness of God for preserving me and mine. I realise what the other people are suffering, the people now under the power of the SS men, I push it into the background and it comes out in my dreams . . .

Radio: Since we can look on the 'Alert siren' as an alert I have been better mentally and have had the radio on a little more. I like interesting life stories, real life, the silly plays and dramatic do's get on my nerves. Life is now so terribly dramatic we don't need the past raked up and served on a platter, often with inferior actors.

Always I like everything ready to go straight down to the shelter if there is a warning. If there is a meal imminent I lay it on the tray as I prepare it. If we are expecting a raid we sit down to the table with the meal on the tray but if we are all having a meal I lay the table and have the tray handy where I can just put the things on it. Our eating habits are just the same. I prepare for myself and child and separately for my husband.

Our working hours: my husband's working hours are much fewer since the air raids. Instead of coming home between 10 and 11 at night as he did all last winter, he is home between 7 and 8. He feels the difference in his pocket but the firm's night shift has been put on to days because they will not pay for 'shelter time' during raids; therefore during the day men do not have to work so much overtime.

After looking inside heaps of shelters I have decided that mine is as much like home as anyone's. I bought a 'Spiral divan' just before the war for taking up and down when we had visitors so that it would leave my child's bedroom freer in between times. Fortunately it fits just into the length of the shelter, it is 2' wide which just leaves room for J.'s little bed at the side which consists of my padded deck chair put very low and levelled up with cushions and a footboard. We have 18" square to stand in, fortunately we are both slight.

My husband has fixed 4 hooks for us and a bullet-proof steel door which we can lock. He has also made us a candle holder out of a 6d gas mask container and arranged it so that it can slip into a holder on the wall . . . The condensation is the biggest problem, the walls run damp and wet as soon as the atmosphere becomes humid. My underneath mattress soaked up all that but left the rest of the shelter bone dry. I have decided to have the mattresses changed over every two days and so ensure that we don't get rheumatism by bringing them in and airing them. From what my neighbours say, having the divan on legs I have the benefit of being able to keep a tin of emergency rations underneath, about 12/6d worth, my leather case with all important papers in and first aid.

9

Driving in London, October–December 1940

Mrs Crawford was a regular diary-writer for
Mass-Observation. She lived in central London for the
whole of the blitz with her two small children and a
household of assorted lodgers and domestic staff. She had
been widowed some years before the war but had
obviously been left comfortably off. Her chief contribution
to the war effort before trying her hand at ambulance
driving (and later mobile canteen driving) was her
hospitality to British and Dominion troops. Her house had
two bathrooms and these seemed to be in constant use by
servicemen who were also entertained with tea, biscuits
and Mrs Crawford's lively company. The Mrs B. referred
to is one of her lodgers, and a fully-fledged ambulance
driver. Between October and December 1940, London was
bombed every night.

Wednesday 2 October 1940
... Mrs B., who is always seeing me typing my diary etc., has
asked me about M-O several times – what does one do, what is the
point of it, do I *really* think it does what it sets out to do, if so, does
it do any *good*, and so on. Tonight she said she'd been reading
Friday's *New Statesman* in the train and had read one article
which she thought was particularly good and valuable – and so
readable and colloquially expressed – had I happened to read it –
it was by – now who was it by? – oh yes, a man called Tom
Harrisson! Of course, she hadn't connected the name with M-O.
She was most impressed when I explained that T.H. is the head of
M-O, and that the article in question was an absolutely typical
piece of M-O stuff, and said she now realised what a good idea M-O
was and that she must look out for more of it.

We had, I believe, no less than 9 raids today, counting a short
one after dark which ended about 9 or 9.30. In fact there was a

raid on far more than half the time. We all lost count of the sirens completely, and took almost no notice of them, though there was a certain amount of gunfire, mostly distant, once or twice.

I've never heard at all from that wretched ambulance-station-head about the job idea. It's quite obvious that all attempts to do anything helpful are doomed to failure from the start unless one is in a position to spend about 12 hours daily hanging round offices, etc., to see people and simply force oneself upon them. I'm quite resigned now to the idea of doing no war-work whatever – I've tried, so I don't feel I need blame myself unduly. Anyhow, I'm certainly *not* in need of occupation!

Thursday 3 October
The ambulance-station-head actually rang up this evening, just when I'd given up the whole idea as a wash-out for good and all! However, she suggested my going round to the station to discuss the whole business tomorrow, about 2, and then going up to the headquarters at Haverstock Hill to place the idea before them and see what can be done . . .

Saturday 5 October
. . . We had an early tea, and then I rushed off to Haverstock Hill for my test, feeling grim enough to suit Churchill but not at all gay. I had a hell of a time getting to HQ owing to the number of detours on the way – more, I think, since Wednesday – which made me hopelessly confused as to direction; then, when I got to the stage of asking people every few yards, they kept telling me I was heading wrong, no matter in what direction the car's nose was pointing at the time – half didn't know about the road-up next door to their own street! Once I'd got right I scorched like anything, but none the less arrived ten minutes late, panting and frenzied – however, it seemed that the woman being tested before me had been half an hour late, so that the instructress hadn't yet come in and my own unpunctuality was covered up.

I felt like hell while I was waiting, and would have swapped places with a dead cat like a shot. Presently, just to add to my 'needle', the woman who'd been tested before me came in, scarlet-faced, and almost in tears with rage. She told me, in a strong Fifeshire accent, that she'd been a traveller for a certain famous firm for over 2 years; was accustomed, therefore, to driving eight hours a day in all weathers, and experienced on all modern types of car, large and small; knew her way round London and the suburbs blindfold. 'But' – in a voice choking with indignation – 'they sent me out to be tested in a 1910 car – *1910*, mind ye, and a reel old wreck at that, with the stiffest and crankiest auld double-declutching gears ye could ever imagine. I can drive most every type o' modern car, but I've never touched such a thing as this; it'd be hard to find such an obsolete affair anywhere now – well, actually, all the cars I've ever driven have been synchromesh, ye see. An' that clutch has fair wrecked ma knee, ma leg's tremblin' yet wi' the stiffness of it! Well now it's not reasonable, is it, to test one's drivin' on an out-of-date auld wreck like that, and withoot any practice allowed at all? And on top of it all, if the instructress didn't seem bamboozled that I couldna' manage better wi' they auld double-declutching gears, if you please . . .'

With all this, my heart – already in my stomach – sank right down into my heels. Moreover, the instructress, who appeared shortly, was plainly in a tearing bad temper – dismissed my predecessor shortly, telling her without attempt at palliation that she would certainly require several more tests at least, and marked her down, in huge angry writing that tore the paper and sent up little splutters of ink, as 'very poor on driving'. When she turned to me, asked to see my licence, and started making out a form on which presently to mark down me also as very poor, I was most disconcerted to realise that she had not, as I'd been told she would, been given the form of application I'd already filled in, on which the special work I was to be tested for was described in detail – she was obviously supposing that I was to be given the ordinary ambulance driver's test, which is necessarily far stiffer since it deals with the transport of sick, not sound, persons. But she seemed so ill-tempered and complained so strongly of being 'frightfully rushed' and 'terribly late' that I didn't dare interpolate an explanation – particularly as much time was wasted while I was giving her all the details which I'd already filled in the other day, and the light was growing worse and worse, and I was in an increasing agony lest the sirens should howl any minute and the whole thing be washed up at the 11th hour.

I was relieved at first when at last the time came to enter the car allotted to me. It seemed a simple and modern enough vehicle (a 12 or 14hp Standard, about 1938, I was told later). Moreover, while the instructress was noting down the car number, mileage, and other details on her report sheet, I fiddled about with dashboard, gears, etc. and was delighted to find that with the exception of the handbrake everything was in more or less the positions to which my own car had accustomed me – and that there was a good space back and front from which to get away; though I was mildly concerned to find that the driving seat was jammed far further back than I like, that the 2nd gear was obdurate in face of all my fiddlings with the gear lever, and that the door next to my seat had a defective latch and was only just caught to by the skin of its teeth, so that had any sudden crisis occurred I would more likely than not have tumbled slap into the road!

Alas, my real grief was yet to come; when, in the moment of getting going (it being necessary to back a few yards to begin with) I found it literally impossible to get into reverse gear. No amount of coaxing, declutching, accelerating, answered in the least; sweating, and feeling myself already damned right at the outset, I tried firmer methods whereupon the instructress screeched, 'Don't force it – don't *force* it, for heaven's sake!' and, forthwith seizing hold of the lever herself, forced it with the utmost violence and a really terrible noise into, not reverse, but bottom gear! However, after about three minutes of sweating hard work by us both, the lever suddenly leapt into reverse with a shudder, more or less on its own, and the preliminary backing was at long last accomplished.

Yet worse was to come. It now proved equally impossible to get into 2nd gear – from which, of course, I'd already encountered resistance when gently fiddling about and exploring right at the outset. I was utterly demoralised by now, thinking that we should never get beyond the station yard and that my case was obviously quite hopeless already after such an impossibly bad start – which I was still guiltily ascribing to my own incompetence. Feeling, anyhow, thoroughly fed-up with the endless declutching, coaxing, declutching again, I decided to short-cut the whole business by starting away in 3rd instead of 2nd (3rd being all right), which was perfectly legitimate since we were on a very steep downhill slope. But the instructress bawled me out immediately – must *not* do that – didn't I know how bad it was for the engine – what was I thinking of – must get into the proper gear – now *don't force it* . . . In the end she herself again got it in, by dint of the most violent forcing imaginable that raised a clatter like the wheels of hell; and *at last* we moved off.

The realisation was by now beginning to dawn on me that all these initial troubles were not my fault at all, but due to an engine so bashed about and in such a hopeless state of repair as to be scarcely fit to take the road at all, let alone serve as a test case – a conclusion confirmed when I realised at the first application that the footbrake was almost non-existent! However, I felt thoroughly despairing and defeatist about the whole thing by this time. If they were in the habit of deliberately using obsolete and packed-up machines to test people on – as seemed to be the case both from my own experience so far and the story of the woman before me – it seemed unlikely that they would make allowances for the difficulties arising from this practice. I felt myself done for before ever I got outside the gates. For this reason, actually, I think I drove really rather better than I otherwise might have done, my anger and frustration having completely driven out everything in the way of nerves; but I don't think anyone could have made much of a job of driving, with maximum speed of 20 mph, a car with almost no brakes, too high 3rd gear to hold the engine back on even the slightest downhill gradients, or to take the clotted-up and pinking old thing up a slope without violent protests in the absence of any impetus, and an unusable 2nd gear! Just to add to the difficulties of the situation, the instructress proved to be as fussy as anyone's grandmother might be, and kept making me jump half out of my skin by sudden and quite unnecessary screams of 'Mind that woman!' – 'Look out for that cyclist, for heaven's sake!' – 'Mind *out* for the main road, do!' etc. Really most aggravating when one is at least sufficiently competent to be able to take note at the speed of 20 or less of whatever cyclists, women, or main roads may be in question!

At all events, I crawled along obediently at 20; I used the 3rd gear for what it was worth as a brake (and in fact was obliged to keep in it almost the whole time, as of course the test course was very up and down and twisty). I made no bad changes on the somewhat battered old synchromesh, doing double declutched both up and down to be on the safe side; I was most careful and clear with my signalling; and I dealt adequately with the usual driving school performances of reversing into side-streets and turning out again, stopping and starting on a steep hill, etc., apart

from the usual gear trouble. The only heinous crimes I committed
– and they were solely because I was being given the wrong sort of
test – were that once – to the instructress's horror – I revved up to
about 25 in 3rd gear in order to be able to change up; and once I
took an extremely gentle corner at 20 (in the ordinary way I
suppose I'd have taken it at about 30) – whereupon the instructress set up a terrible keening about 'think of the wounded people
in the back – don't you realise they *must* not be slithered and
banged about like that – go *much* more slowly . . . !'

Gosh, I did feel mad about the whole bloody setup! Everybody's
warned me that the tests were appallingly stiff – well quite right
if they had been, but as a matter of fact this one wasn't stiff in the
least – just the usual stuff. The trouble was not the stiffness, but
the absolute unfairness; first, I was being tested for something I
wasn't going in for at all, instead of being given the test for my
own special work, and second, it's not any kind of a test, but only a
torture, to make someone perform in a car so smashed-up inside
that it was scarcely driveable at all, and in fact should never have
been allowed to take the road!

The crowning injustice occurred over the final, and stiffest,
piece of the test; namely, once returned to the station, to back the
car up a narrow steep drive to exactly the spot in the parking-line
from which it had been taken. This is exactly the thing I'm bad at
and hate; however, I think I could have made it OK, if only in
relief at getting to the end of the whole hateful affair, but of
course, I couldn't get the ruddy gear into reverse. Nor, incidentally, could the instructress – our combined efforts produced
nothing whatever but a series of angry snarlings and grindings.
After we'd wrestled with it for about 5 minutes in vain, she
suddenly said irritably, 'Well, I shall just have to leave it – I'm so
frightfully rushed, I'm late as it is – I'll give you another opportunity next week . . .' In fact, she was politely failing me, because,
through no fault of my own, she was behindhand and I'd been
given a scrap-heap car . . .

Failing a proper stiff test through one's own incompetence
would be annoying and discouraging, but to be failed like this on a
test that wasn't a test at all made me so raging with a sense of
utter injustice that I just couldn't speak for fury. (Of course, I can't
be sure that I wouldn't have failed anyhow! – but that would have
been a different kettle of fish altogether. As it was – quite

honestly and with no 'sour grapes' about it – I didn't have the ghost of a chance. I don't believe the best driver in the world – a London taxi-driver, for example – could have done any better on that old mess of junk-metal.)

Anyhow, the instructress did more or less promise me that one more test would see me OK – failing any howling bloomers. And when I got back home Mrs B. told me that this was actually quite unusually good. No one had ever been known to pass first time, even on a car test – most people had at least 2 failures, even if not 6 – yes, the cars were proverbially frightful, and one's only hope of passing through quickly was to draw a lucky one – i.e. a comparatively driveable one – by chance. I felt a bit better after hearing this, but the whole affair rankled all evening. Anyway, what about the appalling wastage of petrol spent in putting people through it over and over again in impossible cars, and by the people themselves in going repeatedly to be put through it? Not to mention the waste of time and energy.

The instructress suggested I should take another test on Wednesday morning. I pleaded for an earlier time, and it wasn't for some minutes after I'd accepted 7 p.m. on Monday – the only alternative time – that I realised that the added horror of darkness would then be added to my ordeal.

I had a hateful drive home in the half-light, losing my way several times again owing to detours, and no doubt wasting a lot of petrol by so doing. I did, however, relieve some of my feelings by speeding furiously (for me, that is!) but arrived home still in a vile temper. Being behindhand with things again owing to the waste of time yesterday afternoon and B. and J.'s visit today, I sat down to a couple of hours of savage typing, which left me worse tempered than ever and with a vile headache. I got to the stage of feeling that I'll give that test business another couple of tries, and if these are equally unjust and idiotic, I'll just wash the whole thing out. Heaven knows I'm busy enough as it is, and up to a point I'm offering to do the ambulance service a favour by using my own car and petrol in their service; anyway, after a third visit to HQ, I shouldn't think I'll have enough petrol left to be the slightest use, in any case!

Tuesday 22 October

. . . I was thunderstruck – after all this time and all these rebuffs!

– to receive two letters containing offers of work by the evening mail! I could have been knocked down with the proverbial feather.

As a matter of fact I think one of them must have been founded on a misunderstanding. It was from the head of the Women's National Auxiliary Council of the YMCA and stated that in reply to my letter help was urgently needed in Mobile Canteens, and would I fix an appointment to see her as soon as possible, as she was most anxious to accept my kind offer of part-time service. This neither refers to, nor tallies with, the previous telephone reply to my letter, which stated that permits could not be obtained for part-time work on Mobile Canteens. I shall jolly well find out what *is* the position in regard to part-time work before I commit myself to any appointment, which might otherwise just be another waste of time on a mare's nest.

The second offer was a spontaneous suggestion from M-O of 'semi-full-time' paid work for them. I should love this, if it really is 'semi' and I can manage to fit it in. I don't really feel I want pay for it, but I suppose in a way it's better to take it as it puts the whole thing on a proper footing.

All this is most exciting. I feel quite determined to get and take one job or the other – I should really like, if it were conceivably possible to wangle the times, to fit in both somehow – after all the Mobile Canteen work ought to provide a certain amount of copy for M-O.

Cannon St Station, Saturday 9 November
. . . I was disillusioned to discover that this famous mobile canteen work proved, in the end, to entail neither cooking, driving, nor danger – it was, in fact, only ordinary canteen work under another and more glamorous name! The thing was the ordinary large canteen-vans are, perforce, so heavy and awkward that except in case of absolute emergency they and their two attendants are driven to and from their pitches by male drivers – professional van-drivers; while the little light vans which do the emergency call work (i.e., alas, all the really interesting work: fires, demolitions, sudden raid emergencies of all sorts) are entrusted only to senior full-time members – quite rightly too, I suppose. Nor was there any of the cooking of sausage and mash etc. on a stove in the van that I'd envisaged; nothing hot was sold

except tea – our only beverage. The food was all of the meat pie, sausage roll, bun, and jam-tart variety – with chocolate and cigarettes. So that what the work came to in fact was simply a sort of playing at shop – in this case on a platform at Cannon Street. No mobility about it, and in fact anything harder to be mobile in than the interior of a van, with most of the exiguous space occupied by spare trays of cakes and pies . . .

Wednesday 13 November
Well, I take back all I said about the YMCA work, and its positively dull simplicity and straightforwardness. Today it was gruelling, and for me by no means so darn easy!

. . . I was summoned hastily to the office and asked if I'd mind taking on driving the van, as it would be difficult to find another driver at this 11th hour. Pride made me long to say – casually – 'Oh yes, I'm sure I can.' But in the meanwhile I'd been given the day's route sheet for our van, and it was a very different kettle of fish from the Cannon Street business of the other day. No affair of simply driving to one place and remaining there all day, but a long drive all round back streets between Charing Cross and Euston Road from one bomb-site to another, to feed one after another of the various demolition squads. To drive, without any practice, a large, heavy van over a long and complicated route which was completely strange to me, in a district I don't know at all well, would, I thought, be a pretty tall order – and, which was the crux of the matter, decidedly risky. I had visions of myself packing up the van – or, which was far more likely, getting stuck or lost, and making such slow progress as to be unable to get through half the work. So I said that I really didn't dare to accept the responsibility; it wasn't that I wouldn't myself welcome the chance to get acquainted with vans, but I really did think it was too risky, from the point of view both of the vans and of the work, for me to drive for the first time on such a long, full, and complicated route . . .

They took this well – particularly as the male professional driver attached to the establishment happened to come in just then, and pointed out that 'there's some very tricky driving on Route IV, it'd be a very nasty route for Mrs C. to start driving on, it really would.' So, feeling apologetic but much relieved, I withdrew, and went off to have a cup of tea at the canteen. But my

troubles were not over. I was again sent for in about 10 minutes.
The office had got hold of another part-time worker who had
agreed to help them out, and had in fact already appeared on the
scene – a tall, emaciated, raddled woman with hennaed hair,
wearing MTC uniform – which my heart leapt up when I beheld,
for must she not be a most efficient driver?

Not a bit of it. The trouble was, went on the office sadly, that
this Mrs— had made it clear that in no circumstances whatever
would she even attempt to drive the van; she was only willing to
help out in this emergency as an attendant. And it was absolutely
too late now to try getting hold of any other driver – even if it were
possible to get hold of one at all, our whole routine would be so
delayed as to be more or less useless. So what? So what indeed? I
didn't quite see why my new partner – MTC and all too – should be
allowed to get away like this with a flat refusal to drive; so I
looked hopefully at her and again murmured that it wasn't that *I*
minded, it was the *risk* and the probable failure to get through the
work . . . But Mrs— remained aloofly unconcerned. Evidently it
was nothing to her who drove, or if anyone drove at all; simply,
she wasn't going to have anything to with it herself . . . So I was
cornered. I had to say all right, I'd have a crack at it, then.

It was with a heavy heart and a far from sunny temper that I
inserted myself into the driving-seat of the van – which, as always
seems to be the case with me (who likes the seat as far forward as
it will go) had jammed halfway and had to be levered and then
wedged with the starting-handle. The seat itself was quite the
most uncomfortable I've ever – literally – struck, and it was
almost impossible to see anything at all in the driving-mirror.
The gears, thank God, were standard, but both handbrake and
footbrake were right-hand, which I *loathe*, and also the latter was
so high, and the steering-wheel so low, that, with the seat at last
wedged forward to my satisfaction, I found I couldn't get my foot
up on to the brake without hitting myself a shattering crack on
the knee! After a few extremely painful and unnerving experiences of this, I gave the footbrake up altogether, and drove
throughout the day on the heavy handbrake . . .

Our morning route led us to two gangs of sappers, then to two
AMPs in different parts of Bloomsbury; and finally back to the
centre to pick up fresh tea and a batch of hot meat pies, and to
renew our supplies of cakes. The pies were late, which gave us a

welcome chance to spend pennies at leisure and fortify ourselves with hot tea in the canteen ... One way and another they certainly do break one in by the shortest and sweetest way, according to that method which trains horses by the use of lassoes, and teaches one to swim by throwing one into deep water. There's no coddling of the tenderfoot; I can't complain, as I definitely believe in that method myself; it saves endless time and trouble for both parties, and distinguishes right at the outset between those who are and those who are not capable of functioning in new and trying circumstances. If I hadn't been more or less forced to drive the van today, I'd probably never have dared to risk doing so on occasions when it was possible to avoid it, and so I wouldn't have learnt for ages and would all the time have been haunted by the fear of having to start doing so one day.

What with the lateness of the pies, and the delay in the office and over the float business – and perhaps, I'm afraid, too much loitering over our hot tea in the canteen – we were again somewhat late getting off. And then we were further held up on the way to our first pitch by a brand new diversion which hadn't been allowed for on our route map, which we had some difficulty in negotiating. It was mostly not our fault at all, anyhow, so we were somewhat fed up, on reaching our pitch at last, to be greeted by surly growls and grumbles from one and all because we were half-an-hour or so late . . . I felt a bit guilty at first, thinking of our loitering in the canteen back at the centre; but after all the pies hadn't been ready for us, and it wasn't our own fault that I'd been held up in the office, nor was it the centre's fault that the way had been blocked. If those damned AMPs thought it was possible to be perfectly punctual at each call on a long and complicated route through blitz-time London back streets, they could just think again. So I retorted somewhat waspishly that it wasn't our fault we were late, and anyway they were damned lucky to have us calling at all, late or not; we weren't doing it for fun . . .

On the whole, the day was satisfactory and great fun. The most amusing pitch was with a squad of AMPs at one of the worst wrecks I've ever seen, in a side alley somewhere just off Hatton Garden. Three or four adjoining houses here had been knocked to nothing but a smash; there was nothing whatever to show that the heaped jumble of broken beams, rubble, and jagged and distorted pipes had ever borne any relation to human dwelling-places. I had a nasty shiver down the back as we drew up at this scene of complete and utter chaos, because it was very obvious that the bodies of whoever had been in these houses were still there, underneath all the muck and muddle, and would be there for a very long time . . .

Anyhow, one of the houses at this pitch had been a 'beautician's' of some sort, and the AMPs working there – a particularly merry and friendly lot of men, mostly Scots and sometimes very hard to understand, loaded us with gifts of 'face-pooderr', many boxes of which they'd salvaged. Quite a good kind, and, by good luck, in good shades too. Unfortunately the boxes, though perfectly sound – it seemed unbelievable that they could have come through such a cataclysm with no more than bent and battered edges or stained labels – were not in quite good enough condition to solve the Xmas present problem for us! But what we didn't want ourselves would obviously be a most welcome gift from the gods for maids, etc. I felt rather uncomfortable about receiving it at first – wasn't it looting, and if so, wasn't it dreadful? But the men seemed to regard it as absolutely matter of course and rushed about among the wreckage scrabbling round for more and more boxes and packets of powder, like terriers nosing out rats. Even if we'd really not wanted to take the stuff, we could hardly have avoided it, and it was brought in by all hands from all sides; the men hardly had time to drink their tea in their eagerness over this new game, and they even pelted us with boxes as we were driving off. There we were finding odd boxes among the cakes and in corners of the van all through the rest of the afternoon – one box turned up floating in the milk jug! Altogether we found when we got back to the centre and divided up the proceeds that we'd made a haul of some 200 boxes and packets each – not bad! So perhaps on this particular occasion the Jewboys weren't so far wrong after all about 'fevverin' our nests'.

At all events, I think the present fuss about looting is being carried to absurd lengths. To break into premises that have become unguarded through bombing, and steal quantities of valuable and more or less unharmed property is one thing, and should certainly be severely punished – though even so I don't personally consider that any sort of thieving deserves so harsh a penalty as 'life' or death. But as for taking packets of tea, say, or cigarettes, or any other bits of perishable stuff which are scattered about the streets and among irreparable wreckage, and which would only waste if not taken – well, it would not be human to refrain from doing so . . .

At one of our last pitches of the day in Charing Cross Road again, we had a bit of excitement. There was a raid on again – about the fourth of the day, I think – and suddenly we heard planes and loud gunfire. Each detonation swayed the van astonishingly, and I saw a number of people running on the pavements. Rather to my surprise, Mrs — was out of the van like a scalded cat, and was standing in the middle of the street looking up at the sky before you could say knife. I went stolidly on with what I was doing – some more of our squalid washing up, I believe. Presently Mrs— called out that she could see lots of gun-puffs in the sky overhead so I came out to have a look too. But I'd hardly had any time to see the balls of grey smoke popping into existence in the cold, colourless sky before Mrs— came over all conscientious – she must have thought of her uniform, I think, and felt conscious of her soldier-to-civilian relationship to me! – and positively ordered me back into the van. I went in quite meekly as there was nothing more to see than I've see often enough before and also, truth to tell, I felt just as glad to have a roof of sorts over my head; but I couldn't forbear remarking that really I liked that from *her* after the way she'd bounced out into the street at the first shot!

. . . We actually finished ahead of our schedule, and got back to the centre about 4.15 with all the day's work done except for the final washing out and clearing-up of the van. I must say I was glad to get in. I'd reached the stage of feeling that I should scream if I had to go on inching in close traffic on that great stiff heavy handbrake much longer. And my left foot had quite given out on the job of depressing the vastly long stiff clutch. I'd been wondering for some time why it was that my gear-changing seemed to be going more and more to pieces since this morning when I'd been rather proud of it. Then I realised that it was because this wretched foot had gone on strike . . . I'd never been properly warm all day; now that the chill of the evening was beginning, cold seemed to be creeping more and more into my bones. Besides, spilt milk and tea were swilling all over the floor of the van by this time and we'd been dismally aware as we stood serving that our shoe soles were completely soaked and permeated by the horrid sludge underneath.

After we'd unloaded the van and put away our unused slab-cakes, etc., Mrs— said she'd make a start on the washing up if I'd go straight along to the office with the 'float', which I did. Here I got quite held up for some time, being, quite unexpectedly, praised and made much of! The head was extremely nice, patted me on the back and thanked me and said, 'Go to the top, you deserve a medal! That was really good work.' The professional driver came in and added a tribute; I asked whether it was not just that my van had been a particularly easy one, as it certainly seemed easier than the one I'd been out in the time before, and he said solemnly, 'Oh no, I assure you – we have four or five vans that are a lot easier than that one!' Then the head led me up, like a prize scholar, to the woman who is, I believe, the head of the driving side and said, 'Miss—, I must tell you how sporting Mrs Crawford has been . . .' etc. I really felt tremendously bucked by all this. Everyone had seemed to take this business of sending a complete novice off into the wilds of Bloomsbury and Soho on a strange van so much as a matter of course that it never occurred to me to expect any particular praise for my day's work, and such a nice dollop of it quite set me up . . .

Mrs— had disappeared when I got back to the kitchens and I found the van all beautifully swept and garnished and the dirty mugs and urn gone from where we'd dumped them, so it seemed that I'd sneaked out of my share of dirty work. I felt most guilty about having thus abandoned her in the hour of the washing up; however she didn't seem to mind at all when she came back in a little while. We furtively divided up our spoils in the way of face powder at a table in the corner and then left; she suggesting that we should have some tea together before we went our different ways . . .

10

M-O Report No. 520: Women and morale, December 1940

> This report was written by another full-time female Mass-Observer, Priscilla Feare. The information is taken from the whole range of M-O material: diaries, replies to directives, observations and interviews.

Since the outbreak of war, Mass-Observation has been making a record of wartime conditions, public and private opinion, the reaction of people to events and social change. This unique system of studying society and tracing the impact of war on a nation has given special attention to the part that women are playing. It has been the job of at least one whole-time investigator from the beginning of the war to study the activities of women's organisations, the effects of leisure activities such as the cinema, radio, fashion, the press, all of which provide a background to women's lives and morale, and help to influence their opinions and attitudes to the war. A full and continuous survey of the impact of propaganda of all kinds on women has completed this picture of wartime life; while the differences between men and women and their reactions to news have brought out certain fundamental differences in morale.

The word 'morale' has been used widely by press and Government propaganda to describe the state of the public mind about the war and the principles for which we are fighting. An official definition of morale has yet to be given. Pre-war definitions put the accent on the military or general side; the Oxford dictionary, for instance, defines it as the moral condition 'especially (of troops) as regards discipline and confidence'. Though many of them are now doing a man's job, sharing with men danger and hardship, the morale of women cannot be judged by the same standards as that of men and soldiers. The housewife, though she has not the direct leadership and discipline that the soldier experiences, may have to undergo more danger and put up with more inconveniences than her husband. It is the propaganda of her everyday life which determines whether she accepts war and sacrifice willingly or not. The material, ever-present things of life – prices, blackout, running a home, evacuating her children, worrying about her men – these things are the first impacts of war, the factors which colour the ordinary woman's desire to win the war and faith in leadership.

War 'grumbles' collected during the first half of 1940 during by-elections from Battersea to East Renfrew revealed women's attitudes to the conditions imposed by war. Blackout was easily first, followed by prices, food, transport, inconveniences which made women worried or even scared. Evacuation and conscription added to these difficulties and brought women further worry and loneliness. In March they were grumbling thus:

> 'Only my husband going.'
> 'I don't know. I've so many.'
> 'Taking our boys from us, and our pockets – the prices are so high.'
> 'I grumble all day about everything.'

As time went on, and the war showed signs of intensifying, women put their personal grievances in the background, and worried about the loss of life, the war itself. By June 1940 many were suppressing grumbles, feeling that they ought to accept uncomplainingly the sacrifices demanded of them. At S. Croydon by-election, for instance:

> 'Well, I don't know . . . It doesn't do to grumble, does it?'
> 'No, you just put up with everything, don't you?'
> 'Well, I don't know. We mustn't grumble, must we?'

But all the time, behind their grumbles about the war and its prosecution, or determination not to complain, there still appeared the constant worry as to how to make ends meet; economic worries about prices, wages, shopping; psychological anxieties about blackout, parting from husbands and children.

These are the permanent, inescapable factors which must affect a woman's morale. They are behind the dangers and fears of air raids and bombs; they are more difficult to combat when sirens and air raid shelters begin to order life, or when the news is worrying and invasion puts new fears into a woman's mind. Mass-Observation has kept a detailed record of this year of new successes for Nazi Germany, new invasions, battlefields, threats, and the morale of women as compared with men has been closely followed and studied in many aspects. The invasions of Norway, Belgium and Holland, the capitulation of France, were an unprecedented series of events which impacted violently on the people of this country, leading as it did, up to the Battle for Britain itself. Day to day surveys of feeling and opinion were made from the first moments of each campaign to its conclusion. In every case women were much slower to recover from the shock of the news than men, and more erratic in their changes from depression to optimism. The following table compares male and female reaction during the first week of the Norwegian campaign, taking the index Disquiet/Optimism (with Optimism = 1):

Table 1

	Invasion	Rumours	Naval defeat	Churchill denies rumours	Germans advancing	Narvik victory
	April 9th	10th	11th	12th	13th	14th
Male	·84	·44	·30	·26	·39	·08
Female	3·67	2·00	·50	·70	·73	·33

Editor's Note: Mass-Observation frequently used the device of a scale to measure morale. My understanding of this table is that if 1 = 'optimism', then 3·67 is 'very high optimism' and correspondingly 0.08 = 'very great disquiet'.
Definitions are not provided and therefore these figures should perhaps be interpreted as relative measures rather than absolute ones!

There is thus the characteristic trend of women feeling far more depressed and shocked at bad news, and changing to optimism more suddenly than men. While male disquiet gradually declines, that of women is more erratic, and never drops to the low level of men on the last three days. Similarly, the high percentage of women who could not give any opinion reflects their growing bewilderment:

Table 2

April	9th	10th	11th	12th	13th	14th
Don't know	27%	28%	18%	14%	35%	19%

A peak of disbelief in the news was reached during the Norwegian campaign, and rumours were collected in numbers. Depression, scepticism, bewilderment were shown by women at many points. This can be illustrated uniquely by extracts from war diaries kept by many voluntary observers of the National Panel. For instance, here is a housewife aged 50, on April 9th, describing an afternoon at the local WVS Centre:

> I looked at many 'mothers'' faces – mothers whose boys were far away and in danger and I thought it was not a bad thing that there was a shortage of money and we had to plan little efforts and fiestas to raise money to buy wool and material, for it gave them a 'fixed' job and not a pastime like going to a whist drive or the pictures. I know by myself that the fact I've certain days and certain tasks to do keeps me on an even keel sometimes and keeps me from thinking when I go to bed at night, for I'm always so tired that to keep my letters up to date is at times an effort. I felt so nervy and jumpy after tea – could not settle – I kept turning the wireless to see if there was a news bulletin anywhere in English – *not German* – and wondering if our sailors were winning in the reported sea battle. I asked my husband if the whirr of my sewing machine would annoy him . . . He said, 'Do as you like, my dear – you seem nervy tonight – what is it?'

Diaries kept by women of all ages and classes show more clearly than anything else the deep anxiety and fear, or great relief and optimism that characterises the reactions of the ordinary woman as compared with a man. A young married woman, aged 38, working class, wrote a few days after the invasion:

> Everyone is so much happier now we actually know that we are in Norway. I had a feeling all along that now we have put our hands to the plough we shall not turn back, we have only just gone in time, though, the Germans have a pretty strong hold.

And a middle-class woman who took the news of successes quietly, determined not to believe anything until news was 'official':

> Papers all upset that news they had published as fact was not accurate. Really, it was a pity, as disappointment after exhilaration is chilling. Motto – beware of both.

These few extracts are typical of many. The swiftness of events, the optimism created by wishful thinking of leadership, press and BBC, the shattering disillusion as Hitler completed each carefully planned stroke, created for people, and especially women, a continuous bewilderment, shock, and at times the deepest depression and fear. Overlapping therefore with political crisis, invasion and parachute fear, 'facing facts' and a series of international shocks, these spring and summer months were months of trial and nervous tension for most women. Then Hitler invaded Holland and Belgium, and the process was repeated. Day to day morale studies by Mass-Observation showed a similar barometer of feeling among women: on May 18th they were much more worried than men, and some were showing definite terror of the immediate future. Many were unable to grasp what was happening at all. By the 21st, pessimism was slightly relieved, but the next day women were in a particularly depressed condition. Investigators recorded two in tears about air raid fear during the morning. Comparing figures for the three main groups of feeling throughout the invasion of Holland and Belgium, the same characteristics are shown:

27% males and 31% females expressed Disquiet
30%   30%   Optimism
21%   30%   Doubt

Moreover, the amount of disquiet was greater among upper and middle-class women than among the working classes, who were far more bewildered and unable to give any opinion.

Thus by the end of May many women were deliberately refraining from listening to the wireless, and said they preferred not to think about it. The day to day swings in morale continued. Any small news item that might be interpreted as encouraging gave people heart; lack of news produced a state of suspense, until the Belgian capitulation administered another, unexpected shock.

Extracts from women's diaries show again the depression, false hopes, symptoms of shock. A young cookery demonstrator wrote on May 10th:

> I listened to the 10.30 news, which seemed confused. I did not hear the 1 o'c news, but someone rang up during the afternoon and told me there wasn't going to be a Whitsun holiday. She has a shop and said, 'I don't know whether to open or not – you don't know what to do, do you?' I went to the hairdresser's tonight and his wife looked very worried. She said, 'I expect we shall have them over tonight.'

A middle-class woman of 37 wrote later in the month:

> News fairly good. Apparently we are holding them again and also cutting in on the spear head of their attack – a daring plan which would be a wonderful move if it succeeded – but a mad waste of life if it doesn't . . .

But soon she was writing of the latest news:

> Apparently the lack of news was not a good thing, for shortly after making my last entry in here the news came through that the Belgian Army in obedience to the command of Leopold the king, who acted in defiance of his Ministers, capitulated to the enemy.

Everywhere in women's diaries appeared the tremendous influence of the day's news. Worry and anxiety one day, minor rumour of success causing cheerfulness and hope the next. A working-class housewife in Birmingham wrote:

> A BLACK DAY. We need all our prayers now, and they won't have to be ordered. The 1 o'c news has made me feel sick . . . I don't think France will give in, but neither did I think Belgium would. We *must* win – we *must* win, I could not live beneath a brutal power. I said to my husband Sunday, I would die fighting rather than live the life of a slave.

The process of disillusion began again, even deeper than before, yet soon people were snatching at new straws of hope, and the events that led up to the capitulation of France had many parallels with Norway. There is the same complacency varied with tension and anxiety. Rumour flourished, and women were cheerful or depressed according to the current news bulletin or press report. The end of the Chamberlain era brought new hopes, and the belief that with fresh, vital leadership the war was half won. The Emergency Powers Act was welcomed as proof of active measures and initiative. But as the news grew worse, or the position became more confused and obscure, bewilderment and depression returned, gas mask carrying increased, women writing in their diaries extracts like these:

> Mrs B. was telling me that when the Belgians gave in she felt *terrible* – she felt like sitting down and weeping her heart out. Then she started to plan what she had better do if we were invaded – for she was certain we would be invaded right away and she planned that she and Mrs M. would take the old car, pile all the kids into it and get away – and when she came to think of the old car starting off all piled up with bedding and kids it struck her as so funny that she sat down and had a good laugh – and that was that.

A working-class housewife:

> Germans 20 miles south of Paris – and we are just registering our 28s today. Lord Simon says we shall either win this war or it will go on for ever. The Queen says, 'When we have caught up in this armament race.' Well, well, and we wonder why we feel sick. Around me, people seem to be suffering from the reactions of the present news, depressed and hopeless, everything ending with 'If we win'. Having suffered like that myself when Leopold's treachery was apparent and I had an abscess in my face, I can sympathise . . .

Even the most level-headed and rational of women found themselves worrying about the news, being restless and unable to settle down to anything, on edge with the tension and suspense. Many middle-aged working women found their routine of housework and shopping a physical burden, and several mention headaches and nervous strain at this time. A working housewife of 50 wrote:

> I don't know whether it's the heat or I'm doing a bit too much running round, but today I'd a real black fit of depression – luckily rare to me. I felt a hood of misery over me that

threatened to choke me. I felt my efforts were feeble and doll-eyed, and that *anything* I could possibly do was so futile as to be utterly *worthless* . . .

Diary extracts, as well as direct observation, show a difference in women's reaction to news, especially bad news, according to temperament. Some women are more determined and almost desperately convinced that we can and must win; others, bewildered and apathetic, do not understand what is happening, and are additionally depressed for this reason. The news of the capitulation of France was another tremendous blow. The state of shock lasted longer than on the surrender of Leopold, or the collapse of Norway. Invasion and air raids were immediately expected again, always a more vivid fear with women than men. A girl of 25 said:

So the French have finally given in. People don't seem to be worrying about it. They're waiting for the raids. I think an anticlimax like this is worse mental strain than other things.

The suspense of waiting for more news, confusion about what would happen next, caused in many women acute bewilderment and anxiety for the future. A housewife aged 50, said:

So cruel. I don't know what's going to happen now, I really don't. It seems all up. You don't know what to do for the best. I don't know whether to send my children away, or not. I'll never see them again if I send them abroad. I don't know whether to apply for a shelter or not. I think perhaps I ought to join the ARP; then I think I've got my duty to the home first. Oh dear, I wish there was somebody who would come round to all the houses and discuss our problems with us. I wish I had someone to discuss it with.

This feeling of uncertainty, the tendency of working women to leave all the difficult things such as politics, ARP, opinions about world affairs, to their husbands, has come up many times in our surveys. The average housewife's horizon does not include these extra, unexpected problems; no one explains them to her in a way which shows her that they are as much her concern as a man's. These days before actual raids forced a new routine and problem upon women, caused many to feel worried and baffled, afraid of tackling the unknown, making decisions about their children, thinking about shelters, invasion, bombs. Middle-class women are better educated, better informed, more able to visualise the future and make decisions independently. What happened then when the threats and fears became reality, when the barbarism that shocked women when they heard and read about death and destruction, became part of their own lives? Since Britain came into the front line herself, Mass-Observation has recorded the impact of air raids and danger from many different angles. Older women were beginning to feel the strain of waiting for the expected invasion and blitzkrieg. One woman of 60 wrote in her diary:

> I can't understand it, I go to bed early and I always used to feel fresh in the morning at least – but I suppose it's the war, however much you try not to think about it, it's always there.

The first raid, however, is usually treated as something exciting, though afterwards many women became nervous. An artisan woman of 70 said after the first raid on Thames Ditton:

> I can't bear those beastly things now – every time I hear one I feel quite ill. You know I don't show things much but I was quite upset after the raid – I couldn't sleep that night. I think it was the noise and the suddenness of it all.

Women at first take shelter more readily than men, but after repeated raids they become adjusted to the new conditions and bombs are a matter of routine and inconvenience. A voluntary observer wrote in August:

> My Aunt Bella, who was scared stiff at the thought of air raids when they began about a month ago, had gone as arranged to Mrs S.'s air raid shelter two doors away, and they'd had a merry party, telling jokes, laughing and talking all the time.

There are recorded very few instances of women's morale being seriously affected by raids, though boredom, weariness, upset habits are general in badly hit areas. An observer in Newcastle reported:

> Women are particularly sick of these raids. I've talked to dozens and they all affirm this war is very much worse than the last and they are *sick to death of it*.

Detailed observations were made of reactions to the London blitzkrieg, with particular respect to the effects on leisure activities and habits. In common with other raided towns, it was found that although outside leisure activities such as films, sport and other communal pleasures had in most cases ceased, shelter life and the psychological adjustment created a listlessness and disinclination to form new habits or continue old ones. Many shelters, particularly those of the brick surface type, provide poor light and facilities for the staple leisure occupations of women, knitting or reading. Out of 16 women observed in a West London brick shelter, activities were divided as follows:

Table 3

	Reading	Knitting	Smoking	Doing nothing
Under 30	2	1	1	0
Over 30	2	3	4	3

Thus 50% of the women observed were doing nothing at all or just smoking, while in a brick shelter in the North where light was confined to a Hurricane lamp, during 40 alarms observed during the month August–September reading only occurred twice. On 17 occasions women knitted. In August the number of women knitting at one time varied between 3 to 6 out of a total number of between 12 and 15 women. By September even knitting tended to disappear, being observed in only three cases during the last 20 alarms. Women were too tired after an endless succession of alarms to have much enthusiasm for anything, and night raids usually found most sleeping or dozing after conversation had ceased.

In Anderson shelters or basements, women have more opportunity for carrying on with their usual home activities, in the company of their families, though younger women become impatient and bored by this restriction of outside amusement, difficulties of transport, and dependence on their own homes. Women were more heavily affected by the combination of bombs and travelling facilities, and a comparison in October between male and female visiting habits showed that the majority had curtailed their evening activities:

Table 4

	Men	Women
Go out less	65%	91%
Make and receive fewer visits	59%	82%

Typical replies from women:

'I never see anybody.'
'I never go anywhere now, just go straight home.'
'We never go out at all.'
'I don't get home till fairly late, so there's no chance at all of going out again.'
'Oh my God, I sometimes go as far as the pub, that's all.'

Radio listening and reading newspapers were also affected:

Table 5

	Radio		Press	
	Men	Women	Men	Women
More	12%	3%	29%	12%
Less	47%	55%	24%	36%
No change	41%	42%	47%	52%

Reasons were not always given for decreased listening or reading. Some women said that they didn't do anything now, 'hadn't the time', though people saying this often appeared actually to do less than before the raids began. After the first shock and confusion of air raids, women began to settle down into a passive acceptance of conditions, a life restricted on all sides by blackout, bombs, travelling difficulties, prices. There is still the problem of evacuation, the growing momentum of conscription, the isolation from friends and family. News of international interest does not cause the same worry and apprehension as before. The war has settled down once more into a phase; women have all they can do to carry on their ordinary job, in the home, the workshop or the office, putting up with their own personal share of the war. Among middle-class women there is frequently a desire to do more than they are doing to help the war effort, to take part in some useful, humanitarian capacity. Working-class women have less time and opportunity, though the practical side is again the one that appeals to them: knitting, sewing for the Red Cross, preserving fruit, providing cigarettes and comforts for their men in the Forces. The average housewife has plenty to do in attending to the immediate, material things of life, plenty to worry about in her own children, husband in the army, or family in a bombed area.

Most women would seem to have put up a protective barrier against news neurosis, and circumstances help to localise their interest and activity in the war. In October 1940, shown by answers by the National Panel of voluntary observers, the major changes affecting women more than men were in family and friend relationships (6 times more upset among women), and those caused by evacuation:

Table 6

	Family and Friends	Evacuation
Men	4%	10%
Women	24%	20%

while the latest analysis of diaries (late November) again emphasises the personal factors rather than general war depression or cheerfulness. During a week including important news items at home and abroad – Greeks holding out against Italy; Taranto; Rumanian earthquake; Molotoff's visit to Berlin; a statement by Churchill, the death of Chamberlain, and Armistice Day – only three appeared to arouse spontaneous interest or reaction: the Greek news and Taranto, and the death of Mr Chamberlain. The report states:

> This lack of violent enthusiasms or depressions is typical of the diaries as a whole during this phase of the war. Listlessness, seldom explicit, but evident in long and colourless factual reports of air raid damage from bombed areas, in the lack of positive statements of opinion, in increasing concentration on the purely local, is the dominant feeling.

Some women are saved from boredom by the presence of young children, round whom their diary observations centre. But one middle-aged housewife wrote:

> 4.50 p.m. Rita suggested pictures. Said I: Yes, I'll put Dad's dinner in oven and leave a note; *and for goodness sake let's get out of this house.*

Thus there has returned for many women a state of mind reminiscent of the first winter of war. In spite of the danger and inconvenience of raids, which only serves to increase the sense of endurance and acceptance of the inevitable, for the ordinary woman the factors influencing her life and morale are basically the same as they were a year ago. They are in fact arising from the fundamental differences between the circumstances of a woman's life as compared with a man's. If her children are evacuated, her husband called up, the average housewife is left in the same surroundings, with the same round of familiar routine. Her leisure occupations are restricted, her opportunities for mixing with other people reduced. Wartime conditions have broken habits of work and leisure for most women, without providing the opportunity for compensation. In addition to material dislocation, there are also the anxieties about menfolk and children, uncertainty and tension, personal danger and lack of sleep, rising prices, blackout. Good morale may be attributed to those who accept these worries and difficulties uncomplainingly, those who are willing to make the effort to surpass or overcome them. Most women find plenty to grumble about, not without reason, but the majority are accepting the inevitable, not with a fervour that accepts sacrifice as a duty, but with a quiet endurance and passivity that conserves their energies for the humdrum, everyday tasks necessary for holding together what remains of ordinary life and habit. So much may be drawn from our evidence at least, in our attempt to find out what women are thinking and feeling in this war. There appears no sign of defeatism; a certain amount of worry about the future – the course of the war, always the cost of living, dislocation of homes, the many ways in which war is translated into terms of everyday life. These are the things which are the first concern of women.

FOUR

APPEALING TO WOMEN?

Until 1941 war work for women remained voluntary. Women could, and did, enrol in the women's sections of the Forces: the Auxiliary Territorial Service, the Women's Royal Naval Service (Wrens) and the Women's Auxiliary Air Service. They could work in agriculture as members of the Women's Land Army, or care for the sick in one of the many nursing services. They could opt for Civil Defence work as air raid wardens, emergency messengers, fire duty staff and for various kinds of medical work. Many women at home with families undertook some form of voluntary work which could range from taking in evacuees or soldiers as lodgers to working with the Red Cross or the Women's Voluntary Service. The Home Guard, however, would not accept women except in an auxiliary capacity. No women were trained to use weapons although some formed small unofficial groups to teach themselves self-defence.

The voluntary basis of women's war work shifted during 1941 when labour shortages were becoming serious. A measure to compel women aged 20–21 to register at Labour Exchanges for war work was introduced in March 1941. This was quickly extended to cover all women up to the age of 40. The Essential Work Order brought both employers and employees under the control of the government. Women could not leave their employment (nor employers release them) without the permission of the National Service Office.

The voluntary principle was abandoned altogether in December 1941. The Minister for Labour, Ernest Bevin, was forced to acknowledge that conscription of women was necessary. Women were desperately needed to replace men in the factories and in the support services of the military. Measures to introduce 'compulsion' (as it was known) were welcomed by the feminist lobby who felt that some clear policy on women's war work was long overdue and who were angry at what they believed was the needless waste of women's energies. The National Service (No. 2) Act conscripted single women between the ages of 20 (later lowered to 19) and 30. Mothers of children under 14 were exempt as were certain women running households and taking care of other war workers. The category of 'mobile' women was introduced to indicate women who were free of household responsibilities and who could be moved from their home area into an area where labour was urgently needed.

11

M-O Report No. 615: An appeal to women, March 1941

This report is a typical Mass-Observation critique of government policy. It was probably written by Tom Harrisson based on the research carried out by the female Observers monitoring the press. The report is more concerned with the uses (or misuses) of propaganda than with the needs and interests of women themselves. It nevertheless illustrates the mixed messages which bombarded women in relation to their war work. The consultative committee which is mentioned was a new advisory body which the Minister of Labour had established as a result of continuous active lobbying of women MPs, members of the Woman Power Committee, to take the issue of women's labour seriously. The consultative committee included MPs Edith Summerskill and Irene Ward and members of both trade union groups and voluntary organisations.

After eighteen months of war it is still easy for any experienced observer to notice Government departments and Cabinet Ministers making major blunders in their treatment of public opinion and in their handling of propaganda. This partly arises from the exceptional degree of isolation from mass feeling which most of our present leaders now experience; and partly from the continuing and consistent ignoring of elementary facts in planning voluntary appeals and mass compulsions (e.g. the fact that it is necessary to survey the prejudices, suspicions and anxieties of people on the subject about which the appeal is made, *before* making it).

Seldom, however, do these activities become so conspicuously ineffective that they impact on the inexperienced observer. Usually, moreover, the publicity campaigns and their consequent muddles are conceived and executed in the privacy of the

Government departments; any outsiders concerned with the inside facts are liable to be persons who do not want to make a fuss or are not in a position to make a fuss. Particular interest, therefore, attaches to the recent activities of the Ministry of Labour, in dealing with one of the most revolutionary changes of the past eighteen months, namely the mobilisation of womanpower.

From the very first, analysis showed that this campaign was being muddled, that the women appealed to were confused, that the effect of the appeal was thereby minimised. This was clear by March 11. But it was not until March 20 that the eight independent women appointed by the Ministry of Labour as Consultative committee in the campaign made the front page of the newspapers (e.g. *Daily Express*) thus:

BEVIN EIGHT IN REVOLT
They say he took the wrong line in appeal to women.

The eight women Mr Bevin appointed as his consultative committee have decided to tell Parliament that they do not approve of the way he has approached the women of this country to take part in the war effort.

They met yesterday and agreed his approach was wrong psychologically. They feel the Labour Minister should have appealed to women emotionally rather than give them a series of orders and regulations.

One of the committee said to me last night: 'Women are eager to serve. But they feel they have not been taken sufficiently into Mr Bevin's confidence.

'We are forced to tell Parliament tomorrow that we should have been given fuller details of what is wanted of us, a fuller explanation of the part we might play in achieving victory.'

And this item went on to say:

'Nevertheless he would have got his first 100,000 volunteers within three days of his appeal if it had been on different lines.'

Looking at the press at the beginning of the campaign the inexperienced observer might be excused for believing (as so often) that everything was going swimmingly. For instance, the *Evening Standard* of March 10 had as double-bannered headline right across the front page:

WOMEN RUSH TO ENLIST TODAY IN BEVIN'S ARMY

And there followed a stirring write-up of the enthusiastic
response to Mr Bevin's appeal of March 9. The unobservant
observer might similarly have been excused for not noticing,
three evenings later, in the same newspaper, a much less conspicuous item, relegated to page 7 with the heading:

RESPONSE TO CALL FOR ARMS WORKERS
'DISAPPOINTING'

This item went on to elaborate the disappointment of the Ministry of Labour, and in doing so showed only too clearly the lack of
pre-vision on the part of those who instituted the campaign. For
instance:

A fair proportion of married women have children and may be
unwilling to volunteer until they have made arrangements for
their care.

Ministry of Labour local welfare officers are *recommending*
local authorities to establish day nurseries where these children can be accommodated while their mothers are at work in
the factories.

Meanwhile the Government are calling for *500,000 more*
women to register for training in the munition factories.

Our italics above. It is rather strange to think that on such a
major issue it should be vaguely left to Local Welfare officers to
recommend local authorities to establish day nurseries. This is
one of the elementary things which could and should have been
thought out and initiated ahead of any appeal or regulation
demanding the services of mothers with small children. That is,
provided an advance study showed that this would be the best
way of dealing with the situation.

The *Evening Standard* item of March 13 gave some of the
questions which it was supposed that women contemplating
registering voluntarily were asking, and the answers. These also
reveal a strange situation, a rather naive approach to the tensions and anxieties of women. For instance, one of the questions –
and indeed it is the question that every interested woman was
asking – was 'What sort of wages will I be paid?' To this the
Ministry of Labour answer reads as follows:

It is impossible to answer this question exactly. A lot depends
on whether the firm employing you pays union rates. If it does,
the minimum will be 35s.

But as the women are registering to be allocated to a job to which they are appointed and which they do not select themselves, how can they possibly know in advance whether they will get union rates. Indeed this answer seems as if it was deliberately calculated to accentuate uncertainty on a subject where assurance was essential. It might be noted as strange that these volunteers would be penalised by the accident of being drafted into a non-union firm at liberty to pay lower wages to recruits gained through a Government scheme.

Another brilliant answer to the question 'What are the working hours?' The answer: 'They will vary at different factories.'

On the subject of whether the workers would be sent far from home, they are informed that 'it is essential workers should be mobile-minded'; this ambiguous way of saying it is also grammatically beyond the understanding of many. Again on the subject of whether two volunteers registering together being able to go and work together the reply was vague and unreassuring. And so on.

But what a way to have the ground prepared for a campaign for volunteers! No wonder by March 13 the result was 'disappointing'. Women are not brainless dolts and everyone has heard of so many stories of inefficiency in this war, and of misuse of labour power, supplies etc. that only a small minority will voluntarily go into anything blind. However by March 18 (two days before the 'revolt' of the consultative committee), the *Daily Mirror* had worked the campaign up again, back to the old March 10 success.

WIVES AND MOTHERS RUSH FOR WAR WORK
Labour Exchanges were stormed yesterday by an army of women responding to the Ministry of Labour's appeal for women war workers.

The damage which the press does by phonily writing up campaign successes makes a considerable contribution to campaign failures. The remarkable feature of this appeal is the way in which it was apparently launched without the necessary decisions having been taken as to how those responding should be treated. However urgent the appeal, it was committing propaganda suicide to launch it ahead of the arrangements for implementing its effects. Had the conditions of employment, etc., been announced beforehand, and the Minister of Labour made any sort of survey of the best ways of making the appeal itself, it is very difficult to believe that he would not *at once* have got the 100,000 volunteers he wanted. Yet he was clearly aware of what he was doing, for in his initial Newcastle speech (March 9) he stated that in a few days he would announce the new terms of employment and wages for women, but that he was awaiting the decision of the Arbitration Tribunal on an application from the Trades Union. One can only conclude therefore that the Minister and Ministry of Labour knew what they were doing in fact, but had no idea of what they were doing in propaganda and in manipulating the necessary machinery for democratic appeals – and these appeals are particularly dear to the present Minister of Labour.

At many other points an observant observer would have noted a lack of any clear policy, press guidance, etc., in the opening stages of this crucial campaign for female good will. For instance, on March 11, the *Daily Express* had a front page item starting like this:

TO THE WOMEN OF ENGLAND

Mr Bevin has appealed to 100,000 of you to volunteer for work in war factories within a fortnight. In Europe Hitler does not ask the women to work. He orders . . .

And this item went on to describe in detail how women were conscripted in Germany – in essential facts this description does not differ importantly from what is likely to happen to many women in this country in the very near future. But on the same day, the *Daily Sketch* had as its headline:

CONSCRIPTION OF WOMEN TO BEGIN

The main front page item of the paper stressed the immediate introduction of compulsion – thus invalidating much of the meaning and emotional appeal of the Minister's voluntary demand of two days before. While there is no doubt a perfectly reasonable and logical relationship between the volunteering and the compelling in the official plan, the two things at once became confused in the campaign. The *Daily Sketch* item was quite definitely not calculated to encourage volunteering. And though it had a cross head 'Many volunteers', it ended by quoting the manager of an Exchange: 'We have been unable to give potential volunteers detailed information about wages and conditions of work, and for that reason we have lost some of them.'

The *Evening Standard* said that registration must be done through an employment exchange. But the *Sketch* said with characteristic attitude to the worker problem, that registration was to be done through *un*employment exchanges! But the *News Chronicle* (March 11) said applicants need *not* visit an employment exchange, they 'can seek advice at demonstration centres'. This item in the *News Chronicle* was in itself an extraordinary reflection of the campaign position, in that it again indicated the appeal for volunteers had been made in a somewhat precipitate manner:

PLANS TO MEET THE WOMEN'S RESPONSE TO WAR WORK CALL

Plans have been made to meet the response to Mr Bevin's call for women war workers. It is expected that most of the volunteers will be taught in factories where they are to work.

Two days later on March 13, the Advertising Trade paper *World's Press News* contained the following announcement, which might be calculated to confuse the observer who had by now come to the conclusion that an extensive campaign had already been launched, and in a way calculated to prejudice the goodwill of subsequent activities – an amateur campaign, ahead of the professional one now announced:

BIG LABOUR SCHEME STARTS

As part of the Government drive to get some hundreds of thousands of recruits into vital munitions industries, the Ministry of Labour, in co-operation with the Ministry of Information, is launching an extensive advertising scheme. Press posters, leaflets, broadcasting, films and special local drives will be used. Colman, Prentis and Varley are handling this account, which is one of the biggest schemes yet planned by the Ministry.

And again, two days later, the *Daily Express* front page (March 15), a sort of late surprise (surprising to anyone trying to follow this business) headlined:

BEVIN TELLS THE WOMEN TOMORROW

But by this time there was chaos in the public mind. This was brilliantly accentuated when papers, after the Minister's second speech on the subject within a week, headlined that the 20s and 21s would be conscripted *without exception*. Within a couple of days very extensive exceptions were being announced. And by this time influential intelligent women as well as the young women who are mere pawns in their game, were beginning to get fed up. For instance, the *Daily Mail* had a feature article by Ann Temple headed YOU'VE GOT IT WRONG MR BEVIN and making commonsense proposals which one would have hardly expected to be necessary at this late stage. The article included the following reasonable summary of the general problems:

> The voluntary system *rightly organised* would have given the country its best and speediest womanpower. Women have always responded magnificently to it. In *this* war the voluntary system was doomed to failure from the very start by the stupidity, tactlessness and incompetence that made women draw back in dismay.
>
> And here we are beginning all over again, this time with the compulsory registration of the 20s and 21s – single and married. There are to be 'interviews' . . . 'a few days to think it over' . . . 'more interviews'! Then allocation to a job (perhaps) and in the job hosts of 'welfare nurses' to see the girls are not 'home-sick'. 'There will be a tender regard for everyone's feelings,' says Mr Bevin.
>
> Heavens above! Are we at war? Where's the Minister's sense of proportion? Not tenderness, Mr Bevin, *please*. But *clarity, organisation, speed*.

So, by March 20, even that most regular and loyal of Government supporters, the *Daily Sketch*, had as its main editorial a strong criticism of a campaign which indeed merits a special inquiry into the bungling of leadership; the *Daily Sketch* editorial, with points italicised by us, reads thus:

> It is high time for Mr Ernest Bevin to tell the country precisely what he does mean by his proposals for the conscription of women.
>
> The letters received by the *Daily Sketch* from its readers indicate quite sufficiently that he has, by his vagueness, *caused*

quite enough 'alarm and despondency' to bring [him] *before the magistrates* if only he were a private individual.

The difficulties in the way of conscription of women are obvious enough. It is possible that they could be tackled and solved. *But there is no sign that Mr Bevin is tackling them.* He is simply talking and making the soldier say, as one does in a letter to the *Daily Sketch*, 'We all feel very strongly, and are not afraid to say so, against the conscription of our wives and sweethearts, who are the very people we are fighting to protect from Nazism and all it stands for.'

There is we are quite sure no intention of introducing Nazi methods into this country. Mr Bevin has unintentionally introduced the idea that there is. *He must make his plans, say what he wants done, and when his plans have been approved, get it done.*

At the present moment no woman in Great Britain knows *where she stands and the husbands, brothers and sons of all our women are in the same state of uncertainty.*

12

The diary of Amy Briggs, a Leeds nurse, 1941

This extract is taken from the first instalments of a long diary sent to M-O by a nurse, Amy Briggs, who was in her early thirties. In 1941 she combined running her home and taking care of her two young daughters, Anne and Sheila, with shift work at a nearby First Aid Post. Her next door neighbour, Mrs M., looked after the children while she was at work. She was married (very unhappily) to T., a private in the army, who came home irregularly on leave.

Thursday Oct 16th 1941
Beautiful sunny morning. Up early and decided to work hard. Haven't enough time to do work properly so don't do it at all. My nature – all or nothing! Managed to clear a pile of washing up. Wanted to black-lead. Hadn't any black-lead. Too much bother to trail to the shop for it so didn't do it. Hooray – didn't want to, anyway. Prepared nice dinner for the kidlets – all had happy hour together and then parted. Shan't see them again until tomorrow morning. Blast the war! Never sworn for years until this war came along. Enough to make anyone swear. Have to work until 10 p.m., therefore impossible to go along to my Thursday night meeting. Decide to ask Iris a few things about her escapades. Iris is 40, had twins 20 years ago – never married. A very broad-minded creature but so obviously a case of 'sexual starvation'! Decided as I listened to her that any man could take her out. Can hardly blame the war this time – she's an old hand. Have supper together and try to take in all that she says. Somehow or other, cannot agree with her. Prefer to listen and profit by her mistakes. Leave her at 10 p.m., seeking her married man who hasn't turned up. Wonder what kind of meeting they had at the hall? Wish I'd been there. Wish they'd just 'come across with the goods' which

I'm seeking. Just that 'something different' which I feel every man today is seeking. Wish I could be like Paul – struck on the Damascus road. Wonder if they'd call me Pauline, then?

Enough wondering – sat up until 12.15 p.m. and then almost too tired to go to bed but eventually arrived there.

Friday Oct 17th

Woke up at 9 a.m. and instead of jumping out of bed as I intended, just lay there thinking and thinking. I wish the war was over and for once I could have *all* my own way. Couldn't even tell all the Mass-Observ. people what that would be. Wish I could get the 'perfect' job. Don't know what it would be, yet, but it must be different and it must not be routine work. Something out of the ordinary, such as interviewing Hitler. I bet I could manage him. Bet on? Got up late but had time to romp with the girls at dinner-time. Arrived at work at 2 p.m., wage-man arrived at 3 p.m. Decided to buy shoes and vests and goodness knows what. Then decided I couldn't afford them. Shopping postponed. Went shopping for sister in downpour of rain, but felt so fresh that I walked all the way instead of riding. (Had to break off writing this – 11.15 p.m. – to look for my torch, as I thought I heard a plane over. False alarm.)

Nothing much to report – one of those days which just drift along without any untoward happening.

Going to answer some M-O questions and then hop off to bed. Cat having a hectic time chasing a fly round the house. Wish I were a cat with nothing to do but chase flies and meouw for milk. Hope there's no siren tonight. Too cold to trail across to the post at this time of the night.

War Opinions At a First Aid Post

One night last week, just when I'd been having a good laugh at my children, my neighbour came in with a face as long as a week and said, 'Russia's losing.' Now I don't profess to know much of the higher theories of this war business, but I do know what the working man and woman think and I have my own doubts and fears as much as anyone. One look at her face put me absolutely in the dumps, for the time being, and then a thought struck me – 'I must find someone who thinks we are winning' – and ostrich-like, I wanted to find a covering which would hide any unpleasant facts and so, purposely, I brought the subject up at the supper-table at work and again in the doorway at 12.30 a.m.! Our supper party comprised a St John's nurse, a first-aid worker, a canteen worker and myself. Cautiously, I asked if Russia was losing and waited for a hearty and cheering 'No – not they', but my spirits sank as one after the other confirmed my neighbour's statement. So I suggested that we invade Germany now, but thrashed it out and came to the conclusion that it would be mass murder. Canteen worker thinks that all the countries in hands of Nazis on the verge of revolting. St John's nurse thinks that if we were to march thro' France and Belgium, the conquered people would fall in behind and 'united we stand' would be our motto. Felt like singing 'See the conquering hero comes' as I pictured our men leading the way. First-aider says in doing this, we would distract the Germans and draw them from Russia and thus give them a breather. We are all puzzled and don't really know what to think.

Feeling very despondent, I went to the doorman, an old veteran of the last war and asked him if Russia was losing. He answered with a very throaty, hoarse, 'No, lass! They're tricking 'em and when the ice sets in, in another fortnight, the Germans will be trapped.' And then he chuckled and rubbed his hands with glee at the thought. In the last war, he spent most of his time in Russia, so he ought to know. At any rate, ostrich or no ostrich, I'm going to agree with him, because the thought of what Russia's losing would mean to us, is more than anyone with any feeling at all, could bear!

We have on our staff one of the leading citizens of Leeds, and he is of the opinion that we are by no means sure to win, ourselves, and so I asked him just what difference our loss would mean to me. As he explained how my working hours may be altered, the cinemas and dance-halls closed on certain days, I wasn't a bit perturbed as they do not interest me and so I told him no matter what the Jerrys attempted outwardly, they couldn't rob me of my country walks, as that didn't affect them and they could not therefore kill that happy, calm 'something' within. He looked at me closely and replied, 'No, the best things in life are free,' and after a while he left the office. Next came the wage-man, a very, very nice quiet educated little man. We discussed invasion and the invasion instructions issued house to house by circular. Like myself, he thinks that they are ridiculous. What man or woman, says he, is going to slam the door in the face of a man with a tommy-gun under his arm? It is only natural for anyone, for the sake of the children behind the door with him, whether it be a man or woman, to give in. I said the same, adding that they could even have my tin of plums, which I'm hoarding for Xmas, if they wanted. The man in charge of the fleet of ambulances, an old soldier, said he'd hand the ambulances over and say, 'Help yourself!' Personally, I agree with him. If, as they say, they were given guns, it would be a different matter – they'd fight it out to the last man. Also, they added that we have played right into the Germans' hands by issuing a plain uniform to all Home-Guard and ARP workers. No distinguishing marks of any description – how easy to copy!

Last but not least, we have the opinion of sister-in-charge. She was a Territorial Army sister in the last war. Her opinion is that we, as a nation, are cornered absolutely. If we win, according to her, it will be by some miracle. Every capable man and woman, she says, should be compelled to work a couple of hours a day, apart from the daily routine, in some way or other, to speed up the munition and aircraft work. I agree with her! Fetch them from the firesides for an hour or two a day. They'd enjoy it, even tho' they deny it and the increase in output would be enormous. As for the British army now in training, send them to the nearest munition factories or build a site on their camps and put them to work in some way or other. Every little helps but why won't folk see this point and volunteer?

In the general summing up of the opinions of these people, I come to the conclusion that the situation is very grave – that the general feeling is not one of 'We are sure to win' but rather that 'We must not lose'.

Saturday Oct 18th
Sent first M-O diary off. Hope it comes up to standard. Nearly broke my toe, rushing to unlock door to let Anne in – must put less polish on the floor! Very quiet night at work, complete with usual cattishness from staff. What a rut to get into. Must be the continual waiting and waiting for sirens.

Very trying time inwardly. Wish I could have all my own way. Decided that the perfect job for me would be to work in a station refreshment room. Trains – people – suitcases – fresh faces – how grand it must all be! Decide to say nothing about this particular day – boring and long and trying.

Monday 20 October
Up to 5.40 a.m. Arrive at post 6.40 by mistake. Seems funny to work in starlight. Is the whole world upside down – morally, spiritually and materially? Begin to think it is, including myself. Not much to do at work. Home again by 2.45 p.m. Took Anne [for] a walk. Have decided that she must see a specialist. Stripped and washed her, prior to infirmary visit. Went to meeting at 7.15. Excellent! Home at 8.35, decide to make myself some chips. In the middle of making some when the siren goes. Jolly good fun making chips by torchlight (blackout not too good so had to put light out). Can't eat chips. Heavy gunfire. Not on duty so stood in doorway, watching flashes and searchlights. Wish it was all over, with my heart! All clear at 12.10 p.m. Into bed and blotto.

Tuesday 21 October
Back at work at 7 a.m. Count up my £.*s. d*. Shocked to find myself nearly skint. Everyone tired at work, therefore grumpy. No phone calls. Anne taken to infirmary. Comes home with bad report: 'No good signs about lungs'. Went to bed very worried. No sense in trying nowadays. Can't get right food or right hour for children in wartime.

Wednesday 22 October
Up early. Work in starlight and bitter cold. Not much doing at work – let's skip it and arrive at teatime. Go home to empty house. Wish some kind fairy would light me a fire before I come in. More bad news – Anne has to go to hospital. Out with my knitting to finish her jumper! Decide to go to bed early. Partially undressed when lousy sirens go again, about 8.30 p.m. Back into my togs once more. Must report at the post. Got halfway down garden path when guns begin to roar and blaze out. Stand stock still, wondering if I dare go. Two miles is a hell of a long way when guns are going! Decide that I can't afford to be out of work, so kiss the girls goodbye and pick 'em up and sprint for a tram. Tram halfway there when policeman hops on and stops it. Some bright spark suggests we are OK while the planes are overhead. Don't feel OK myself. Jump off tram and run for post, wind whistling round my

tin helmet. Terrific gunfire. Oh boy! What a life. Arrive at post very hot, very triumphant minus shoulder straps on my ?s [bra] and a pin somewhere else. Such is life! Sat talking to the post chaplain, decide to form a dramatic society. Gunfire, piano-playing, talking & laughter – what a mix-up it all is and what a tragedy. All clear and no bombs at 11.32. Home to bed, after I'd made and eaten some more chips . . .

Friday 24 October
Pay day and Sheila's birthday. She is 9 today. Seem to be getting an old woman. Take them both to see *Fantasia* as a birthday treat. My long weekend off. Leave work on Sat at 2 p.m. and should go back at 10 p.m. on Tuesday. Should have a pleasant time with just the girls and I. Hubby away so all should be quiet.

Home from cinema at 6 p.m. Find hubby at home. Hell! Sees that I'm very, very annoyed and so we fall out. Tears and no tea for me. Can't help it – wanted to be alone!

Saturday 25 October
Taken very ill at 5 a.m. Decide that I'm going to die and jolly well feel like it. No work. Instead have a half day in bed. See Dr at night. Tells me I have all the signs of a duodenal ulcer. Rats! Ring Sister, tells me that I must go to work on Sunday as she's marked Sat as my day off. Go home and have a real, good cry. There goes my long weekend!

Sunday 26 October
Work at 7.10 a.m. Late but glad to get out of T.'s way. Home at 2.40 p.m. Dinner ready for me. Fall out immediately we meet. Wish I could hide my feelings but I just can't. Have a nap, no tea – can't eat any. T. leaves at 7.30 p.m. Wish he'd leave for good – all three of us. Go to bed early ab-so-lutely fed up.

Monday 27 October
Receive letter summoning Anne to hospital. What a rush! Got her to infirmary at 1.30 p.m. Leaves by ambulance for Knaresborough at 3 p.m. Go home utterly disheartened. What's the use of trying? Feel like ending myself. Got Sheila's tea and pack her off next door to bed and try to snatch a sleep before going on duty. No

use! Arrive at work at 10 p.m. Quiet night – no calls or anything. Home at 8 a.m. and hop into bed.

Tuesday 28 October
Bed at 8 a.m. Sleep until 4 p.m. Feel absolutely lost without Anne. Put Sheila to bed and have a trip down to mother's. Both have a cry over Anne. Leave mother at 9 p.m., armed with a lump of meat pie and go to work. Everybody in the worst possible mood or is it me? Night over at last, go home and eat my pie, ulcer or no ulcer. Jump into bed at 8 a.m.

Wednesday 29 October
Up at 4 p.m. Only Sheila and I. Simply awful! By the time we'd had tea and washed S., time for her to go to bed. Only me now. Don't know what to do. Dr's medicine makes me ill. Can't eat any of the free supper which is provided at post for night staff. Night staff in terrible mood. Miss G. absolutely bad-minded – can see no good in anyone. Can't stick it any longer and tell her off good and strong at 6.30 a.m. Suggest she tries kindness for a change. Imagine me, 32 years old, telling 58 yrs old G. just where she's wrong. Can't help it – can't stand this continual back-biting and injustice. Go home feeling as if I deserve a medal. Into bed at 8 a.m. . . . .

Friday 31 October
Get up feeling full of beans. Black-lead & do some small jobs. Go to work for my wage at 2 p.m. and then go to see my sister at 3 p.m. Try to get some oranges for Anne. Nothing doing. Get home about 6 p.m. Find Sheila has tried to get tea ready for first time. Bread 2″ thick, smothered in jam ration. Fire halfway up chimney. Have a good laugh but mustn't let her know, bless her. Send her to bed at 7 p.m. and have a nap myself and then work at 10 p.m. . . . .

Sunday 2 November
. . . Get up and get ready for Knaresborough. Go to town without a bite to eat. Miss bus, an hr to wait for next, eventually arrive at Knaresborough in 3 hrs time. Usually takes at the very most 1 hr. Bus service absolutely disgusting! Find Anne playing about in ward but looking very pale and wan. Informed by sister-in-charge

that we must blame the wartime food for her condition – no eggs, no meat and nothing which goes to keep children strong . . .

Wednesday 5 November
My day off. Bad news – T. is coming home for 7 days. Clean the house upstairs and down and wait for him to come home. Doesn't come on Wed. Three cheers! One more night of peace and quietness. Wish I could run away for 7 days. Bed at 11 p.m. full of foreboding.

6 November
Letter from Anne to say that she is coming home on Friday. Thought it was Friday and went to fetch her by mistake. Very disappointed. Did some shopping in town. Get into house and followed in by T. Been at home just 20 minutes when the trouble begins. Suggests that I had had my day off on Wed. on purpose to avoid him. As if I could! Burns his dinner which includes 1 person's meat ration for one week. Go to work heartbroken. Dread home time and think very, very seriously of ending myself. Met at 10 p.m. by T. who mutters at me all the way home and then starts on me as soon as I get in. If I had no children I'd run away. As it is, I can't bear it any longer. I wonder what I'll do when the war is over? Went to bed in tears.

7 November
T. fetches Anne from the infirmary. Plays absolute h––l with me, because I've arranged for them to sleep at home for 2 nights. Crazy because he can't watch and spy on my movements, which, to his distorted mind, won't bear watching. Insults the person next door who looks after the girls for me. Now I'm in the soup alright. Refuses to mind them while T. is at home. Go to work in tears once more. Decide that the gas oven will be an easy way out. Home from work at 10.25 p.m. and more arguing and arguing.

8 November
Get up to be met by more jealous insinuations. Don't answer at all. Useless trying to talk to anyone who won't listen to reason. Go to work in tears once more. This is getting above a joke. Counting the days of his leave, every night and every morning. Arrive home from work at 10.25 p.m. to find T. sat with the clock facing him. I

could kill him willingly! Still swearing at me at 12 p.m. because I *refuse* to talk to him. Anne wakes up and screams out with headache. Thank God for an excuse to get out of his way. Fetch her downstairs, make some strong tea and nurse her. I wonder – can she have done it on purpose? Before I take her to bed, place 20 Players on table for T. to see whilst I'm upstairs. Come back downstairs. T. very quiet. Fancy quietening down for 20 cigarettes. Wouldn't quieten for £200 myself if what I was saying was right. Made me a cup of tea and looked very sorry. Don't know what time I went to bed – too tired and broken-hearted to look.

9 November

. . . When he's gone back I'm going to do all that he accuses me of – flirting on the way home and having male friends. I wouldn't care a damn if it was true but I never go out. One thing I'm certain of, instead of turning down all these offers, in future I'm going to accept them (maybe!) . . .

13

The volunteer war worker, Bradford, October 1941

Mrs Trowbridge was a middle-aged housewife living in Bradford. Her one son, Stephen, was about to go to Oxford as a student and her husband (whose occupation is unknown) lived with her. She was evidently comfortably off and was active in a range of voluntary capacities: she belonged to the local WVS, the University Women's Federation (which helped professional women refugees from occupied Europe) and a local community organisation which funded and administered the neighbourhood nursery. The extracts begin on the day a soldier arrives to lodge in her house.

1 October 1941

The ordeal is over – my soldier has arrived. Very mild and inoffensive – very thin and delicate-looking. I suspect a tendency to asthma. Wonder if a smoky room suits him – though he should be acclimatised to smoke and dirt – he comes from Burnley. I'm so thankful my son was at home to receive my visitor – Stephen has such a way with people that they feel at home at once. In next to no time they were deep in questions of cricket – and football. Both have gone to bed as pleased as Punch, because they both agree that Willis Edwards of Leeds has been the greatest halfback in soccer.

Had no time to think about the war today, but I did notice that there was a report that the Rumanians were 'ratting' – as though the Germans would let them!! If the Rumanians retire successfully, we shall have the Finns, the Hungarians, and the Italians doing the same.

10.05 p.m. – and I believe that is the sound of AA gunfire. Must see to my water-buckets, and warm clothes for the family. They won't.

2 October 1941

I was right about enemy air activity last night – they had the alert at Leeds. My fire-watch tonight 11 p.m. to 1 a.m. The 12 o'clock news has just announced 3 bombers brought down tonight – 2 in the N.E. – they must have made an early start tonight.

My soldier seems quite at home now. Of course, Stephen is a great help – he is so friendly. If today has been a sample of Army ways, it looks as though my gas bills, far from being less, will be infinitely greater. Dinner ready for 1.10 p.m. – message brought that the soldier wouldn't be up till 2.15 p.m. or thereabouts. He arrived at 2.30 p.m. – oven on till then. Tea hanging on till after 7 p.m. – washing up at 8 p.m. I shall have no time for anything at this rate! What a prospect!

The food situation is just as I prophesied. The grocer in Heaton refused to give extra rations to some of the women who are entertaining soldiers. He says he has had no intimation from the Food Office of any extra arrivals in Heaton, therefore he can't be expected to have any supplies for them. But what is the poor housewife to do? My soldier seemed surprised when I remarked that the fruit and tomato situation was serious in Bradford. They are going begging in Southport.

The billeting allowance question is again to the fore. My soldier hasn't mentioned the subject; neither have I. But other women have already had violent arguments about it. They have rung up the billeting officer, only to be told that it isn't his affair; or that they are being robbed and that it is their own fault.

My soldier tells me also that dozens of fellows were turned away from the addresses they had been given. Evidently the occupiers had acquiesced when the billeting officer called, but had no intention of being saddled with a soldier, so just turned him away when he arrived! The Government's powers!! Where are they?

Just heard today that the Assistant MOH inspected the Nursery yesterday, and was so satisfied with it that our grant is coming through without any more delay – dating back to April 1st. Almost too good to be true! For we were nearly on the rocks financially. Another muddle revealed by the new Milk Rationing Scheme. At present the children who are allowed free and cheap milk get it at the Nursery. With the new scheme in force, unless the whole of the child's family is registered with Nursery milk-man, he will be unable to deliver milk for that child. That means that the Nursery will have to apply for milk under a catering scheme, and pay full price for it, thus cutting right across the plan for milk for the children. The Food Officials here simply will not help the matron out of her dilemma, but pass her on from clerk to clerk, and the 'boss' is unreachable.

7 October 1941

Have had no time for almost a week to do anything but feed and entertain relays of youths and soldiers. What with a soldier who is humbugged about by inefficient superiors; nobody's mealtime coinciding with anybody else's, packing for Stephen's departure on Thursday, youths coming in to say farewell etc., etc., etc., there hasn't been a minute free for me to sit down and read a newspaper even.

I never had a very great opinion of the Army and its officers, but after the last few days I don't know how we shall win this war. At least I do know, that the Army, as now run, won't do it. Total war! And we hear still, of interviewing officers who ask a prospective officer from an OCTU what the best white wine is to serve with oysters!!! As though he were interviewing an applicant for a chef's post! And the petty Hitlers! My soldier's duties since Sept 28th have been: 1st Sunday whole day picket – walk – no buses – wet through to skin – no change; Tuesday night – all night picket – terrible cold; Wed – travel to Bradford; rest of week – day picket, finish 7 p.m.; 2nd Sunday – whole day picket – no buses – walk 3 miles for 8.30 a.m.; Tuesday – all night picket. Who is dodging?

Why do we continue to deal with the Germans as though they were like the rest of the civilised nations? They show every sign of low breeding – they have no idea how to give way gracefully – they must be granted every concession – they demand the delivery of their wounded, to be transported in our ships (not theirs) before our wounded are released. It's a cruel disappointment for everybody, but I agree that we shouldn't cave in to the German demands. I also think there's something in the rumour about their demanding Hess. I'm also disgustingly pleased that the women internees have had to remain here – I should give them plenty of hard work to keep them occupied.

Deep gloom at the Nursery today. They expected that I should turn up flaunting the cheque from the MOH. I haven't seen it yet. Committee meeting tonight of University Women's Federation.

Arranged Autumn Meeting at which refugee graduates are to be entertained. Heard that our German 'science' woman has arrived safely to join her family in S. America after her internment in the Isle of Man. We are thus relieved of having to find funds for her support.

Reactions to billeting coming in from all sides. Some boys are banished to the kitchen; others are presumptuous. Some want a private room for 18/6 per week and others offer all their lodging allowance except for 3/6 bus pass. Evidently all the soldiers on this road have agreed to pay 25/-, coming in to all meals. I think they are 'getting at us' but as my soldier is very quiet and unassuming and has a ridiculously small appetite compared with my family, I couldn't in all fairness demand more. One of my friends is seething with rage about her lodger who has lived on the fat of the land for a week for 25/-, requested that her spare bed should be reserved for his pal, and then calmly informed her that he is leaving on Sat, because when he and his pal 'tossed' to see who should move, my friend lost!!! As though they were doing her a favour by patronising her home!!!

9 October 1941

Attack of migraine this morning – no wonder! – What with the news and Stephen's departure for Oxford at 9.30 a.m. Heard some interesting news about the Joint Recruiting Board before whom Stephen was [presented] last term. The Air Ministry officer evinced great surprise that anyone should prefer to go into the Air Force – the fact that Stephen had already joined the Air Cadets weighed not at all – at which the Chairman of the Board pointed out that evidently the hopes of thousands of young men were being raised because of the ATC scheme, only to be dashed to the ground at the University. The Naval representative seemed to be asleep most of the time – remarked that it was strange that a young man from land-locked Bradford had put down the Navy as 2nd choice – ignoring the fact that many young men like Stephen have sea-faring forefathers – great-grandfathers who sailed the tea clippers from China and relatives on all the 7 seas today! The final impediment was Stephen's glasses. So, he is doomed to the Army. And what an Army!

I've heard enough this last week to make me despair of our ever winning the war. Debate on manpower in Parliament – Army shrieking for men – Industry clamouring for them. Men in the ATC despairingly applying to be given a job worthy of a man – appealing to the colonel above the heads of the section-leader – result, transfer to a department where girls and less skilled men stick pieces of paper on bigger pieces of paper. And then the Minister for War gets up and babbles about 'no square pegs in round holes' nowadays – psychological tests and the like. The fact of the matter is that the people who are running this war are the same as ran the 'peace' – they still seem to think that their 'peacetime' methods will win the war against the Germans. There's no sense of urgency – extreme urgency – about anything they do, and when we have lost this war, the verdict will be that the people of this country, meaning such as I, never realised what a powerful enemy we were fighting, and what was necessary to defeat him. It's not the ordinary people who don't realise our danger, it's the administrative and executive staffs.

10 October 1941

I see there's a new plan – another one – to distribute food for the benefit of workers in heavy industries. It's only right that miners, blastfurnace men, dockers, shipyard workers, agricultural workers etc. should have the lion's share of meat, cheese, sugar and butter, but I do not agree that the 3rd and lowest grade of workers should be described as 'Sedentary workers and everyone else who eats at home, *or in restaurants* and luxury hotels'. People who eat at home (and people who live in luxury hotels, surely) have only the food for which they have coupons. People who feed in restaurants and canteens have their rationed food at home, and what they eat in restaurants and canteens is *extra*. This is absolutely unfair. For 7 or 8 months this year I, along with several other housewives, helped in a canteen, reserved for ARP workers and police – the staff of a Control Report Centre. We helpers were astounded and disgusted at the quantities of food which were always procurable, and for which they paid ridiculously low prices. They had cups of tea, with sugar, in season and out. After a jolly good dinner at midday, there were cups of tea again by 3 p.m., and from about 4.45 p.m. to 6.45 p.m. we were harried to death cooking and serving egg and chips, sausage and chips, fish and chips, and scones or biscuits, or jam tart. They turned up their noses at salad or sandwiches – they must have a cooked tea, and all this without tipping up any coupons. Our husbands, on the other hand, didn't see an egg for months at a time, nor a tomato, and we couldn't afford to buy such things as cucumbers. And these people aren't 'heavy workers'. I know they have long hours of duty, and if and when there is a blitz they work like Trojans, but here in Bradford, the ARP workers at these centres spend their time playing cards, table-tennis, sky-larking with the police and the male staff, painting faces and finger nails, and attending to coiffures – to say nothing of an afternoon at the 'Lido' bathing and sunbathing. I resented the state of affairs very much, but as a member of the WVS I wished to help where I could be of most use, but I never could understand why the ARP staff couldn't patronise the cafe which is situated on the same premises, next door to the canteen, and which the soldiers in the district were obliged to use. Things are altered now – the full-time ARP girls attend to the meals and so earn their money, but their food at the canteen still costs them no coupons.

12 October 1941

Alert at 11 p.m. Planes over very shortly after – making in the direction of Manchester. Going very fast for bombers. If there's nothing doing here by 12 p.m. I shall go to bed. Husband and soldier already there.

Letter from Stephen Sat. evening. Is still in his old rooms at College. Trunk keys which were missing when we wanted to lock up at this end, reposing in his writing case at Oxford!! I guessed they were. One of my keys unlocks but won't lock his trunk.

I ought to feel less depressed after Beaverbrook's effort but for some reason I don't. Everybody's attention is turned on Moscow – nobody seems to attach an importance to the 'spearheads' that [are] moving quietly along the north shores of the Black Sea. I can never understand why these motorised 'spearheads' can't be annihilated when they penetrate such a long distance ahead of the main body of the attackers. Motor vehicles can't run without oil and lubricants, and I'm sure if we adopted the German tactics we should be full of excuses of how our tanks were immobile because our supplies had been cut off by the enemy behind our front line.

13 October 1941

. . . My neighbour was very disgruntled this morning about last night's alert. Fancy Hitler upsetting her routine again after having been such a gentleman all summer!

14 October 1941

So sorry I missed the 'funny turn' on the wireless last night. But how can any intelligent woman be expected to switch on for a programme for women containing such inanities as 'Confessions of favourite stage and screen stars'. Horrible thought! 'Beauty in battledress' and 'All-weather faces'. Utter tripe! I noticed when I switched on for the news at 9 p.m. that there was the 'dithering' in the background which we had last winter, and thought it came from the Italian stations. The programmes for tonight don't seem to offer much chance for the Germans to chip in, unless they do it in the News, or Evelyn Laye's programme, and who on earth wants to listen to Evelyn Laye?

Weekly visit to Nursery. Learned that Government grant will not be sent to me until passed by the local Health Committee. Wonder when their next meeting will be? From the Nursery went on to a meeting of the full committee of the Community Centre, of which the Nursery is the most flourishing part, at present. The Nursery part of the committee had somewhat of a shock when we gathered that our Secretary was toying with the idea of a 2nd Nursery in another part of the estate. What plan has she for our present Nursery – now that we have managed to have it recognised, too? But for the war, the committee's plan of having a Centre for babies, young people and adults would have materialised – a plot of land had been set aside by the City council, but owing to conditions everything has been held up. A week or two ago the Council issued what was virtually an ultimatum – either the Community Centre committee proceeded to use the land for a Youth hut or the Council would grab it for the purpose. So – our impulsive Secretary has a grandiose plan to acquire a pre-fabricated building at Government expense to be erected on the vacant plot, if – IF – the local Health Committee give the plan their blessing. At any rate, the MOH has suggested a Round Table conference between his committee and some of the Community Centre committee. The result should be interesting – the Bishop is Chairman of our committee!

15 October 1941

One of my friends opened her heart to me yesterday about the war. She said the anxiety was getting her down, but she daren't say anything at home because her husband upbraided her, accused her of 5th Column leanings etc., etc. What a lot of husbands belong to the 'It'll be alright' school of thought! I'm afraid when the winter raiding starts again morale will fall with a thump. One of my friends was so upset on Sunday night at the sound of the alert that she had what I think is an apoplectic fit – still unconscious.

Today's gem! Woman on tennis courts heard to remark that she wasn't particularly worried about the war – her husband worked in a bank, and even Hitler couldn't do without banks!!!

16 October 1941

What is to be done about getting girls to join the ATS? The colour of the stockings frightens some of them off, but for the most part the girls in this district won't have anything to do with the ATS because of the tales they have heard about the officers. It is unfortunate that so many of the officers have loud, unfriendly, patronising voices, and speak what they think is King's English with so much affectation and over-emphasis. Neither the King nor the Queen show any sign of this affectation. The officers seem to think that if a girl speaks with a Northern accent she is uneducated, uncouth, insensitive – in short a barbarian, and proceed to treat her as if she were a kitchenmaid being interviewed by an ill-bred duchess. As very few self-respecting girls in the West Riding would dream of going into domestic service (they look on it as degradation), they resent the haughty, patronising ways of the ATS officers.

17 October 1941

Very interesting meeting of the University Women's Federation. We entertained 5 refugee graduates who are working in the district – domestic work, teaching and hospital work. Only one of them seemed disgruntled – a Czech lawyer who was disappointed because she had to look after her 'war-working' husband instead of practising her profession. One of the medical women gently chided her by suggesting that the unhappy refugees should try to recapture their feelings when they were granted their visas to come to England!

The Viennese teacher told me an interesting story behind the visit of J. B. Priestley to the North for the purpose of inspecting the Army's Educational system. One day our Mrs Wirth was asked by the Army Education Officer in the district if she would take a German class for officers and men, starting the following night. She thought the sudden request rather strange, but consented. A number of officers – all ranks, and men appeared, so did J. B. Priestley, and so did the *Picture Post* photographic outfit. After that session, nobody turned up again except a corporal, a teacher himself, with whom Mrs W. continues the course by post. She was somewhat loath to criticise, but she can't understand such an Army Educational System. We can!

18 October 1941

Start a week's holiday today, but my soldier complicates matters. Husband very disgruntled – he thinks it all wrong that he should have to be responsible for rousing a soldier every morning at 7.30 a.m. – and whilst my husband turns out 'on a siren', this guy stays snug in bed! He's a good example of a 'Mother's darling' – must have been waited on hand and foot, like so many North-country men. Afraid he'll miss it here. My menfolk have to be self-reliant – I don't believe in making a slave of myself for any man.

19 October 1941

Suggestion today that Bevin should check up on women in uniform running canteens etc. Good idea. We have lots of women round here sporting WVS uniform who spend a long time doing very little. An interesting light was shed on the methods of these women supposed to be running canteens and feeding centres. My sister-in-law spent some time in the South with her husband at an OCTU. She helped at a feeding centre run by Lady This and the Hon. Mrs That. The non-titled ladies went early to prepare the vegetables and do the cooking – the 'titles' arrived with the cooked dinner, passed the plates to the children with a profuse sprinkling of 'darlings', and disappeared in their cars when dinner was over, while the non-titled continued with the washing-up etc. And so it goes on.

20 October 1941

Last bus from Town to Heaton 9.22 p.m.! It won't affect me, but what about the war-workers who have to go on duty, and those who are coming off? The soldiers who are billeted here can't understand the stagnation in a city the size of Bradford – they think it is worse than any village. Our Tramways Manager has always been a believer in early to bed – before the war our last bus was 11.20 p.m. – and he is another of our collection of petty Hitlers. He came here from somewhere in the south where snow rarely falls, and the first thing he did was to get rid of our snow-ploughs!

10.30 p.m.: Gunfire from the direction of Leeds – planes over immediately after – no sirens in B'ford, although planes loitered overhead for quite a long time. Thought we were 'for it' this time, but they have gone further west, to Manchester and Liverpool again? Going to bed as usual.

21 October 1941

Somewhat astonished on reading the summary in the October Bulletin [from Mass-Observation] about menus. It surely can't be based on information gained from the N. of England – probably London and coastal districts. Honey!!! To 'eke out' at breakfast! Absolutely unobtainable here. The one jar I *have* seen lately cost 5/- per lb. Eggs for breakfast!! Porridge replacing cereals! I can't get either at my grocers. More fruit than in May!! What sort of fruit? Who can afford even apples at 1/3 per lb? And what is there besides apples? Nothing here. The only department where we compare favourably with the rest of the country is in the meat department. When fish is procurable, I refuse to pay such fantastic prices as are asked. We still stick to high tea – anytime between 5.45 p.m. for my husband and 7 p.m. for the soldier.

The farce of our Mrs Wirth and the Army Educational Dept more amusing than ever. Refugees are not allowed to help in canteens for soldiers, but her request that she should be allowed to take the Army class in her flat (a bed-sitting room) was granted!!!

22 October 1941

8.40 p.m.: sirens at Leeds – none here. Heavy gunfire – planes immediately. Usual route 8.45 p.m. Our sirens with planes over-

head. Very heavy gunfire – not ours, for we haven't any. I wish we
had. I find it very comforting – the heavier the better for me – at
least we are hitting back trying to get at them. Why we don't have
some nightfighters on this route to Manchester and Liverpool I
can't understand. The Germans always come and go the same
way – why not try to down them before they reach their targets
and so prevent damage? There's plenty of uninhabited spaces
between here and the Mersey, where a few 'liquidated' German
planes could fall and cause very little damage.

23 October 1941
Soldier very late for tea – after 8 p.m. – came with the startling
news that he had to report in London on the 28th inst. – in
connection with POW camp accounts. 60/40 chance of his returning here – had requested the Billeting Officer to keep this address
free for him if he should return!! A respite for me, at any rate!

Contributor to newspaper asking today why there is such
abysmal ignorance about and indifference to the Empire in this
country. That's easy! Elementary school teachers, particularly
men, are usually the duds among their contemporaries – have
gone all Socialist, therefore against anything to do with Empire –
especially since they had cuts in salaries (the same as everybody
else) some years ago. Secondary and Grammar School teachers
having gone all 'Red' at the Universities deliberately infect their
pupils with the same disease – deride the Empire even to the
length of distorting history. I find that the older generations know
nothing and care less about the Empire – or any other country
under the sun.

25 October 1941
'Eggless' week again! Yet shopkeepers are selling eggs 'off the
ration' at 1*d* each. Woolton must have discovered a huge consign-
ment hidden away – eggs which should have been offered to the
public before they went bad. No thank you! I'm not buying his
rotten eggs.

Have heard another reason today why many parents are most
unwilling to allow their daughters to join the Forces – and I agree
with them. A young married acquaintance of mine, on leave from
an Air Force station, was heard, at a mixed party, describing with
great glee the hundreds of girls there were at this station – 'pick

where you like' style of thing – what a 'stunner' he had picked up etc., etc. – sickening! Particularly to parents who object to such things, and some of us are still quite 'provincial' when it comes to fornication and adultery. My young friend looked quite surprised when he knew what I thought about him – he didn't think his wife would take that attitude! Perhaps not, but I do, very strongly.

27 October 1941
Very busy weekend. Golf Sat. morning – allotment afternoon. Sunday morning in bed – afternoon tidying the garden, now that all the leaves have been blown off the trees. The magpie's nest also landed in the garden – they aren't very expert builders, for their 1st attempt was blown down before they had finished it. Jerry-building even in the bird world!

Fancy! We have been at war for over 2 years, and we still read in the papers: 'The call *now* is for energetic leadership skilled in modern mechanised warfare' . . . 'tradition and red tape should not hamper them' . . . 'The appointment of a number of energetic generals in the "forties" with mechanised experience and skill would do much to dispel such lack of confidence as exists in and out of the Army'. Indeed it does! Our General Staff absolutely ignorant of mechanised warfare, and a section of the population howling for the government to throw masses of PBI against mechanised hordes of Germans.

28 October 1941
Weekly visit to Nursery. No news of the M. of H. grant – have had to fall back, for the salaries, on the donation earmarked for the Nursery salaries. No news of any result from the Round Table conference held by the committee and the Medical Dictator of Health. Found two of the children had returned to Hull, of all places. Parents should be jailed for taking children back to such danger areas.

The Police and Billeting Authorities don't play the game. As an example, they have fined a woman in Baildon for refusing evacuees. She is a widow from the last war – supplements her pension by taking boarders, and so quite rightly refused evacuees with their paltry allowances when she knew that very much bigger houses, and very much wealthier people were free of evacuees. Naturally she was fair game for the authorities. She is taken to Court. It won't do.

29 October 1941

At last we are beginning to find out where the eggs have gone. 150,000 in one Black Market prosecution alone, and there's probably 150,000 other cases that ought to be brought to light. The news yesterday that the transport of food is to be curtailed and kept 'regional' isn't very pleasant reading to us in this part of the world. We produce nothing eatable – what are we going to do?

30 October 1941

No news of my soldier. Has he gone overseas? To the Isle of Man? Or where? My conjecture that he was a 'spoiled darling' was quite right. One of his friends remarked to me that he wondered how my soldier would fare in a P. of War camp after his coddling at home!

The snow shifting season has begun! Snow fell heavily this morning. Two inches in depth by noon. It looks as if we are to have a longer winter than usual – 9 months instead of 6. Our southern APC are aghast at the thought of this weather for another 6 months or so.

See that Lady Allen of Hurtwood, in charge of Nursery Centres, is afraid that the scheme of War Nurseries is in danger of falling between departmental stools. Don't we know it! I gleaned a little information this morning about the Round Table conference of last week. The local Health committee can only pay us as child-minders because our matron is not a fully qualified State Nurse, and our Head is not a fully qualified teacher. But that is entirely the Health committee's fault. If they had been willing to co-operate with us a year ago in the question of recognition we could have offered higher salaries and so have obtained fully qualified staff. With casual donations as our sole source of income, we daren't launch out with an expensive staff. The MO thought he had helped the Nursery quite a lot – he had actually allowed a child of under 2 to be admitted, and had passed the 1/- per day grant for him, although in so doing he was breaking rules.

14

M-O Report No. 1151: The demand for day nurseries, March 1942

By the time Mass-Observation produced this short report urging the government to do its own consumer research, there had already been considerable nationwide agitation by women for more and better day nurseries. The responsibility for nursery provision was shared between the Ministry of Health and local authorities but as the previous extract suggested, the local Medical Officers of Health could prove extremely obstructive. There was still widespread antipathy to the idea of mothers with young children working, and this, together with the grudging release of the necessary funds and facilities, meant that most mothers still relied on private arrangements for their childcare. In *Out of the Cage*, Penny Summerfield suggests that at a generous estimate, only a quarter of all pre-school children of women war workers attended nurseries by 1944. Even in areas where nursery places were available, the hours were often not designed to fit in with factory shifts.

I got a letter from my husband's old firm only this morning asking me to work for them. But when I went down to the clinic some time ago, they said the nursery wasn't open. (Hampstead housewife, aged 30.)

Well, I'd go if there was anywhere nice to leave baby. (Kilburn housewife, aged 25.)

My little boy goes to school, and they don't take them till half past nine. Nobody will take you for work at that time. Lots of them round here say they'd go on part-time work too. I tried at the factory I used to work at, but they said I'd been out too long, 14 years. (Wandsworth housewife, aged 30.)

Well, I tried to get my children evacuated. I've got a girl of 4 and a boy of 2. But I waited 8 weeks and then they said he was too young to evacuate, and I was in a position to stay home and look after them. My husband's in the police force and I was doing box-making. I don't think it's fair. If they want women to do the war work, they should look after the children. (St Pancras housewife, aged 30.)

These remarks are typical of hundreds collected by a recent Mass-Observation survey of human factors in industry. How far do they indicate that there is a substantial reservoir of labour waiting to be tapped if the Government would provide enough day nurseries? How many of the women with children who say they would go into industry if only somebody would look after their children would in fact do so if day nurseries were provided?

A sample enquiry in four London boroughs, where day nursery waiting lists were substantially in excess of available accommodation, showed that more than 1 in 10 of the women with children either had their names on waiting lists or had made enquiries about day nurseries or some other means of having their children minded during the day. Nearly another tenth were already helping to look after someone else's children. On the other hand, one quarter of the women with children encountered said they definitely would not like to go into war work even if day nurseries were provided in the district.

These figures do not give any quantitative illustration of the number of women available for war work if their children could be looked after during the day so much as indicate the two opposite extremes of feeling on the subject. In between those who have actually taken steps and those who have made up their minds against the idea come two considerable groups, those who would be prepared to go out to work if something *were done for them*, and those who have no definite ideas at all.

The main difficulties that women find in becoming war workers by putting their younger children into day nurseries may be listed as follows (not in order of importance):

1) Long waiting lists at existing and projected day nurseries.
2) Existing and projected day nurseries too far from home or work.
3) Day nursery hours too short, e.g. opening at 9 a.m. after the factory opens, and closing at 4 p.m. before the factory shift is over.

4) What to do about younger children of school age whose school hours are equally inconvenient from the factory point of view.
5) Dislike of anybody but mother looking after the child.
6) Alleged red-tape attitude of official concerned.
7) Belief, often originating in doctors' prejudices, that children will catch epidemics in day nurseries.
8) Fears aroused by clumsy handling of day nursery propaganda, e.g. in some places women have got the idea that they are to be conscripted into industry and their babies put into day nurseries.

In spite of these adverse factors there is widespread welcome to the idea of day nurseries among mothers with young children. On the whole they realise that their children will be properly cared for and looked after. The prejudices that still exist, and it is regrettable to say still propagated by members of the medical profession, against day nurseries could easily be dispelled by a simple propaganda campaign explaining the purpose of day nurseries, how they are run and what the babies' routine there is, with the precaution against the spread of disease. Day nurseries should be open at stated times for parents and prospective war workers to inspect them.

The remaining difficulties are problems of organisation, of opening sufficient day nurseries to satisfy the demand. The Ministry of Health has complained that it does not know how many day nurseries to open because it does not know how many mothers have children they want to put into them. Has it not heard that the Government now has a piece of machinery for finding out these sorts of things? Why does not the Ministry of Health ask the Wartime Social Survey to investigate the demand for day nurseries in any area where there is any doubt?

There are far more areas in which the demand for day nurseries at present exceeds the supply. Where, as at Cardiff, it is alleged that day nurseries are open and half empty, it will usually be found that large proportion of the mothers with young children in the area have never heard of the existence of the day nurseries.

One final word may be said on the subject of childminding. Eighty per cent of the mothers in the London area studied were against having their children looked after by neighbours. This may be surprising to those who know the strong tradition of childminding that prevailed in many northern towns, but it is a factor that must be taken into account. At any rate the Ministry of Health's scheme for registered daily guardians has so far only been adopted in five towns of which London is not one. The prejudices to be overcome here are much stronger than in the case of day nurseries and it seems even more desirable that the towns where it is intended to adopt this scheme be surveyed beforehand by the Wartime Social Survey.

15

War factory, Aston, July 1942

These extracts are taken from a much longer report (No. 1496) which was based on the work of two female Mass-Observers, Veronica Tester and Marion Sullivan. The arrangement of sending an Observer (now called Investigator or 'Inv' by M-O) to work alongside other employees was first tried in a Bolton cotton mill. During the war, the device was used at least twice. Early in 1942 Celia Fremlin worked in a Gloucestershire factory which manufactured parts for radar equipment. Her conclusions were published in a book published a year later by Gollancz: *War Factory*. In the Aston study, Veronica Tester was not asked to observe on the shopfloor itself as Celia had done, but to look at the support services. She spent four weeks in a large factory in Aston. The first week was spent in the kitchen and canteens where she helped with cooking and washing up; the second week was spent as an assistant in the Welfare Office; the third week, she worked as a typist in the accounts department and the last week as a clerk in the Progress and Planning office.

The factory was engaged in the production of steel tubes, mostly for the Admiralty. Women made up 25 per cent of its labour force (as against 15 per cent before the war). Many of the workers had been recruited from as far afield as Scotland and Tyneside but the single largest group was Irish women who came voluntarily (that is they were not affected by the conscription laws which regulated British women).

Mass-Observation had, by 1942, developed a shorthand system for designating the sex, age and class of people observed. 'A' meant 'rich people', 'B' meant 'the middle classes', 'C' meant 'artisans and skilled workers' and 'D' meant 'unskilled workers and the least economically or educationally trained third of our people' (from *War

Factory). F40C therefore referred to a skilled
working-class woman, aged 40.

Unfortunately no additional papers have survived
which show how the Investigators were received by the
other workers. The impression given is one of complete
acceptance and perhaps this was indeed the case. Two
factors may have helped Veronica to ease her way in:
firstly, she was presented as a trainee. Secondly, people
inured to the vagaries of wartime bureaucracy may have
been quite used to the sudden appearance and then
disappearance of a new employee. And women of different
educational and class backgrounds found themselves
thrown together either through direction by the
Employment Exchanges or through the need to
supplement husbands' wages (the wages of private
soldiers were notoriously low). Nevertheless, there still
has to be a question mark over exactly how much a
participant observer might learn in just one week; there is
also the ethical question of the Investigator 'spying' for the
government. The purpose of M-O's work was to assess the
efficiency of the industry and the part played in that
efficiency by the morale of the workers at all levels. In this
study, there was a particular interest in the quality of
management. The Aston project was part of a fuller M-O
study published the same year: *People in Production: an
Enquiry into British War Production.*

Canteens

Most of the married D women who are working in any of these
departments are in the habit of going out to work. This does not
mean to say that it is necessary for them to be in regular work –
frequently this isn't possible because there are children to consider as well as husbands – but they are used to casual employment and their present jobs are not merely taken because there's
a war on. Reasons for 'going out to work' seem to be varied – some
admit that 'the extra bit of money helps along', or 'it's a bit to put
by'; others have brought up children who are now married, so
have the time; another attitude is: 'I've always gone out to work';
and yet another: 'You get a bit of fun and it makes variety.'
Besides these there are a few younger married women without
children who have been conscripted into either full- or part-time
work. All these married women are thoroughly independent
about their jobs. They know they can get work elsewhere if and

when they want it, and it doesn't hurt to be out of work a few weeks.

There are only 6 unmarried women working on the canteen side, all C class. 3 of these are of call-up age, but not conscripted so far. All 3 are engaged to be married, and when the war is over have no intention of working. 2 are girls of 15 in their first job – to them work is an accepted part of existence. The remaining one is over 30, but conscripted from tailoring because single, and work is essential for her in order to live and support her mother.

The majority of these women, both C and D, whether working for their own choice or because the war prevents them from getting married and leaving work, take a good deal of pride in doing their jobs well. The most listless are the 3 or 4 conscripts, who don't get beyond bare efficiency. (That is probably explained by the mere fact that they allowed themselves to be sent to particular jobs. As appears later on, the more general thing is for women to find their own jobs when ordered to start, or change work, sooner than be sent anywhere.) For instance in the works canteen, F30D, who kept the tea urns clean would polish them up till they shone and said to M30C who was getting hilarious with tea dregs over the counter, 'Don't you get a spot on my urns. They're extra bright today.' F40D, scrubbing the floor at the end of the day: 'It's a shame to walk on it when it's wet. It don't show up nice after.'

Boxes in which utensils are taken down to the works for making morning and afternoon tea are always kept well washed out, and always covered with a clean cloth. Salt, pepper and mustard pots are kept well wiped and washed, and the sink is kept very clean. All this without interference from the overseer. Even F15C/D, who uses a sink down in the works when making tea there said: 'It looks horrid and dirty. I must get some Mirro down. You remind me, I can't remember things. It wants a good clean-up.'

On the staff floor F19C organised the washing of all the new trays, only recently in use and usually just wiped over. Asked if she had been told to get on with it she said, 'No – I just thought it was time they got done. They needed it.' On this floor there is very much more supervision than among the older women below; this brings up two of the main points encountered in the attitudes taken to work. One is Interference and the other Enjoyment.

Enjoyment

With some of the married D women a factor in deciding them to go out to work appears to be the pleasure of company there, and enjoyment of working hours. F45D comes 20 miles into work every day – and she doesn't need the money particularly, she has brought up and married off her family; she doesn't mind the distance as her husband does it as well, but she does like the people she's working with: 'We get a good laugh here and a bit of fun.' Incidentally she is a hard worker and always on time.

In the kitchen section the D women on the vegetable side, the unskilled labour in fact, prepare and cook the potatoes and cabbages, clean and wash up from 8 a.m. to 5 p.m. with an hour's break for dinner from 2.30 to 3.30. They do find the work hard and tiring: F40D: 'It's the heat down here, it's not proper air or anything, you do get tired, and we're on all the time. There's not many of us keep it all going. You're tired at the end of the day.' F37D: 'It's real hard work and it takes it out of you in this underground place.'

But all the same the women are usually very cheerful. They gossip all the time as they get on with things and help each other when anything's behind. Some days the cabbage arrives late, so when it finally does come, someone from another job goes over to give a hand. They don't feel the work is too monotonous and when drains go wrong or there is some sort of overflow, as happened 3 days out of 5 spent with them, the extra work and mopping involved got no grumbles. F40D: 'I'm quite happy here. I don't mind what I do, muck out lavatories or anything. I like a bit of variety – it's no good doing the same thing all day everyday.'

On the Works canteen floor the workers are a cheerful unit on their own. As in the kitchen they are all of the same class and they get on really well together. They co-operate in their work without being chivvied, and if they're one short, things still get done. In the mornings they come in at 8 and get things ready to take down to what are called 'tea points' in the factory. These are places where urns have been installed and boiling water is available. One woman goes out to each point taking tea, milk, sugar and bread and butter (for the women workers) and the factory workers line up with their own mugs for it. When the canteen workers return from this and have cleaned their utensils, they have a slack time and their own 'lunch' which they take very easily. But from 10 or 10.15 onwards there is a grand rush – first cleaning everything, then getting dinners up ready for 12 o'clock, and finally serving at top speed until things slack off a bit towards 1.15 – then there's all the washing up, etc., to be finished before they get their own dinner at 2.30. Round about 2 o'clock come the complaints of tiredness, but the atmosphere is cheerful and usually full of jokes. Afternoons are started with tea points again at 3.30 and final clearing up takes till 5 or after. This is done at a slower speed, there's more time for gossiping and not the freshness or energy to rush through the work in order to get out punctually at 5 as a rule. One or two do manage this, but some others always stay on an extra quarter of an hour or so to get quite finished . . .

Interference and Supervision

A remark that came from both girls and women, Cs and Ds, when asked if they liked their jobs was: 'I like it when I can get on and nobody interferes.' In the Works canteen, where the happiest atmosphere prevails, and the work is done perfectly well, there is least supervision. The woman in charge is on a level with all the others and works just as hard as they do, but she is generally liked and things go smoothly. When she had her week's holiday everything continued to go well. The Chief Supervisor and her canteen assistant are not always popping in and out of the department – the overseer just goes up to their office to get her supplies of tea, sugar, etc. The Chief Supervisor is very well liked on the whole – partly because she's not too much in evidence.

F35C: 'She leaves you to get on with it.' F40D: 'She's very straightforward – very nice to have dealings with.' F30D: 'She'll tell you what's wrong plain like and then it's over. Not like that other one, always comes round with a smile but can't leave you alone.' F22C (whose immediate boss is the canteen Assistant Supervisor): 'I'm quite happy when I'm left alone to get on with things, but my boss . . . She's been down 4 times this morning, all about nothing, and it's been like that ever since she came here. Miss G. (Chief Supervisor) leaves you to get on with your work and you know where you are with her. If anything goes wrong, there's a row, she tells you to your face and that's that. But this other one – always interfering, always coming round after something. You know she doesn't trust us. I certainly don't trust her with that smile.'

In the kitchen taken as a whole, the atmosphere is not very good – it's unsettled. This is partly because the 2 cooks have too much to get through and the assistant is not suitably chosen for the job. Though a nice enough girl and liked for herself, 'she's frightened of making pastry and she won't try at anything like that. It's no good with a girl who won't just try her hand' – (F35C). M30C: 'I'm here late every evening – we have to get on with things for the next day – we need another person here.' M35C: 'I never can really stop for a minute. You want another cook here and there aren't enough women really, not to keep the place as you'd like it. When my friend was cooking here too it was lovely. She's left now. One thing was, she found the air down below here too trying for her. You know, it's awful how tired you are at the end of the day, and always being late going home.' But down here also the question of interference arises: 'I'd do anything for Miss G., but I don't like a lot of others coming down and interfering. I've got plenty to do and I can't waste time with them – (F35C).

On the staff floor canteen the question of supervision is most difficult. Where young girls are employed, as the two F15Ds, they do need more looking after, but as the supervisor's office is on this level and they use the canteen, there is a great deal of extra wandering in and out and what the girls feel to be unnecessary fault-finding over little things: F15C/D: 'It seems as if she can't come by without having something to say – she's got to pick a fault. She says it smiling and nice, but you get fed up. F19C: 'Mrs R. (Assistant Supervisor) wants some tea taken in now. She's always wanting to be waited on. Why can't she come and fetch things for herself? Other people have to. You get fed up with running after her.'

It is a fact that the Welfare and Canteen office does tend to treat the staff canteen workers as little maids; where staff from all other offices have to come in and get their morning teas, the canteen office frequently ask for a tray to be sent in, or at least got ready, for them. Again in the afternoon, where there is a rule that a few people have tea taken to their offices, the canteen supervisors are inclined to take advantage of their special circumstances to get that bit extra done for them – tea at odd hours and so on. The girls don't say anything about objecting as a rule, but if they're in a rush, or it's near going home time, they do get annoyed, and the feeling is, 'Why can't they do it for themselves, or come and give a hand?'

Welfare and First Aid

The Welfare department has only recently come into existence so the work is growing continually. At the head is F35B who is also at the head of the Canteens. Her work is mainly done in the office and seems to consist largely of dealing with ledgers and forms, and engaging staff.

The Assistant on the Welfare side, Miss S. (F38A/B) deals with the human side of the work and is in continual contact with the Works. She arranges for the provision of overalls, clogs, caps for the women, and deals with billets, ration books, Labour Exchange visits and every sort of personal problem for the imported Irish labour. 'The job just grew of its own accord. I've never had to look for things to do, they just arise. Of course it is the Irish girls that form the greatest part of the work.'

The ambulance room is a department entirely on its own, presided over by Sister, F40A/B, with 3 trained nurses under her, so that there is always a nurse on duty. Formerly Sister was on her own, just helped by the First Aid man, who had been at the factory for years. When he died a few months ago the nurses were engaged, and there is also an old sort of pensioner known as Corporal who has been with the firm for years and is now unfit for heavy work, who gives a hand. The First Aid dept. has been very well fitted out – it is bomb-proof and gas-proof and has cleansing rooms for gas attacks. One part can be turned into a small hospital at a moment's notice. Drugs and surgical instruments of all kinds are there, and all the equipment is beautifully kept.

Attitude of supervisors to work and workers

The chief supervisor appeared to have very little to do with the actual welfare work, and not a great deal of contact with the workers other than her canteen staff . . . the assistant welfare officer's approach to work and people is very different. She is frequently on the job till 10 o'clock at night and invariably interrupts her meals if she does not miss them altogether whenever there is a query. Other members of the staff are constantly lecturing her for working too hard, paying too much attention to the girls and bothering over every little detail. F35B from another dept: 'It's really ridiculous, those Irish girls run to you with the most ridiculous things, not to mention troubles right outside the factory, like this business of getting marriages fixed up even. Any of the staff would be ashamed to run to you over such things.' Miss S.: 'But that's what I'm here for – to deal with all the little personal problems and try to smooth things out for them a bit. It's my job. Anyway, I'm very fond of all my Irish family.' She certainly takes enormous pains to make the girls settle down happily. 'So much of my work is smoothing the girls down when they first come. They're not told that it's heavy dirty work when they're in Ireland – it's left to me to deal with smoothing that down at this end.'

On one occasion 4 girls had asked for their release from the firm and did obtain it. 'I didn't mind about two of them, they weren't any good, but the other two had the makings of good workers, only they were very troublesome. I worked really hard to get them to stay, but finally they had to go to the Labour Manager's office as they had definitely asked to be released. Unfortunately they weren't treated very tactfully there, their Irish pride was aroused so they took the release. I took them out to a meal that evening and gave them my address at home in case they felt they'd like to come back after all.' She visited the Catholic hostel where the girls had spent a few nights, but the girls had left there, and tried every way to get in touch with them again. Finally the girls phoned her and asked to be taken back after all. 'We're very lucky with our Irish girls on the whole – they're exceptionally nice. We've only had one or two complaints from landladies about dirt and drunkenness. Some of them do take time to settle into billets and in the end prefer to find their own. It will be so much better when we can get the club going. There'll be bedrooms so that I've always got somewhere I can put girls who have to leave billets suddenly or anything. At present that's so difficult. At [the hostel] there's so much soft soaping to be done before a girl can go there, though they're very happy and well looked after when they are there. There'll be rooms for washing and ironing, another difficulty in billets, and they'll be able to meet their friends in nice surroundings and have somewhere to go in the evenings. It'll be an absolute blessing. And then when there are personal matters they want to talk to me about, it's much nicer to do it quietly in a place like that over a cup of tea. There's nowhere here when the new girls come and there's all that Ministry of Labour visiting, form filling and so on to be done. I feel so sorry for them left in a corner of the canteen here while I'm called away for a bit. I shall do all that at the club and there'll be a housekeeper in charge there too.' Among other improvements she's keen about is the opening of the new cloakrooms for the girls: 'I do hope they'll be ready soon. It'll be an enormous improvement. But you've no idea how difficult it is to make men understand the need for cupboards. I've fought a hard battle to get lockers for each girl and a cupboard for me to keep the stock of overalls and things in, and I've won at last though they wouldn't do things quite as I wanted. At present there's nowhere they can safely leave belongings – it's very hard for them.'

Overalls are issued free, but coupons have to be given up. This is often very difficult as new arrivals come with no coupons left. Miss S. has started a pool of her own for these cases in order to get a few in hand. One improvement she'd like to make is concerned with wages: 'The women frequently grumble when they get their pay packet because they can't understand why they've got such varying amounts from week to week. If only the Wages Dept would put on the packets how the exact money was arrived at it would save a great deal of ill feeling. I must see what can be done about it but I'm afraid it will be a very uphill business.'

Inv. assisted at a paying out during which 5 women [came to be paid] headed by hard-working but belligerent F53D who said: 'I only done 2 hours short of me time. Why's it so much less than last week? It's not right, I'm only 2 hours short, oh it's no good going to the Time Office, they keep you waiting hours and then you're no better off. Oh, it makes me fed up.' F25D: 'It's happened before this. You go and hang about the Time Office and they don't bother . . .'

Opinion of morale and absenteeism
The opinion of the Welfare people seems to be that the girls work pretty well on the whole. Regarding absenteeism, Miss S. does not go out of her way to deal with it or seem particularly concerned about it except when it is rather glaring. For instance, in the case of F20D who stayed away frequently and then kept her friend away too. These two were frequent offenders and Miss S. called at

the house, dealt with relations and by exerting her charm on the girls themselves did a great deal of improvement. Such details over arrangements to have bread and butter at dinner time instead of a whole meal when they had been feeling rather sick helped a great deal. She herself looks on her own job as war work but says of the Irish girls: 'I'm afraid very few of them are here to do "war work". It's the money that brings them over – they're eager to earn as much as they can. That's why most of the Irish girls work pretty well on the whole. There's very little evidence of their having the right spirit towards their work . . .'

Attitude of workers to welfare
. . . When clogs were being issued – coupon-free but paid for by the girls themselves – there was quite a rush for them. There were invariable disappointments and misunderstandings about people who put their names on lists and then weren't there, or had ordered the wrong sizes. But Miss S. overcame all this sort of thing very well and calmly. F30D: 'You're like mother to us, you are really.' There was a chorus of agreement. There was quite a bit of excitement over receiving the clogs, and next day, and even that afternoon, several girls turned up with the soles of them painted red or green.

One woman, F32D, had worn the soles of her shoes right through, her only pair it appeared. She asked Miss S. if the issue of the clogs could possibly be half a day earlier so she could send her shoes to the menders and have them to wear for the weekend. Miss S. did arrange it and served the woman first – certainly this sort of consideration gives the workers great confidence in the supervisor.

Regarding the actual services, not a great deal was heard, but these were spontaneous remarks made in conversation: F35D (a crane driver): 'It's the ventilation that's so awful, and it's worse when you're up on the crane. You get all the fumes up there and the heat's terrible. We used to get milk to drink up there, then they stopped that with the shortage and we got a cold drink. It wasn't so good but it helped. Then they stopped that – they reckoned up the cost, and found it came to more than the milk – it's healthier to get that, it sort of gets rid of the germs. I don't know why they want to go spending a lot of money on lavatories for the men when they've done without for 40 years – it would make more sense to spend it on ventilation – have sliding roofs for the blackout like they do in some other factories. All the crane drivers in the next shop to me have died of consumption. It's a terrible thing . . .'

An incident illustrating Miss S.'s treatment of the workers
F18D had been a great source of trial over the size of her dungarees. Miss S.: 'I'm going to try size 13 for her if I can get so large a size. She's a very big girl – nurse says there must be something wrong with her glands.' The dungarees were procured and given to the girl. A few days later her landlady called to say that the girl was in her 8th month of pregnancy and the landlady was afraid the child would be born on the doorstep. All Irish girls are supposed to come over with a medical certificate but this was one of the last lot whose certificates hadn't arrived.

Miss S.: 'I can't understand it at all. She's such a slovenly messy looking girl. If it had been one that used lipstick and dyed her hair it would be different, but this girl, she's most unattractive.' Miss S. collected the girl and drove her to town to fix her up in a home for unmarried mothers. 'Do you live with your parents at home in Ireland?' F18D: 'I live with my sister.' Miss S.: 'Well, would you like to write and tell her where you are going to be and that you'll be looked after?' F18D: 'No, I don't want her to know about it.' Finally Miss S. persuaded her to say they'd write together and tell the sister the whole thing. F18D (to Inv.): 'I don't mind if I go to a Catholic or a Protestant place – there's good and bad of both, isn't there? I want to come back to work after it. I like it very much here, I wouldn't want to leave . . .' She then went on to talk about clothes rationing and how she minded that much more than food. All this was when sitting in the car waiting to know where she'd be sent. She took it all very calmly – just accepted everything that happened with no comment. Remarks among the Welfare and Canteen A/B staff and their B secretary cronies were typified by 'I suppose she's got no shame' and 'It's disgraceful really, they get out of all the complications at home by coming to work knowing this.'

Relations between Welfare and First Aid
. . . The Ambulance and First Aid is an entirely separate unit. F33A/B (Chief Welfare) in answer to an enquiry from Inv. about

spending some time down there: 'That's a department quite on its own. We have nothing to do with it. Sister's in charge down there.'

No wishes were expressed in the Welfare Office for closer co-operation here but a case did arise when it seemed necessary. The assistant welfare supervisor was told in the works that F20D and her friend were absenteeing again so she called on their homes but was told they had medical certificates. 'I must have an arrangement with Sister to cover this sort of thing. We have got a system for other things when it's necessary.' However, the whole thing is regarded in a rather different light by Sister herself. In addition to her nursing training, she has also done a social science course and has done a great deal of social and administrative work. Also she has been at the factory longer than the Welfare department. 'Of course it's ridiculous that these two departments should be separate like this – it's quite against the nature of things. It makes me wonder sometimes what I'm here for. I'm used to the working classes and I love them. These women come to me with their troubles a great deal, the married ones and all. There's always something about a nurse and the uniform that makes it easier for people to speak out. They do feel it's in confidence. As a matter of fact I get a good deal of that sort of work here, but I just keep quiet, in the background. Some time ago there was a case – one of the women was pregnant and I was keeping an eye on her, but I was told it was not my job, that came under Welfare, so would I please cease to do anything. Isn't it ridiculous? However, it's no use arguing so now I just go on doing things but keep it quiet. I really can't be bothered with Miss S. at all. She's deliberately rude to me – now that my title is Sister, she makes a point of calling me "nurse" in front of people. And another thing – I suppose she did this through ignorance but she could have asked me – she put all her top floor canteen staff into the American nurses' caps. Hardly suitable I think. I was already wearing them because obviously veils are unsuitable in the works – so now I've had to buy new caps.

'Of course I get staff down here as well as the works. One or two of the old hands who think they're too superior to come down near the works don't come, but most of the others do now. It's silly for this to be called First Aid. We do so much more than that from dosing for colds to massage . . .

'Really, though it sounds a funny thing to say, I'm glad when a man has a slight accident – it takes him off work for a week and he gets a rest, and you should see the difference that makes to him. The hours are definitely too long in the works. A lot of these men look worn out, and then they have allotments and firewatching or wardening to do as well.'

The offices: behaviour at work

On the whole, the atmosphere in the offices is very free and easy. In spite of the clocking in system, punctuality is not an unfailing virtue. Then of those that are punctual, some go to their office, arrange their work for the day, then go to the cloakroom for a gossip. Others just blatantly stay in the cloakroom doing their hair until it's nearly 9 o'clock before they go down to their offices. Which is done depends on the departmental head. One of these, M55B, is very strict. His girls are always in their offices on time or very near it, and they start work right away. This is the 'snob' office and most of the girls don't even put their coats in the cloakroom but keep them by their desks. This is done in other offices a bit as it facilitates leaving punctually, but in this particular case it is more general and there is a definite 'superiority' atmosphere. The line is set by a couple of rather 'smart' seniors and the more junior girls, who would probably behave differently in other offices, adopt their attitude. These girls certainly get on with their work in the ordinary way, keep regular hours, don't go to the cloakroom to gossip, and in fact, on the surface behave in the most exemplary manner. But actually, while the juniors do have to keep up a good flow of work, the more senior girls manage to get their gossip in all right under cover of doing work together, whereas in other departments it is quite open. Also, those that go in for 'face repair' do it in the office, not upstairs. Inv. remarked on this difference to one of the seniors. F28B/C: 'We've got a very strict boss. Anyway our work is done for the directors and we have to get it done for the time they want it, so we can't play about and slack like those others.'

The 'others' and their talking were looked upon with great disfavour. Incidentally this is a very unfriendly office and not at all pleasant for a newcomer. F20C, who was new to the firm and put there, asked for a transfer after a few weeks because of this, and it has a bad reputation among the other girls. F19C: 'They're a snobby lot in there – you're unlucky. You should have been put in with us, we're all friends together.' F12C: 'I shouldn't like to be in there. One or two of them are alright but they're not a bit friendly are they?'

All the same, this model and hardworking office was a different story on Saturday morning when the boss wasn't there. The whole atmosphere was eased – conversations were held without so much pretence at work, but these were still very cliquey and newcomers were left to get on with the work. As the office shuts at 12 on Saturdays, there is no break for morning tea and biscuits, so on the one morning in three when the departmental head is away, a couple of girls nip across the road to a cafe and bring back a jug of tea. It's all done with much hiding under coats so that no other office even suspects. Certainly the very much slacker office next door doesn't do this.

In the other office, also all female but with a lower average age than the previous one spoken of, things are cheerful and chatty all day. A certain amount of work gets done, but long conversations are carried on quite openly and the senior or supervisor is thoroughly matey with all the girls and is very popular. F17C: 'It's nice in here – we all get on ever so well together and we talk as much as we like.' F18C: 'We're not allowed to go to the cloakroom in working hours, but we do. When we get fed up with sitting in here we go up for a chat. You get a lecture every now and again, but we don't mind.' At most times of the day there were girls up in the cloakroom (where there is little welfare supervision), the chief occupation being combing out curls. All the office girls, between 18 and 30, spend an enormous amount of the firm's time on their curls, either combing out each twiddle themselves on arrival in the morning or again after lunch, or else standing and talking while another girl operates on them. There are the usual couple of 'experts' who are much in demand for doing curls or making new styles – in this case, both F17Cs . . .

Relations between men and girls

From the girls' point of view, whether they work in all female or in mixed offices doesn't seem to make any difference. Those in the female office do not express any desire to be in a mixed one, and those in the mixed ones do not take any interest in the men there. They behave exactly as they please and the men might not be there at all.

In one office where there are 3 girls of 15, 17 and 18, they are extremely rude to two of the men, M40C and M60C – call them silly twirps to their faces. The men just smile indulgently and don't mind the girls at all, and put up with it when they're working and the girls start reciting such rhymes as: 'One fine day in the middle of the night, two dead men got up to fight', and more schoolgirl stuff, or flick their heads with handkerchiefs and so on, and tell the men they're slow old fools and have made a mess of the books. There is an amazingly free and easy atmosphere but nevertheless what work there is to do gets done.

In a larger office, the girls carry on their conversations among themselves as if the men did not exist. M40B in charge here says: 'The girls do chatter a lot but I quite like having them on the whole. They've improved some of the crusty old men a great deal – made them quite human. We did try to have one girl next to each man, and that split them up and worked quite well, but we can't do it now. It's no good being too strict with the girls – they have been stopped from spending a lot of time in the cloakroom but that hasn't done any good – they talk here instead.'

16

Welders' letters, 1942

In 1942 one of the M-O diarists sent a batch of 54 letters to Mass-Observation with her diary. She was employed as a welding instructor in her father's firm in Sheffield. The letters were written to her by two groups of her former pupils who, having done their training with her, had been placed in other Yorkshire towns to work as welders in tank production. Just two of the letters have been reproduced below, from two different women. The first is written by a single girl in her late teens, working in Huddersfield. The other is from a slightly older married woman on a journey in Scotland. The letters are a wonderful insight not only into factory life (and young women moving into 'men's' jobs) but also into the friendship networks of the girls. Unfortunately, the welding instructor who kept the letters didn't keep copies of her own side of the correspondence which must have been just as entertaining and testimony to a lively and affectionate relationship between her and her pupils.

Huddersfield
Wed.

My Dear Little Hedgehog,
Thank you very much for your most welcome letter, I thought somehow I should get a letter today but there were three waiting for me. Glad to hear you are sorry about us being separated, but it will not make any difference to the war effort because we have worked very hard this week. We cut five plates each in turns as there are only two machines and one of the men is away poorly, so E. and I join. We cut seventy plates out on Monday, eighty plates yesterday and ninety-five today so there will be plenty ready for welding when the plant is ready. I am very upset about being

alone amongst all the men but I shall have to face it, I expect. It would not be so bad if there were some more girls in the room. One of the welders at H.'s put a weld on our new device and what a slag-hole. I said, 'My word, if Mr P. saw us do a weld like that we should be sacked!'

I am very pleased to hear you are making good use of the girls before they leave you – have you been out with them for a farewell do? Good old A. getting her hand in, but it is as well she is learning how to wash things for a start, because she might be busy washing nappies if things don't turn out for the better. I hope her sweetheart gets some digs for her, and then maybe he will be able to finish the job off right, and bring forth fruits.

Talking about fruit, I have just had some prunes for my sweet tonight and I was reading your letter at the same time, and did I laugh. I think mine would be much sweeter than yours, because the day I wet myself, with laughing, I had some Prunes up my knickers slop, and I threw them under the saw somewhere, but I am in good condition so you will not be poisoned. Poor Mrs F., we think about her quite often, especially when we are thirsty because we can only get water, but I don't fancy it these days. E. says if I want a drink at Ilkley, I shall have to go alone, so it looks as though I shall have to be teetotal because I dare not go alone . . .

Yes I realise I was a naughty thing five-timing but I am one-timing now, and strange to say I have to meet my one and only tomorrow night. Oh boy will I love him you bet I will. I wish it was tonight because I am in the mood – but not to be loved properly. He would never do such a thing as go with another, because he thinks too much about me and if he ever gets in any girl's company, he always tells me, and that only one interests him, that is me. He wrote and asked me to see him at 7.00 p.m. – is not it a good job I am not working over, I would have knocked though, I would leave home for him I love him that much, I do wish the war was over . . .

I shall be over in three weeks time. You see, I shall be on days after the holiday I think, so that means I will not have a Monday for a month so please wait for it, and keep it dark it's a black pudding [secret], and I want to come alone, but I will write you when I am coming definitely. I shall have to have a short sleep in your office though in the afternoon because I shall go to work at

9.00 p.m. I will now close trusting you are in the pink and feeling none the worse for sleeping out and also after spring-cleaning.

Goodnight and Godbless
Yours very sincerely
A . . .
With love

My Dear Friend,
. . . but here it is Saturday night, and I am still in Glasgow. I am residing at some hotel, I forget its name, but what looked like a catastrophe, has really materialised into a beautiful adventure. One I could well imagine you to be the participant of. Here, as near as I can tell you, are the details. I left Huddersfield at 11.15 last night, and I found Daddy Brown had put me into the wrong train. Rectifying that mistake, I eventually started my journey. Arriving in Manchester the Glasgow train was filled to capacity, so consequently there were about 30 of us, stranded. We were placed in a train to Wigan, but when we arrived at Wigan, we were still unable to board the train for Scotland. We were waiting for a train to Preston, when I jumped on, and asked if I was right for Preston. The guard very brusquely said, 'Hell no, this train is non-stop to Glasgow.' Imagine my joy when quite by accident I had boarded the correct train. The journey was long, and tedious, and it was 10.45 a.m. before we arrived at Glasgow. I parked my case, and I went in search of this elusive bus station J. had spoken of so often. I was directed to one, I was told to go to another. I retraced my steps, and arriving at the second bus station for the bus to Furness, the inspector said, 'There are only two buses, you have missed the morning bus, and the next is 4.50.' J. had said it was 3.15, but the man said it was 4.50. I nearly bought Lewis's in the course of this day, walking in sheer exasperation to the bus station – only to my chagrin to find my bus had gone at 3.15. Imagine what I felt like stranded in Glasgow. I let that inspector have it I can tell you, and then he said I told you where to catch your bus, which he never did. I eventually dissolved into tears, and as plainly as I could, I told a policeman my story.

The policeman and the sergeant brought me to this hotel to secure me a night's lodging. They have managed to squeeze me in. The son here is charming (just as I was writing that he came in to tell me my room was no. 18). He also said he would like to take me for a glimpse of the Clyde when he is finished his work, but I told him I was going to bed, he said I had a comfortable bed – a single one, and he would stand guard at my door all night to make sure I was safe. Anyway to continue my running commentary. After I had been signed in, I sat on a settee, and before I knew what had happened – I was asleep. I was really fatigued. I awoke with a very soft deep voice saying, 'Blondie, Blondie.' I sat up quickly and found myself looking rather puzzled at the handsomest face, and the bluest eyes, I have ever seen. In my confusion, I thought it was the son, but as I apologised for falling asleep, he said, 'Please don't – I have only just come down from bed myself.' So I knew I had not met him before. We conversed quite naturally – and I soon learned he was a Canadian. We became quite friendly, and soon we were joined with still another Canadian. Before I knew what had happened, I was having tea with them, their names are Eddie and Robert respectively. Robert was meeting a lady friend, and I am going with Eddie (my blue eyed boy) to make the foursome, am I really wicked? I can't help but keep thinking what J. is wondering and doing right now. He will be worried about me I know. I would rather be with him than here but I might as well make the best of a bad job.

Eddie has just come downstairs and pulled a wry face when he saw me still writing. He said, 'Golly, it sure must be some letter, and some person to whom you are writing.' I said, 'How right you are – to both of them.' Anyway I will finish this later.

If I make any mistakes now blame it on the Scotch and sodas I have had, and the piano player right behind me. It is 10.30, and I feel just fit for anything.

Eddie is really something, yes here it comes, I'm fascinated to death with his eyes, and his truly cross-atlantic drawl, which seems to come right from his boots. If you could only hear the cracks he is making at this letter, he is making Pauline cry with laughing. He just said if my pen was a horse he would back it, he has never seen a pen fly like mine does. By the way he still calls me 'Blondie'.

Charlie (the son) has just been to me and sarcastically asked me if I'd enjoyed my night in bed. I said 'Certainly I had', but his anger was assumed, for he called me Flower, and chucked me under the chin. I wonder which flower I remind people of. It must be a cowslip. I have never seen anything as fascinating as a Scotchman, in a kilt. I was watching four this afternoon as if I had never seen a Scotchman before. The swing of their kilts, their legs, and bits o' things are not to be sneezed at. (They could be if they had pepper on.) Well, dear, I really must close now and join the company. Don't forget to give my best regards to Mr P., D., and W., not forgetting John Thomas Buffalo. Please convey my thanks to Mr P. for the lovely day I had last Tuesday. I've had a card from E. Goodbye and God Bless You. I am just going onto the piano. Goodnight and best of luck. I Remain Yours . . .

17

Joining the WAAF: the first three months, 1943

Joan Arkwright began keeping a diary for Mass-Observation in 1940 when she was employed as a personal secretary to the manager of a paint manufacturing factory. For a few months, her conscription was deferred because her work at the factory was considered important (the paint was used on war vehicles etc.) but she became impatient with office life and decided to volunteer for the Women's Auxiliary Air Force at the end of 1942. She was 27 years old and before joining up lived with her parents near Altrincham.

Tuesday 5th Jan 1943
It was snowing thickly as I walked to the station at 7.45 a.m. wondering what lay ahead of me. The platform was almost deserted unlike the scene at 8. The few passengers walked soppily up and down in the slush until the crossing gates clanged to, and the train arrived. It was warm inside, and when I got out at Oxford Road it seemed a pity to stand around freezing until a bus appeared so I tramped along Oxford Road to the Recruiting Office and kept my circulation going. It was still snowing and quite dark. There were several girls already waiting. We talked about the trades we wanted and so forth until it was our turn to fill in the form and file into the examination. My only doubt was my eyesight as I wear glasses regularly, but they tested me without and I could read down to the third row of the chart, and then with, and I got to the bottom row and they seemed satisfied. They weighed me and measured me and kept saying 'good' all the time. I haven't had rheumatic fever, ear trouble, TB, any serious illness or an operation, my family have no mental weaknesses. In fact I was almost a model recruit. Anyhow I passed. After waiting twenty minutes or more the officer informed me I was accepted,

asked me about my education and said that so far as she was concerned I had the necessary qualifications for Admin. but I should have to go before a psychologist and only one in twenty passed so I must not be disappointed if I did not. Then she said, 'Come back here at quarter to two and we'll enrol you.' It seemed a pity to roam about in town and I caught the first electric train back home. The folks were mightily surprised, not expecting me until tea time. Mother was relieved to hear that I should not be drafted until Friday week. After lunch I went back and we all sat around waiting for an hour and a half, during which time an NCO filled in on the fourth form our size in hats, shoes, birth place, next of kin and so forth. At last we were all shepherded downstairs and sworn in, and paid one day's pay plus a ration allowance, and given a few words of advice about the journey. I wonder how many of us realised the import of the statement we signed. It is not just another job, or a new experience, to be tackled thoughtlessly. We belong to the Armed Forces of the Crown. Loyalty to the Country and its traditions should be the backbone of service. I hope I shall still feel like this after several months as a WAAF.

Thursday 14th Jan
Last day at home. Up about 8.30, did the *M/C Guardian* cross-word after breakfast. Repacked my bag to squeeze more in it (small weekend case). Cleaned up a greased bicycle. Walked into Altrincham for stamps.

Friday 15th Jan
Up at 7. Checked my watch at 7.30 – Frank Titterton was singing 'Always'. The morning was very dark. Everyone else on the train seemed to be making a routine journey to the office. I bought a Workman's return and gave it complete to the ticket collector. At the recruiting office there were 9 of us. The officer put me in charge and took us to the station, where we had a cup of tea in a WVS canteen and were put into a compartment of the Birmingham train. I was given our railway warrant and a large envelope for the Depot. The train ran well. We talked a little, and watched the countryside. We were in Birmingham ahead of schedule, found the RTO and the Platform and caught our connection comfortably. On one station there was a block of American soldiers – what a tough looking gang, grownup dead end kids. At

Gloucester we filed into an RAF bus with a crowd of others. At the Depot they issued us with cutlery, inspected us, fed us and then tested our intelligence. We make our beds – dark blue blanket over biscuits [thin mattresses], and leave it that way in the morning although we fold up a blanket, a sheet, a blanket, a sheet and wrap a blanket round the lot.

Saturday 16th Jan
6 a.m. Sweet bugling issued from the loudspeaker, then the lights flicked on and we all leapt out of bed. I was not listed for fatigues so I pottered around. Breakfast at 7 – I've never seen so many gathered together to be fed. It was the queue 2-deep round the room that impressed folks most. Good food and big helpings.

The day has been spent – as an officer warned us after the psychology test last night – in waiting. Waiting to be interviewed, waiting to be photographed, waiting for pay books and 101 things. I am accepted for Administrative. Quite a few girls having failed for the trade they want have refused the alternative batwoman or cook and been discharged.

Sunday 17th Jan
There are 3 girls here who have come from USA to join up. They are British and could enrol only in England. They came over on the same ship and were delighted to meet again here.

We got our kit during the afternoon. There was considerable hilarity when it came to trying the undies on in our hut – they weren't all the right size.

Tuesday 19th Jan
What a busy two days. Marking dozens of articles, and some of them have to be taped first. Everyone has been running around asking for marking ink (Sunday we could not buy it), borrowing from the lucky few who had it. I waited until I could go to the newsagent's and buy some. Then I hardly got time to use it because there was a parade for rehearsal for a recruits' concert, and a parade for uniform alterations, then the concert itself. Still everything is done now and tonight lights out is 9 p.m. because we have breakfast tomorrow at 5.45 a.m. and leave for our training depot.

Wednesday 20th Jan

We left Gloucester in the dark so I know no more of the town than I did before I went. We had a special train to Compton Bassett – 6 in a carriage – so the journey was comfortable, and the NCOs brought cake round. It was raining when we arrived and the camp looked desolate. The stoves in the hut wouldn't light and we all felt thoroughly miserable.

Saturday 23rd Jan

Inoculation morning. We lined up with left shoulders bare and the MO performed. I've never spent such a hilarious afternoon. It was probably a mild form of hysteria. Angela had the utmost difficulty to reach her mouth with her fork during tea and we all howled with laughter. The stove in the hut was well and truly stoked all evening and we went to bed nicely roasted about 8.30. The arm is definitely stiffening more.

Wednesday 27th Jan

There was a lecture in the NAAFI Reading Room. The Tannoy announced it at tea time specially. Jill and I went along to find ourselves the first arrivals – almost the only arrivals. When the lecturer arrived we drew easy chairs round the fire and made it a fireside talk. (There were 2 officers, 3 corporals and us.) The subject was N. Africa and the lecturer really knew all about it.

Friday 29th Jan

There is to be a cabaret in the middle of Tuesday's dance and I have volunteered to do a solo dance for them. The question is what to wear. I think slacks and a blouse would be best, tho' a wide long skirt is the ideal, but that means sending home and there is very little time.

Saturday 30th Jan

For the first time since I left home I have had real tea, out of a pot. A. and J. and I went into Colne and found a lovely cafe. We had tea, toast (properly buttered too), and cakes (both jam ones and cream) and the charge was 10*d*.

I had to rush back to camp because I was on cookhouse fatigue – cutting bread on a bacon slicer. After that I visited someone in sick bay, had my supper and washed my hair. A pretty good evening's work.

Monday 1st Feb
I do loathe first aid lectures. I listen hard and try to remember all the advice but the description of some of the wounds is nauseating.

I have a lovely green silk kimono to wear for my tango. I pressed it in the wash hut and hung it out so as not to crush it. The hut NCO will put it on her bunk tomorrow as it can't be around during hut inspection.

Tuesday 2nd Feb
My vaccination is beginning to ache. I did PT today with one arm because I didn't want to be crippled tonight.

The cabaret was a distinct success. My turn was much appreciated. It's as well that corporal lent me a pair of white pants. The skirt swung out in a lovely fan during the pirouettes.

Wednesday 3rd Feb
The CO talked to us this afternoon about his experiences in the Middle East. Later we went for a 'route march' – 3 miles at the most to some woods and back where we collected deadwood for our fires.

Domestic evening – meaning that we stay in quarters until 8 polishing our lino and washing the shelves and lamp shades and mending.

I went round to NAAFI at 9 – no lemonade, no tea – only vile cocoa so I came away again. An early night will do me good.

Tuesday 9th Feb
The weather was sopping. We all expected to have a scratch parade in the gym but at the last minute a watery sun broke through. So we marched onto the parade ground to martial music. Every one of us afterwards admitted we felt proud enough to burst. We were reviewed by the Station Commander who spoke to every girl. After lunch there was great excitement, those who were travelling more than 8 miles away paraded for subsistence. I found I was posted to L— oh whoopee. The actual Posting Parade was not until 6 p.m. The short distance girls learnt their destination then. A. and J. are on disposal (which means odd jobs) until

their postings arrive. Packing is a sticky job in a kitbag and case.

Wed 10th Feb
4.30 a.m. I had to wake the hut, being the only one who could be sure of being awake. We assembled in the NAAFI and were tucked into buses. I had to change at Bristol (the buses took us to Chippenham Station for the early train) and found a WVS restroom – very cosy and welcome. At B'ham I changed again, but there the train was already in the platform. A couple of soldiers fought their way across the station with my kitbag and case. At L—there were 3 airmen also for the camp and we waited hours for a transport, amusing ourselves by drinking tea in the local canteen. I arrived on camp after dark and was put temporarily into a hut and given a meal. Tomorrow I see the Admin Officer.

Tuesday 16th Feb
Am I cheesed? This afternoon the claim site Guard Room returned their unclaimed mail and amongst it was a parcel and letter for me which should have been at the Waafery Guard Room on Saturday. Anyhow it was worth waiting for. Yards of news from Mother and newspaper cuttings, a packet of Lux and some filled choc. blocks. Tonight a domestic night. We are supposed to stay in our huts and spring clean them, do any washing and mending etc. And at 6.30 we heard that there was a lecture in the NAAFI which we must attend. It was about USSR and how the government fought against illiteracy – very interesting but it upset my programme.

Wednesday–Sunday 7th March
For two days I visited sick quarters. The flight sergeant hadn't the least idea what to do with me so he posted me in the kitchen one morning to study sick diets. Very easy, lean against the wall by the stove and watch the cook run around. I did help wash up the tea cups. A lot of time I spent in the staff restroom talking to the orderlies and MT drivers. They have a very low opinion of Admin WAAFs because on this station no one seems to care about welfare so much as putting girls on footling charges. When I'm a fully fledged Admin I shall remember many of their comments. On the second day I was told to see the ward and the corporal on

duty explained some of the procedure of reporting sickness and accidents, then one of the orderlies suggested I looked around the officers' ward. She began making two of the beds so I lent a hand and when we had finished she complimented me on the way I had folded the corners.

Monday–Wednesday 10th March
Complete with case and respirator I hitched to the main camp for 8.45 transport to G— B—. It arrived at 9.45 and was already packed tight with equipment and airmen. Anyhow they squeezed up and Brenda (one of the station hairdressers) and myself scrambled over the tail board and perched ourselves where we could. Talk about the rocky road to Dublin – the road went over a series of hump bridges.

I am here for a week in the guard room as part of my training. Brenda is the duty hairdresser (G— B— being a satellite station a hairdresser is sent out for 3 days each week). We are both in the same hut and have palled on. Monday night there was an ENSA concert 'The Gang Show' in the WAAF NAAFI – it was an A1 show – some of the boys made lovely girls.

Last night we went into the Airmen's NAAFI for supper and got talking to some erks. They were trying to guess our trades and where we came from. They were miles out. 3 of them thought I was London. I suggested Devonshire. Today the sergeant said surely I'd found a boyfriend, in the same tone as she would say, I suppose you've had tea. In the forces a boyfriend seems to be one of the necessities of life.

Thursday 11th March
It is 12 years today since I began my first job. Makes me feel quite ancient. I told the sergeant. She said, 'Is it your birthday?' I said, 'No, I shan't be 28 until June.' That shook her rigid. Like most people she had taken me for 21.

Sat 13th March
On my day off I hitched into Derby, rang up Avril at the office and went to the Kardomah where she met me and we walked round the shops and up to her digs – a lovely house, big rooms and very clean, there are 6 girls in it. Avril's bedroom is cosy, modern

furniture, an Indian rug – really attractive. But the cosmetics she has strewn about!!! A real glamour parlour.

We went to see *In Which We Serve* and had dinner at the Midland – hors d'oeuvres, chicken and spinach and roast potatoes followed by an ice cream sweet under a fancy name – price 5/- plus 1/- house charge. There is a special forces bus to camp at 9.45 and I made it comfortably.

Sunday 14th March

I loathed having to come away from the satellite station. Sgt Horrocks is a gem and there's not an NCO alive who can touch her. Without banking on it I was much comforted by her suggestion that I might be posted back there after my training. I travelled back in an RAF lorry and got to the Waafery about 2 p.m. I was planning to do so many things, but I walked into the Guardroom and was informed that 'Admin' has been scrubbed. The Air Ministry have decided to cut it out as an independent trade and give an Admin course to every NCO. I could have cried. It took me about an hour to come out of the panic. Now I feel quite resigned. I don't know what to remuster to and I'm waiting until the Squadron officer tells me officially.

Tuesday–Thursday 18th March

. . . It seems queer somehow, I feel unanchored, they don't worry what I do. I walk in and out of SHQ without any questions being asked. Actually I am trying to find the Education Officer, who is irritatingly elusive. The Docs clerk has had me helping him to enter leave on the docs. Everyone in the OR calls me Miss Arkwright – it annoys me a little. I'm not an officer and 'Arkwright' is correct, but I said nothing because the other girls call the ACs Mrs so they must have a civvy street complex.

Friday 19th March

Day off. I trotted down to the Waafery cookhouse wearing my pullover without collar and tie because I wanted a bath after breakfast. Apparently it is incorrect even on day off, but the cookhouse girl had no need to impersonate a Flight Sergeant and strip me off loudly for being Admin and knowing no better than to go on parade (a meal being a parade) improperly dressed . . .

Saturday–Sunday 21st March
I found the Education Officer at last to ask permission to continue
this diary. He was uncertain about the matter and offered to see
the Squadron Leader Admin. (Within quarter of an hour he came
into the Orderly Room to tell me the Sqd Ldr will vet it.) We also
discussed WAAF Education. He thinks there is a lot too much
leisure time wasted in the forces. I was considering taking the
postal course for Matric. but he assured me I should find it a bind.

On Sunday I trotted the dreary streets up to the S.Ad.O.
[Squadron Admin Office]. He OK'd them and assured me I
can write more fully without getting tangled up in Security
Regulations. [The next line is blacked out of the original diary
presumably by the Squadron Leader.]

Monday–Thursday 1st April
This week I am in Equipment Section – clothing stores. It is
interesting insofar as I am learning how to fill in all the issue and
replacement forms correctly (the corporal is a super instructor),
but it is filthy sorting out the cast off tunics and things for
disposal.

Today is the 25th birthday of the RAF. Our celebration was a
party at the Waafery. Everybody was going and there was a
queue for the baths after tea. Janet and Carol came back with
news that they had used the same bath and scrubbed each other's
backs. When we reached the NAAFI there were not many couples
dancing but quite a crowd in the 'beer parlour'. Later the floor got
very crowded. I was amusing myself watching folk swing into a
corner by the band and let go with a jitterbug exhibition.

(According to the AMO, Admin is not scrubbed but drastically
reduced. Anyhow the date of effect is not yet announced and
knowing government departments it may be months before the
reduction takes effect. So far I have met not one airwoman who
doesn't hope that the Admin Flt Sergeant will be among those
remustering. She is far from popular, being unsympathetic and
often unreasonable. The general opinion is that most of our
Admin NCOs think far too much about the airmen to be
interested in the airwomen.)

The buffet at the dance was wizard. Rita from my hut had spent
all day in the bakery making the cakes which were very short and
adorned with jam and cream. As the evening wore on the smoke

and heat made my eyes ache so after a dance with a blonde young man of extraordinary plainness who was extraordinarily affectionate I vanished from the 'do' and went up to the hut. I was fast asleep when the others came in and never heard roll call at all.

Friday 2nd April
Today is the Clothing Store corporal's day off. I had the place all to myself. When I arrived I lit the stove, not so difficult as there were chips in the coalbin. Then I found a deep cardboard box and went out to collect coke in it. Next I swept the floor and began the serious work of the day. 300 overalls, combination blue to be stacked in sizes on the shelf. About half past ten I organised a cup of tea from the technical store and took a rest while I drank it. Sorting overalls and other things kept me busy all day.

At night I got busy packing my things for leave – clean shirt to be collected from the drying room and ironed, stockings to be darned, soiled undies to be taken home for washing (it is impossible to keep white woollies white in the hard water on the Station).

Saturday 3rd April
Today is the day. I smiled very charmingly (I hope) at the Flight Lieutenant in charge of the stores and he signed me an early chit. Never have I been so pleased to go on PT parade. It is held at noon and one gets lunch earlier than you do if you leave your section at 12.30 as usual. The weather was gloriously blue and white. I cycled back to the Waafery with Mary who is one of the PT display squad who are travelling around the local towns for Wings for Victory week. She was in a march past this afternoon and had to parade at 2 with buttons and boots shining.

I changed into my best blue and put all oddments into my kitbag so as to leave the bed space clear.

The train ran well. From Stafford I travelled with 5 airmen who talked about their instructors and compared notes on their opinions.

I was home by 5.30. It was wonderful to walk into a real room with photographs on the piano and ornaments on the mantelpiece. All the familiar books were in the bookcase and it looked like home.

FIVE

TOWARDS A NEW WORLD
FOR WOMEN?

One of the points which Mass-Observation often repeated in its various reports to government and government agencies was the need for some kind of positive image of postwar society. Belief in a better Britain was seen as crucial to morale while the war itself was being waged.

What did women want? What did they hope for? How far did wartime women see their needs as *women* separately from those of men? The evidence – from the Mass-Observation papers – is contradictory. Perhaps women themselves were contradictory. Men and women were tired out after coping with the demands of wartime. For many women, war meant extra hard work and the sadness of being separated from people they loved. Young women had postponed marriage or starting a family. Mothers juggled part-time work with childcare and domestic work. For these women, the return to 'normal' meant the dream of having their own home and being there full time if at all possible. They saw the war period as a temporary condition even if they had enjoyed aspects of it – the comradeship, the excitement, the shared experiences of danger, hope and fear. But these hopes for the postwar years must be set against what was possible: the job market shifted as the war economy was dismantled. Women who had been able to find work in their local area during the war found themselves unemployed or unable to utilise the skills which had been so necessary in wartime. Priority was given to demobilised men. Women with young children found it especially hard to find work which they could combine with childcare. The nurseries were closing down and the idealised image of mother at home dominated postwar planning. Rebuilding the family had been the cornerstone of the 1942 Beveridge Report, the document which laid the foundation for the Welfare State. The vision of the supportive new Britain, despite all its reforming aspirations, enshrined the woman as a dependant of the male worker. Even then, for working-class women who might have wanted to stay at home to bring up children full time, it was not always financially possible. As before the war, women from poorer families had no choice but to try and get work to supplement the male wages. Single women had to support themselves. Struggles for fundamental changes – equal pay, for example – were defeated in the immediate postwar years.

Despite the retrenchment, however, things could never be quite the same again and some of the extracts in this section (all written *during* the war) show the small ways in which changes occurred. Perhaps the most that can be said about the war period is that it began to raise women's expectations of what might be possible. After all, the young women of the war period were the mothers of the 1970s generation of feminists.

18

M-O Bulletin: Women in public houses, February 1943

This extract is made up partly from a Report produced by Mass-Observation to be included in its fortnightly Bulletin and partly from observations made by Edith Loeb, a full-time Investigator who carried out a number of M-O's projects later in the war. The Bulletin was circulated to all the members of the volunteer panel and to interested members of the public as well as to potential M-O clients.

The increasing numbers of women enjoying a drink in a public house were seen by M-O as an important indication of how far women's role had been changed by wartime. However, as their quotation shows, they were well aware of attempts to ensure that after the war, women would be expected to return to their pre-war social position.

This war, like the last, has made fundamental changes in the social habits and position of women in this country. We intend, in future numbers of this bulletin, to discuss various aspects of these changes. In particular, we shall consider shortly people's feelings about the place women should take in postwar Britain, comparing men's attitudes and those of the women themselves, and indicating some of the tensions arising from wartime accelerations in equality of status between the sexes.

The subject of what shall happen to women after the war is becoming a very live issue today. Mrs Corbett Ashby, addressing a recent conference of the National Council of Women, told her audience: 'There is an enormous force of public opinion which is already marshalling its forces to push women back to where they were before the war.'

Just how enormous or otherwise this force is, we shall be discussing in a later bulletin. But it is clear that there are a great many places out of which women will have to be pushed if they are to return to the 1939 position. War jobs are not by any means the only places in which women have become entrenched during the war. They have not only taken over men's activities in working hours, but to a very considerable extent in leisure hours too. Perhaps one of the most significant changes is the extent to which they have entered during the war into the life of public houses. We give below the results of a small survey undertaken last month in one London borough into the changing position of women in pubs, and people's feelings about it . . .

Slightly more than fifty direct interviews were made in London in various public houses. Both men and women were approached and questioned as to their attitude to women frequenting public houses, with specific reference to young women.

Rather over half the people interviewed could see no great harm in women drinking in pubs, either by themselves, or in company of men or other women. A little less than half disliked the idea of young women going into pubs by themselves, and a few remarked on the increasing amount of young women who drank more than they could hold.

Tolerance of women in pubs

As stated previously, the majority of pubgoers did not object to women going into pubs. Most of them were tolerant of women in pubs, and felt that as long as the women behaved themselves, there was no harm in it. Remarks of this type are typical:

F30C: 'Well, why not; it doesn't worry me at all.'

F40C: 'I don't see why the women shouldn't have a drink same as the men. Just the same as women in restaurants. A public house is for all classes, and men and women alike . . .'

The majority of inn-keepers and their staff seem indifferent to women coming into pubs:

F55C: 'Yes, the war has made a great deal of difference; I don't mind girls drinking in the bar alone or otherwise. Usually when they come in alone, they don't go out alone, but who am I to criticise – my job is to sell the liquor and be pleasant to customers, not to be nosy about their comings and goings.' (Fulham)

A publican has also noticed the increase of women drinking in pubs, and thinks it is because they earn more money than they did before the war:

M50C: 'Lots more now than before the war – I should think it's mainly because younger women are earning more money than ever before. A good third of these new customers would come anyway, once they were old enough. Makes no odds to me.'

But he certainly has a bias in favour of men, and goes on to say:

'Of course, quite a lot of them drink spirits but if I'm short, I serve men in preference. Too much isn't good for these youngsters. They usually behave quite well too. I have nothing against it.' (Fulham)

Several women stick out for the equality of women, feeling that since women are doing men's jobs in this war, they ought to have men's privileges as well:

F30B: 'All this old-fashioned prudery – it's disgusting. Women are doing just as much in this war as the men. Why should they turn up their noses and look Victorian because we walk in, in trousers, and order beer. Sheer stupidity.'

A publican (Fulham, Barclays) feels much the same way about this question:

M65C: 'I'm broadminded about it – if a woman wants refreshment, why shouldn't she have the same rights as men. She's entitled to be free.'

A fair number of women, who themselves at times go to have a quick one, can see no harm in women drinking in pubs:

F35D: 'I don't see no 'arm in it – it's 'ard to get stuff to take 'ome nowadays and pubs are nice lively places for a body to go to. Those who don't drink or smoke, there's something wrong with; that's my honest opinion.'

F30C: 'All this old-fashioned prudery should have gone out with the bustle. I see no harm in it and it's only evil-minded folks that do.'

A few people feel that it is far better for young women to come into a pub by themselves than to hang about the streets, or, if they are married, to go about with other men while their husbands are serving. There's also a feeling that, after all, there's a war on, so why shouldn't people enjoy themselves while they can:

M20D: 'Why not – let's have a good time while it lasts.'

F50D: 'I am sure there are lots more than before the war. Poor dears, life's so dull; I think it's much better if they come in alone than go around with other men while their boys and husbands are in the forces somewhere.'

M25C: 'Doesn't matter a bit to me – I certainly think that more women have done it since the war, but I don't see why not. They need a drink occasionally, same as a fellow. Some of the factory girls make a bit of a barney – but I'm all for it myself.'

M40D: 'I sees nothing against it – of course, women can't hold it like men and a drunken woman is not a pleasant sight, but the more women as can drink, the less drunken women one sees. Better that they should drink alone than go gallivanting round with other men if they're married or suchlike.'

Even older women seem little prejudiced against girls drinking by themselves, and want the younger generation to have a good time:

F60C: 'I'm not against women drinking alone – why should it be supposed that they need an escort – lot of good men are as escorts, I must say. I'd rather have a dog any day. Of course one doesn't have to go out alone even if you come in alone – you are only young once; enjoy yourself while you can.'

The war has certainly broadened people's outlook on these matters, and as shown by the remark of this middle class man, who before the war would have probably objected to the idea of women drinking by themselves in pubs, old prejudices are dying fast:

M40B: 'I see no harm in a girl drinking in a pub – alone or in the company of either sex, before the war I was a bit old-fashioned about such things, but war broadens one's outlook somewhat.'

Objection to young women drinking in pubs alone
Roughly a third of the people interviewed expressed themselves
at least a little doubtfully about women drinking alone in pubs.
Some were outright antagonistic, others didn't think it was 'quite
nice' for a woman alone to enter a public house. Some of the
remarks made were quite mild, disapproving only slightly of this
new wartime habit of young women entering pubs by themselves:

F60B: 'I think it's a great mistake for them to start as young as
      that. If they're accompanied by their husbands or
      sweethearts, it's different, but on their own or girls
      going together, I don't approve of that. I think it's a
      great mistake and a pity.'

A few people objected to one girl going into a pub by herself, but
thought that two or three girls together could quite well enter a
pub:

F50C: 'I think it's alright if women know how to keep within
      bounds. My husband and I have a drink together at one
      of the public houses we know every Saturday or Sunday.
      There's a bit of music and it's gay and lively. And
      nobody gets what you'd call sodden drunk, they're a nice
      properly behaved set of people. There's no harm in it at
      all. But I must say I think it's better when there's a man
      in the party. I don't like to see women drinking alone,
      though two or three is alright . . .'

Several older women mentioned that they themselves at times
went into a pub for a quick one, but were disgusted to see so many
young women there:

F45D: 'I go occasionally myself to a pub, but I think it's
      disgraceful to see so many young women there. And it
      isn't as if they were having soft drinks, but whiskies,
      mind you. Half this careless talk comes from these
      young women. They have a drink or two, and then they
      meet other young women and begin telling them that
      they've just had letters from so-and-so and mention the
      different places that they've moved to. I've heard it
      myself.'

One man complains that women don't know when they've had enough, and generally behave badly when they come into a pub, either by themselves or with other women. He does not object to women accompanied by men, since men are supposed to be looking after their ladies:

> M50C: 'Don't approve of it myself – most of these youngsters get more than they've ever had in their lives before and just come into a pub – don't know when the limit's reached – but then war does funny things to people, doesn't it? I don't mind if a girl comes in with a man, then he usually takes care of her and she behaves properly, but when three or four girls come in and all start singing and shouting, it's the limit.'

A middle-aged woman in the same pub complains of the age of the female drinkers these days, saying that a lot of very young girls come in and drink spirits:

> F40C: 'I don't hold with young girls of 17 or 18 coming in pubs alone. It's all wrong, even if they've mothers came in with them, it would be better. They shouldn't really drink at that age; it doesn't do them any good, continually soaking. And so many of them drink spirits nowadays.'

A young man thinks it 'unnatural' for a girl to be drinking all by herself:

> M25D: 'I may be old-fashioned, but I don't like to see a girl drinking alone – it ain't natural to my way of thinking.'

And this feeling is echoed in several other remarks:

> M50B: 'I've nothing against being in pubs, but I feel they should have some sort of escort – it's not really respectable to go round pubs on one's own if one's young and a woman.'
>
> F55D: 'Well, I shouldn't like my Emmie to go running around pubs on her own – indecent I calls it. I don't mind if she goes with her bloke, I know he'll take care of her. Of course, if you goes in with other women, you never know what will happen; people think you're cheap. It's alright for an old body like me, but youngsters, no.'

And this young man, who doesn't care what most women do, but who feels most strongly that he wouldn't like his girl to go into a pub on her own:

> M20D: 'I'm saving up to get married – only go into a pub at Xmas. I don't care what other girls do, but if I thought my girl was going into a pub – I'd wring her neck, honest I would.'

Two middle-aged men mention that they dislike women coming into the public bar, but would not mind them going into the lounge or saloon bar:

> M50D: 'It's alright women going into the saloon. I don't question that. But what I do object to is their coming into the Public Bar. I don't like that . . . I don't think the young ladies ought to come in unaccompanied by men, even if they are in couples.'
>
> M45C: '. . . Young women should be allowed into the ladies' bar, but not into the mixed bar.'

Accompanied women
A few mentioned that they had no grievance against women coming into pubs, accompanied by husbands or boyfriends:

> F60C: 'I don't think young girls should drink on their own, certainly not. My relative, she goes with her husband, and that's a bit different, but I think it's terrible for young girls to drink . . . if women just go with their husbands for like a friendly drink, I think it's alright. A lot depends on the place, don't you think?'
>
> M40C: 'To tell you the truth, I've never really thought about it. It never occurred to me to question the presence of young women in pubs. They always have been there. It looks better for women to come in the company of men. Otherwise there is no tone.'

Female drunkenness
Some people mention that they strongly dislike seeing women who have drunk too much, several thinking that female drunks are much worse than males:

F60C: '. . . And I think the sight of a woman who's had too much to drink is terrible. I don't like to see it at all. But as I say, times have changed.'

Even a woman, otherwise unprejudiced against female pub-going, dislikes to see a woman drunk:

F50C: 'I think it's a very good thing, just as it should be, women going into a public house same as a man would do. You might as well say, should women ride on buses? You can't build special pubs for women any more than you can run special buses. We're all just people nowa-days. And I don't think men resent it; they like to be able to take their girls to a pub without it being thought low. It's a great improvement on the old days, so long as women don't overdo it. I don't like to see a woman drunk.'

M40D: 'Of course women can't hold it like a man and a drunken woman is not a pleasant sight . . .'

M50C: 'Well, a mature woman who can hold her drink there's nothing against that. But girls in there drink Red Biddy and that filth, and lose all self control. That's where the trouble starts – this disease and everything else.'

M25C: 'I don't mind them coming in, it wouldn't be sociable without them, but there is one thing I object to, and that's a woman who has had too much for her own good. It's OK for them to come in alone or with whomever they like as long as they behave themselves decently.'

Some complain of the high amount of female drunkenness these days:

F40D: 'It's alright if women know how to behave themselves. But some don't. The in-betweens seem alright, you don't often see them so drunk they don't know what they are doing. But the old'uns and the young'uns are the worst. They take too much and they don't know it.' (Chelsea)

M35B: 'I hardly ever drink at a pub without a woman with me; I like drinking with women, and you get some interesting conversation. But I do think there's too much heavy drinking among the girls in the Forces, and also among

women of sixty and seventy. Night after night I see
them reeling about the tube stations, dancing Mother
Brown on the escalators – and I must say, I don't care to
see it. I feel that the quite young and the very elderly
have lost all sense of proportion in this war: the young-
ish, middle-aged people seem much more balanced. I
don't know why it is, I haven't evolved any theory about
it.'

Apart from this man, several other people think that female
drinking has much increased during the war, especially among
women in the Forces:

M30D: 'Women drink a fat lot more than they did before the
war – even I remember that. You never saw so much of
it till the war started. Women in the Forces especially.
Not that I mind a woman having a drink at a pub, take
no objection to that, not at all. But some of these lasses
don't know when to stop. Do you know what I saw only
last night? I was coming home by District from Victoria,
and there was three American soldiers, young chaps all,
with their arms round two young ATS. All twined in a
circle, they was, and hardly able to stand, not one
among them. One of the girls was sick in the train
before we got to South Ken. Sick as a dog she was. The
other gal came across to her and took off her cap and
tried to comfort her, but she was so drunk, she could
hardly keep on her feet. Now that's not right to my
mind.'

Some complain that young people these days know no moderation
in their drinking:

F50C: 'Well, you can't make youngsters listen to advice. Drink
taken in small quantities never did anyone any harm,
but these youngsters nowadays don't know where to
stop. They'll learn from experience and then it will be
too late.'

Increase in female drinking
A few people state that they have noticed a definite increase in
female drinking since the outbreak of the war, and comment in

various ways on this. Some explain the increase through the higher earning power women command these days; others think that since it is easier today for a woman to enter a pub than it was before the war, more come:

> M50C: 'Lots more than before the war – I should think it's mainly because the young women are earning more than ever before . . .'

Similar remarks have already been quoted. There is also some feeling that pub attendance by older women has fallen, but their place has been taken by the various uniformed younger women:

> F35C: 'Nearly three times as many young women coming in than before – girls in uniform who didn't drink before and girls who are earning big money. They mostly come at night. The older women have dropped off somewhat, afraid of the blackout, I dare say. But wait till the nights are longer, then we shall have a change.'

> F35C: 'There do seem to be far more women drinking in pubs alone than before the war – but it's understandable isn't it . . . what with air raids and men in the Forces . . .'

The pub as a pick-up

Several people comment that girls seem to regard the pub these days as a place where acquaintance can be made with men. Sometimes they consider this as harmless, sometimes they dislike the idea very strongly:

> F35C: '. . . Of course, they do sometimes come in solely for pick-ups, but that has been going on for time immemorial. That's nothing to do with the war.'

> F50C: 'I don't think decent girls go in them much myself. There's a certain type who just go in to pick up men. Get what they can, sort of thing. Those you'll never stop. It's the sort of homes they come from and everything, and the upbringing they've had. But they're the ones who go after Canadians and Americans and spread disease.'

> M25C: 'You don't get a lot of young women drinking unless they are with soldiers, Americans or something like that, or else because they are on the pick-up; which quite a few do round here.'

M40D: 'With all their faults, the place wouldn't be the same
without them. About young women, well, they use the
pub as pick-ups. But there's not so many about now with
American soldiers going two for a penny. Any decent
girl would come in accompanied, not alone. It gives
their game away if they do. They all hunt in pairs.'

But even about pick-ups in pubs feeling is not really strong, and
though some people obviously dislike it, and perhaps would like
to see it stopped, they do not, at any time, make vehement
remarks on this score alone.

19

Four sisters, Kent, March 1944

The decline in the birthrate seen all over central and
south west Europe and in North America in the late
thirties and forties caused considerable concern.
Mass-Observation set out to examine the attitudes of
British women towards having children and its results
were published in *Britain and her Birthrate* in 1945.
Research for this project depended heavily on the panel
of volunteer writers who responded to an in-depth
questionnaire with considerable candour. The composition
of the panel, especially by 1944, was heavily middle class
and the Mass-Observers were concerned to collect opinions
from working-class women. They analysed letters received
by birth control clinics and they carried out a number of
interviews. The extracts below are taken from reports of
interviews made by Celia Fremlin in Kent. The women
are all the daughters of a Mrs J. who had 13 children.
Celia Fremlin reported that Mrs J. had married a farm
labourer when she was 19 and that her family had been
born in two stages: the age range was very wide.

Mass-Observation concluded that women were opting
for smaller families out of a concern for the quality of life
for their children, feeling that they could not offer the
same emotional and material benefits to a large family as
they could to a family of, say, two children. The favoured
method of birth control was still coitus interruptus despite
the growing but uneven availability of mechanical
methods of contraception.

Freda
Freda is a dark-haired, rosy-cheeked young woman of 27. She has
two little boys, Charlie aged 8 and Billy aged 2. Her husband is
now in the army and she lives in Snodland by the river with his
parents. She married when she was barely 19, the marriage

being, as Mrs J. [her mother] puts it, 'a case of have to'. Charlie was born only a few weeks after they were married, and there was quite a scandal about it in the village at the time, and Mrs J. was very upset about it all. But now all is forgotten and forgiven and the marriage seems to have turned out happily enough. The only reminder of the past now seems to lie in the fact that Freda is much fonder of the younger child than of Charlie. She does not say this, but it is obvious from her manner to the two children, and also by her account of how jealous Charlie was when Billy was a young baby:

> It was terrible, I just didn't know what to do with him. I could never leave Charlie in the room with him a second – he'd have had the carving knife to him, he would, honest! My, he hated that poor little mite. He'd pinch him and hit him – anything he could when my back was turned. I do believe he would have killed him if he could. In the end I had to send him to his Gran's for a bit until Billy was a bit older, and when he came back it was alright, he seemed to have forgotten about it.

The trouble seems to be over now anyway. When Inv. arrived, Charlie was trundling his little brother about in a go-cart most amiably, and later took him on his lap to give him tea.

It was not possible to get much impression of the house or of Freda's housekeeping capacities, as it happens they had had all the windows blown out by a bomb last week, so that the windows are all blacked out with wood and linoleum and paper, and naturally everything looked rather a mess. The shock of the event colours most of Freda's conversation. She says she wouldn't dream of having any more children until the war is over:

> Take last week, for instance. Whatever'd I have done if I'd had another of them to worry about? The two of them were in their beds when it happened, and I rushed upstairs and found them all covered with glass – every inch of Billy's cot, it was a mass of glass. It was a miracle he wasn't killed, but he never had a scratch. He was right under the clothes you see. My, but it gave me a shock. I still keep trembling when I think of it, what might have happened. And then think, suppose it had been a tiny baby there, it would have been killed wouldn't it, that's certain. No, I'd never have another baby while this sort of thing's going

on. Since we've had that bomb I've had them both down under the stairs every time the warning goes. That's the best place, they say, under the stairs.

Then again, I keep worrying, suppose they was to drop gas, then what would I do? Charlie knows about his gas mask and that of course, they have it at school, but what would I do with Billy? He'd scream himself silly if I was to try and put anything over *his* face. It doesn't make you want to have kids, does it? There's so much worry to it nowadays.

Inv. tries to find out why Freda didn't have any children for six years between Charlie and Billy. She laughs uneasily:

Well I dare say Mum's told you all about how it was with Charlie, all that fuss and palaver. Well, it kind of put me off all that kind of thing you know. I felt I'd had a mouthful over Charlie, I didn't want no more of it. Silly because of course I was married and all that afterwards but that's how I felt. Just I didn't want any more to do with it. I'm not like that now but I wouldn't have no more, not with all these raids on.

Joan

Joan is a pretty, gentle girl of 25. She is tall and slight, and has always been delicate, having had pneumonia three times during her childhood. She married at the age of 19 to a mill-worker in Chatham. He is also delicate, has stomach ulcers and is thus exempt from the army. His job is a skilled one and well-paid so Joan has never had to go out to work since she married. For the first three years of their marriage they had no children – not intentionally – and Joan was very distressed about it, and had almost given up all hope of ever having any when Cathy started. She was very ill when the child was born and the child too was very small and feeble for the first few weeks and no one thought they could rear her. However, after she was three months old she began to gain strength and by nine months she was the prettiest, healthiest-looking little girl imaginable, though still on the small side.

They live in a six-roomed house near the river at Chatham. The house is one of a row of similar houses and Joan is not fond of it. She says:

I do wish we could get somewhere further out. It's a nice little house but I don't like being packed in like this. I'd like a little house standing all on its own right outside with a nice piece of garden and a few trees round about. I don't think it's healthy, poked away in a row of houses like this. Especially so close by the river. It's so foggy and misty always even in summer time.

The house however is their own. It had belonged to her husband's mother who had lived with them till she died and left them the house, furniture and all. Joan doesn't care about the furniture either – it is mostly heavy, rather ornate mahogany, very good quality but not to her taste.

Often when I'm going round doing the work in the mornings I think to myself just how I'd like this place if I had a lot of money and could start right from the beginning. I'd have nice light furniture everywhere – you know, the new kind of wood that you don't polish or anything. It would all be very plain and I'd only have just a few pictures that I really like. I don't like them all over everywhere the way we've got them. And I'd like lino not all those heavy rugs and that to catch the dust. And nice low beds – oh, I know just what I'd do if I had a couple of hundred pounds!

I don't know, it's a bit wicked of me to talk like this really. Old Mrs Richards, she was a sweet old lady, I wouldn't like to alter it too much, she loved it just the way it was. Anyway I haven't got my two hundred pounds, so I needn't worry. (She laughs.)

In spite of her complaints, Joan takes a tremendous lot of trouble to keep the place looking nice. The elaborate carved mahogany is polished like glass – it must take hours rubbing in and out among the complicated patterns of the carving.

She is devoted to Cathy – now nearly two – and by all orthodox rulings has completely spoilt her – spends all her spare time playing with and talking to her, rushes to pick her up at the first whimper, and gives her as far as possible everything she wants. But the results seem to justify the method; Cathy is a happy, contented little thing, enchantingly pretty and very alert and intelligent. She can talk extremely well for her age, and though she is barely two can do all sorts of household jobs, like drying and putting away crockery, tidying books up to their right places, sweeping up crumbs. Owing to the anxiety of her early weeks, Joan is still very solicitous about Cathy's health – quite unnecessarily so, from the blooming appearance of the child now. Joan plans her whole day's work in terms of whether it is going to be fine enough for Cathy to go out or not, and if so what time of day would be best for her.

Inv. asks Joan if she means to have any more children. Joan laughs rather ruefully:

It doesn't look as if I'm going to have much choice. It took three years before she started and it looks as if it'll be another three years before Johnny decides to come! I did think for a little while there might be something, last autumn, but it didn't come to anything. I wasn't sorry really. I don't feel up to another one just yet. I was terribly ill with Cathy, you know, and it seemed to pull me down so. I still don't feel quite right yet, even now. And I keep thinking, if anything was to happen to me, what would happen to Cathy? Jack couldn't look after her, being at work all day and I wouldn't like her to go back to Mum's. No I think it is just as well the way it is.

Inv. 'If you felt quite well and strong, would you want a big family?'

Well, that's hard to say – I wouldn't want a big family like Mum's, not thirteen of 'em – My Goodness! But sometimes I think I'd like three or four, and then again I think, well, if I had the others to look after, I couldn't give so much time to Cathy, could I? And we have such happy little times together, Cathy and I do, and quiet the way it is with just Cathy and Jack and me, we can do what we think we will and have such good times together. I don't think I'd like a crowd of kiddies the same way. Then Cathy is such a quiet, good little thing, I couldn't expect they'd all be like that. Look at her dress now. You wouldn't think she'd worn that all week, would you, a kiddie of two?

Inv. certainly wouldn't. The dress was a white wool one with tiny pink rosebuds round the neck and sleeves, and it is absolutely spotless as if it had just been put on.

She's that kind of kiddie you see. I haven't had to force her into it – she's always kept herself clean like that. If she gets a speck of dirt on her hand she'll run to me at once and say, 'Wash, mummy, wash'.

Inv. 'You don't think she'd be better with a brother or sister?'

Well to tell you the honest truth, I don't know that she would. She's such a funny little old-fashioned thing, she seems to be just as happy with grown-ups as with other children. She's real company to me you know, when I'm here alone all day. And there's the little girl next door, I can always have her to play with Cathy if I think she's getting a bit lonely. But she's a funny kid, she'd just as soon be with me.

Inv. 'How do you feel about all the propaganda about the birthrate?'

Well, I think it's alright, for those that are strong enough and have money for it. But I don't think it's right to have children and then find you can't look after them properly. I think it's better to have one and give it all your attention than to have a dozen and never be able to care for them as you should do.

Beatie
Beatie is the eldest of Mrs J.'s children. She is 43, and married to a factory worker in Gravesend. They have never had any children – Beatie knew before she married him that he would never be able to have any children owing to an injury received during the last war. At the time she didn't mind; when Mrs J. warned her against marrying him she said, 'Do you think I want a house full of kids like you, Mum?' and Mrs J. replied: 'You wait, my girl. You'll cry one of these days, when you see all your sisters with kids and you aint got none.'

This is Mrs J.'s version of what happened 25 years ago. Beatie herself never speaks of it and seems quite content with her childless state. She is a queer-looking woman, very gaunt and haggard – she looks quite as old as her mother, and without any of her mother's vitality and cheerfulness. Beatie dresses still in the styles of 1930 – long skirts, low waisted blouses and sloping shoulders. Her manner is more working class and uneducated than any of her sisters. She works at an unskilled job in an aircraft factory and seems very tired and worn out with it:

> The doctor put me on half time a while back just to do mornings, but I don't seem to feel no better. My head's terrible and my back too. I never get no peace with it.

It is impossible to talk to her about children and families and Inv. felt it would be unkind to press her too far on the subject. She got the impression however that her lack of communicativeness on the subject was due to genuine lack of interest rather than to excessive depth of feeling about it. Mrs J. however says that on one occasion, Beatie seemed very upset – when she saw her sister Joan's baby, a very pretty little girl. Mrs J. says:

> She (Beatie) never troubled before, she'd seen all the other kids and never turned a scrap, but when she saw little Cathy, she sat down and cried. I got quite a shock: 'Beatie,' I said, 'but I thought you never wanted no kids!' 'No, mum, I didn't,' she said, 'and I don't now, but she's such a pretty little thing, aint she?' She is too, the loveliest little kid I ever laid eyes on. Yes proper upset my Beatie was when she saw Joan's Cathy. I think it was she remembered how she'd had Joan as a baby – wonderful with babies Beatie always was, a real little help she was to me. It kind of came over her how Joan was growed up too like the rest, and had kids of her own. Well, it's a bad job, aint it? I told Beatie, I told her, 'Don't you marry that young fellow,' I said. But she would do it and now she's sorry.

Inv. 'But Beatie doesn't seem to want any children now?'

> No, she don't *now*. Well, I mean she's better off without, isn't she, her health being how it is. She's on the change, you know, it's taken her early. It does with single women and women what haven't had no children, you know. It takes 'em terrible early, and terrible bad. That's Beatie's trouble. Well, she's got a good husband, she's not so bad off as some, is she? It's a lot if you've got a good husband.

Nora
Nora, aged 22, is the youngest of Mrs J.'s daughters. She is like Freda to look at, dark and rosy-cheeked. She is very clever, and in spite of having had only a village education to the age of 14 has managed to pass all her exams for becoming a qualified nurse, and is now specialising in midwifery. She is unmarried, and

declares herself to be totally uninterested in men, and never wants to get married. She is certainly very keen on her job, and very good at it, but whether her resolutions about marriage will persist it is difficult to say. At the moment she has no boyfriends and makes no effort to get any – never goes to dances or anything of that sort.

Inv. asked her what she thought about all the talk about the falling birthrate in the papers. She says:

> It's only because they want men to fight in the next war. The more babies people have, the more they'll have to fight for them in the next war. I think it's horrible. They don't want the babies for their own sakes at all, just for wars. If it was for the people's own sake, well there's too many people in the country already. Look at the horrible great towns, millions and millions of people all packed together. I think this country would be a much better place if there were only half as many people in it. Then there would be proper houses for them all, and everything.

Inv. asks what led her to specialise in midwifery. She says:

> Well, it's interesting work, you know, you really feel you're *doing* something. Not like the chronic cases, you know you can't do any real good with them.

Inv. 'You feel like that about the work, even though you disapprove of so many babies being born?'

> Yes, I do. I mean, I think babies that *are* born should have the best chance you can possibly give them, and that's our job. Like a little while ago, we had a little Prem born – it didn't weigh above two and a half pounds, and nobody thought it would live. But we worked at it. We did everything we knew – it was under oxygen for nearly a week, it couldn't suck or anything, we had to feed it through a tube. And you can't imagine the thrill when it first began to suck! I was on duty at the nursery that morning and I was putting the tube down its throat and all of a sudden it got hold of the tube between its little gums and started to suck like mad! I was so thrilled I could have just danced about the nursery. I gave it one of the bottles – one of the very easy ones – and it sucked down nearly an ounce right off. And when it was

finished I dashed off to tell Sister, and she was as thrilled as I was. We could neither of us hardly speak! After that it went ahead lovely, and we sent it home weighing five and a half pounds. I haven't heard since but I expect it is getting on fine, they do once you get them up to five pounds. Well, it's that kind of thing that makes me love the work. You feel it's really worthwhile, if you can save a little life like that that doctors have given up.

20

Married women and work, January 1944

The January 1944 'Directive' to members of
Mass-Observation's panel contained the following
question: 'Should married women be able to go out to work
after the war?' The question was put to both men
and women but only a selection of the women's replies
has been reproduced here. In fact the range of views was
as wide among the men as it was among the women. The
only difference is that slightly more ambivalence was
expressed by the women who believe that a woman's place
is in the home than was expressed by men with similar
views.

**Housewife with one child, temporary radio valve
maker, aged 45, Wembley**

I hope the return of women to the home will not be made a grave
issue after the war. Speaking for myself, I shall be sorry to leave
my job, and the part-time hours I work could be continued ad
infinitum as far as I am concerned. I have not enough to do to
occupy me intelligently in the house, and after years of voluntary
'good works' a small regular pay packet is very welcome.

Married woman, munitions worker, aged 46, Bolney

I think married women will be able to go out to work after the war
and see no reason why in certain cases they should not do so. A
number of points will be involved and I feel each case would
depend on individual circumstances, but think it usually a
mistake for women with children to go out to work.

Single woman, nursing and domestic worker, aged 39, Leicester

Married women well trained and fitted for their job will be allowed to continue – i.e. teachers and nurses etc., where there is need of them. But going out to work is incompatible with the proper care of children. Even before the War one saw the sad result of mothers working in the factory in a certain manufacturing village near here. The children ran about the streets wild and uncared-for with no home life. Sometimes women had to work because their work was needed rather than their husbands'; a few because they were used to factory life, and liked the independence their earnings gave them; staying at home looking after a family seemed to them a dull affair. If the men have work reasonably well paid, many married women who worked before the War will be glad to stay at home.

But others will be loath to relinquish the independence and interest in life which war work has given them. But I cannot see how work will be found for everyone if the majority of married women have jobs; and one hopes for such a revival of family life as can only take place if women begin again to take their bigger and more exacting full-time job of home-keeping seriously.

Housewife, casual farm labourer, aged 43, Argyllshire

I feel that it should always be possible – things *should* so be arranged that no woman need feel that marriage is going to drive her into domesticity. There should be just as many openings for women as for men, and just as many openings in *domestic* work for men as for women. Women do men's jobs in this war – let men take a turn at women's jobs after the war. What I mean by this is that husbands ought to accept the sharing of domestic work so that the work can be done quicker when both of them are at it. My own husband does this so I know what I'm talking about. Also men should not feel that it is lowering to take on domestic jobs if they happen to be good at such work and like it – some of them are and do. This is what *should* happen, but I am afraid that domestic work is on the whole so unpopular that men will do their damndest to push women back into it and keep them from 'outside' jobs – and women must fight hard to hold their present positions.

Single woman, science teacher, aged 30, Brentwood

If they want to I see no reason why they should not, and I think there should be a state scheme to enable them to have time off to have children. But I hope it will not be necessary for any woman to have to work simply because her husband's wages are not sufficient to support her and her children.

I think it should be made easier for a woman to have a job and a family at the same time. Otherwise the offspring of some of the best women, who when faced with the choice, choose their careers, are lost to the country and we are not in a position to be able to dispense with the breeding of the better types.

Married woman, company secretary, aged 28, Purley

I am longing for the time when I can stay at home and I know many married women who, like me, are doing a war-job, and would be only too pleased to give up their jobs when the war is over, providing their husbands can provide for them comfortably of course.

Single woman, stenographer, aged 36, Birmingham

This is one of my favourite problems, in the sense that I think and wonder and argue about it quite a lot, and can't decide just where I stand about it.

In the first place, generally speaking I don't really think married women should want to go out to work. The proportion of women with a real flair for business or talents for the professions or arts, to the ordinary ones, is very small. The others may be quite competent, but it isn't evident why they should want to be in business rather than running a home and bringing up children – or if children are lacking, doing voluntary political, charitable or cultural work. Surely there is much more scope for self-expression about running a home, where you are, not so much 'your own boss', as the Managing Director, Matron, Commandant, Star and every other sort of eminence rolled into one, than about doing an ordinary job under an ordinary boss?

Here I'm going to digress a bit and say, though I believe the above is a sound point of view, I admit that very many women are bored by their homes and long to get back to work. Typical is the remark of a junior girl at my office, whose mother works in a factory part-time. I said, 'Doesn't she find it a big effort to run the home, to look after you and your father and go out to work as well?' Said the child, 'Yes, she does, of course, but she likes the company.' And I'm sure that's one of the important factors. Women in modern, small, labour-saving houses, have small families and no domestic help, so much of their working time is spent in loneliness and isolation. No wonder they gossip in shops and enjoy standing in queues! Bigger houses, bigger families and adequate domestic help – given these I believe most women really would get far more satisfaction out of careers as Wife-and-Mother than out of a business career. And I think it ought to be so, so that the customary relationship between man and wife – breadwinner and home-maker – can be maintained, *unless* we are prepared to be really revolutionary and remodel society on the Russian plan. The objection to that, however, is that I can't see that there is scope in this country for infinite industrial expansion to absorb all the woman labour that would be available if the usual home-and-family pattern were abandoned. The crux of the question to me is: if the economic emancipation of women goes on, what will compensate men, in the marriage relation, for the loss of their status as breadwinner to the family? I don't want to be a reactionary and adopt a 'Kirche Küche Kinder' doctrine, but I do believe all the points I have mentioned, and many more, want thinking out seriously. And lastly it seems to me absolutely obvious that the chief reason why young girls of fifteen or so now go wrong and get into trouble in such appalling numbers is that family life has gone to pot. Parents have been afraid, for the past 20 years or so, of exercising any authority and keeping children in their place; they have also, understandably enough, been reluctant to have large families, so that there is no circle of brothers and sisters to play or work with, the child goes out at night just as she wishes, and pleases herself and has no spiritual roots and being naturally silly at that age, gets into horrible trouble. Two ways of tackling the thing: go totalitarian, pump politics into the young people, conscript them into state-organised groups and keep them well under control, *or* rebuild family life.

Married woman, housewife, aged 50, Nr Wrexham

In certain classes the woman has always had to work as well as her husband. I don't see why in all classes women should not work if they wish to, and feel the home will [be] better with their joint incomes. Very maternal women would obviously stay with their young children. The other sort would send them to nursery schools where they would be much happier than with someone who was not very interested in or patient with them. Many women who love their children dearly are yet incapable of coping with them all day and every day.

Married woman, mother and housewife, aged 54, Gateshead

Married women and work. Let them go out who wish. There are hosts of women who are naturally domesticated, hosts have lost their men. I think the 'Woman problem' after the war will be great. Already the teaching profession is crowded with some grand, healthy, women who'd love a home and children. *I know.* They'd make grand homes but they are weary in schools of caring for other folk's badly neglected children.

The wrong, stupid women appeal to young men – until it's too late. Yes, it's the fool, ignorant, selfish women who often marry the decent men. After the war I don't know what can happen. There should be room for married women to continue in the jobs that suit them, and for domesticated women to look after homes. But these women cost too much – a domestic help is a problem.

No! I cannot answer this question generally. I know I had to give up doing a good job of teaching *because I was a married woman* in 1922, and I had a good girl working for me who did not want to leave me. I *know* I was a good teacher and hate mucky, dirty house-work. I love *managing* a house and children and the domestic workers. Poor women, and lots would love to have a home and stay and work there.

Married woman with 3 children, aged 33, Epsom

My feelings are that a great number of married women are looking forward to the day when they can give up their work. But

I feel strongly that there should be *no ban* against married women working. There should be freedom of choice and while there is so much to do in the way of reconstruction, part-time work for married women may be continued.

Single woman, companion and home help, aged 56, Bristol

I feel sure that many women will go out to work after the war; some of them may be obliged to in order to make both ends meet. I am thinking here of women with semi-invalid ex-Service husbands. Other married women will arrange to have their home run for them while they carry on with the career for which they were trained before marriage. Personally, I think that marriage is a full-time career, though not as exciting as one outside the home, perhaps; and a woman cannot give of her best to two careers. But on the whole, I think that married women will be only too glad to make their home the centre of their life, especially if they have had to rough it in the services, or share accommodation during the war. Sometimes I think of the stupendous cost of all the postwar plans proposed for the betterment of everybody and everything. Then it seems that rates and taxes, to pay for the carrying out of the schemes, will absorb so much of the ordinary man's income that his wife will have to earn money, too. I feel that, were it to happen, the home-life of the country would be ruined, and because so much depends on the way that children are influenced in their homes, the wonderful plans would be made to no avail.

Married woman, aged 45, secretary, London

I do not think any woman who is married should have to go out to work; I think those that really wish to, and have no small children (or can put their children in a Nursery School if they are little), should be able to. A man should be paid sufficient to support a wife, and there should be adequate family allowances. If the wife really wants to do some work which is of interest to her, I think it is a good thing for her to feel free to do so, provided she doesn't neglect the home too much, and that her husband really feels happy about it. (Husbands are getting used to it in wartime, and may be educated to agree to it in peacetime!) I am sure *every* married woman needs at least some *interests* outside her home if she is to lead a full life.

Married woman, aged 53, poultry farmer's wife, Nr Reading

The operative word is 'possibility'. A lot of women will *want* to have their cake and eat it (i.e. have a husband, home and children, and a job) but will it be possible on any large scale? Middle-class women with professional jobs (doctors, writers, etc., *if* they can find labour to employ) but what if the so-called working class themselves want the kind of interesting jobs they have had in war? How will *they* 'employ labour' to set them free to go out to work? It seems possible in Russia, with its universal crèche system, and everybody more or less on a level. But England isn't Russia, nor are English Trades Unions comparable to Russian ones. I don't mean the Russians are better, far from it, but the aim of Russian unions is to get the most and the best work out of the worker, for the good of the state, which, in the last resort, is the individual; here the Trades Unions' aim is mainly to do the best for the workers – more wages, less hours, etc. And our Trades Unions will certainly want first and foremost to get their men reinstated in their jobs, and the women – well, they can take what's left. Personally, I think a job should go to the person best qualified to perform it, whether man or woman, married or single, and be paid on that basis. But women with young children should, I think, feel their responsibilities to their children first, and not go out to work while they are rearing a young family. (At present, I could cite numerous instances, some in my own family, in which young mothers, not forced to do war-work, are so keen to do it that they leave their children to the care of the grandmother! As some of these grandmothers are no older than I am – 53 – I think this most unfair! If I had a daughter nothing on earth would persuade me to take over her responsibilities to her children. It is I who would like to do war-work – I've done my child-bearing and child-rearing and I certainly don't want to start all over again!) It is when the children reach school age that the mother (and the children) benefit by mother having a job, possibly part-time, provided she can find the domestic help that having a job would enable her to afford. But will there be any domestic help? I am not impressed by schemes to make domestic help an 'honourable' profession. If too well trained it will command wages that ordinary people can't afford. At present I pay £1 a week (the very utmost I can afford) for most indifferent help. I have to be the brains of the household all the time, do all the cooking, and a lot of the rest of the work, and all the washing. What time have I to do the paid job that I'd simply love to have? Yet I am, I think, a good employer, have always given holidays with pay, plenty of time off, and a lot of consideration – and I have always kept maids for several years – till the war of course.

Single woman, aged 21, WAAF, Norfolk

I have every wish to work after the war so cannot disapprove of any women who think the same. I consider that when their children are less than five years old mothers should not work but devote their whole time at home, but after that age I am sure by a few adjustments in our methods women can have a career without it reflecting badly on their homes or children's upbringing. Having seen so many women frustrated when their children have grown up and no longer need their care; I feel that this would have been avoided if the mothers had had a career of their own and not devoted all their attention to their families.

Another point is will there be enough work for women and men? I can see no reason why there should not be, it is surely only a matter of skilful organisation of the manpower of the country.

Married woman with baby, aged 38, Lincoln

This provoked an interesting bicker on the meaning of the wording of the question. It is a good example of the questions you word purposely vaguely to get various points of approach.

My husband thought of woman and employer, and talked of the inconvenience of women leaving to have babies. My working housekeeper (widow) talked of women and husband, and would the man want the woman going off to work. I talked of woman and man fellow-worker, men returned from the front and wanting the jobs.

Of course in a Soviet England there would be work and to spare, for everyone who wanted. And my thoughts of unemployed disappear. I *want* the women to retain this independence. Anyhow I believe a good proportion of women will fight to hold the jobs they have won, and a proportion of those will win (against fellow-worker, husband and employer).

I read the question as referring to jobs not done in peace by women, and women not going out to work in peacetime. I didn't count for instance Lancashire cotton workers, or servants. There are certain jobs which *ought* to have a proportion of married women: e.g. midwives, architects, schoolteachers (I have seen it said that celibacy is the handicap of schoolmistresses as compared with schoolmasters). I call to mind a case in a women's paper where the higher wage-earner was the woman, and had the breadwinning, while this husband was content and capable running the home!

Single woman, aged 34, teacher, Thornaby-on-Tees

There will be a general increase in the number of married women going out to work after the war. Science makes huge strides in wartime and facilities for running a home and working will be much greater. Canteens and British Restaurants in one form or another, day nurseries and Nursery Schools have come to stay, and these will all have their effect in encouraging women to stay at their jobs. Probably immediately after the war there will be a reaction towards home life on the part of the women now, but the increase will be noticed later. Of course a great deal will depend on whether there is employment for all, the type of government in power, and the social progress taking place. There will be more women in certain professions and trades than in others. I feel sure that married women teachers will be generally accepted and welcomed, as the supply will be so short. There will be more and more women in most of the professions, but the number of women in industry will depend very much on the type of government we get.

Married woman with baby, aged 29, Early, Berks

If they have houses I don't believe married women will want to go out to work. I think for childless women a part-time job is excellent, broadens the outlook. But I do not agree with the idea of parking babies in nurseries while the mother goes out to work, at least it should not be encouraged; some women are not suited to home life but are brilliant in their professions and should follow them if they want to.

Married woman, aged 34, factory worker, Bowden, Cheshire

I think married women will go out to work if they possibly can, but it depends on the economic conditions. In times of mass unemployment public opinion is very much against the middle class women 'doing a man out of a job'. Working class wives have nearly always worked for some period of their married lives.

Single parent, aged 37, civil servant, Purley

I think most married women will cease to work outside their homes after the war. Their main job is to make a home and family and it is an exceptional woman who has the energy to do both. But there will be many exceptional women. A woman who can do both or who has a vocation outside the home should be able to do as she wishes. It is sheer waste of ability to prevent it. It is also waste of a good machine to prevent a woman who is keen on her job from marrying and in particular from having children. I think most women will give up outside work, but it would be an advantage to them and to the community if more of them took on part-time paid or unpaid work according to their income. Running a simple home with the labour-saving devices we hope for should leave some leisure once the children are at school, and everyone is happier doing congenial work than killing time at bridge or shop-gazing. Part-time nursery school or infant welfare work, running youth clubs, local government work, and so on, should attract more and more married women. I believe that the wider a woman's interests are, up to the limit of her ability, the happier she is.

Housewife, aged 33, Newport

If women can make themselves useful in war industries why should not they in peacetime if they want to. I am hoping myself to do some coaching, or teaching, when children need no longer my full attention. I will thus be able to keep my mind alive and occupied, and earn my own respect instead of being dependent on husband.

Single woman, office worker, aged 46, Newcastle

Not too good unless we can produce a Socialist Revolution in this country. In the first place, for the most part most married women in this country don't want to work, in the second their husbands don't want them to, and in the third all men and nearly all unmarried women are also against it. Of course it depends to a large extent on the number of casualties as many widows and women with dependent husbands will have to work. There is no doubt in the minds of those women who have studied the subject, that the position of women in regard to jobs had steadily deterio-rated in the ten years between 1929–1939, due doubtless to economic pressure and to the spread of Fascist ideas. 'Many a man has passed Seraglio[?] Point and failed to mind Cape Turk.' Unless therefore this war brings with it the same broadenings of opinion that the last one did I don't see matters improving for the married women workers. I think an exception may be made in the case of teachers who are at present employed as married women – I think they may be kept on a temporary basis as there will be such a colossal shortage of them.

Married woman, no children, aged 28, aerodynamicist, Winchester

I consider that part-time work is ideal for young married women with no children, or for women with no children, or for women whose children are at school, and I hope that part-time work will be a feature of post-war planning. Where women have had careers, and where they are more suited to continue working than to spend time housekeeping and baby-minding, I think they should work. It is far better for a woman to continue with the job for which she is suited, and to pay the right type of person to look after her home and children, than to become a drudge herself, if housework is drudgery to her. But I do not think that a married woman should ever work very long hours (I suggest a 40-hour week as sufficient) and I think that she should always consider her family before her job. For instance she should never refuse to have children because it would mean giving up her job temporarily. I am very much in favour of the Russian attitude towards women. I am hoping for a development of Day Nurseries, all jobs open to married women, and maternity grants on the Russian lines.

21

VE Day, May 1945

The following accounts of the run-up to Victory in Europe Day show how the last months of war dragged. After the Allied invasion of Normandy in June 1944, the end seemed in sight. In September 1944 the Civil Defence outside London had been disbanded. The same month the blackout was reduced to a 'dim out'. In December the Home Guard stood down. But even as the war machinery geared down, the dreadful V2 silent rockets were falling on parts of England. The last one fell as late as March 1945. It was hard to believe that the war could really be over. The announcement of Hitler's death on 1 May 1945 seemed to be a certain sign. Official Victory in Europe Day was to be Tuesday 8 May and a public holiday was declared for the 8th and the 9th. The King made his broadcast to the nation at 9 p.m. on Tuesday 8 May. As the extracts indicate, however, many people felt uncertain about celebrating the end of the war while fighting continued in the Far East.

The first account of VE Day is taken from the diary of Amy Briggs, the nurse from Leeds. Between 1941 and 1944 Amy took on various jobs including one as a nurse in the first aid post of a factory. By 1945, however, she was back at home full time taking care of her two daughters, Anne and Sheila. Her husband T. has been invalided out of the Army.

May 8th

Got up with every intention of attending service at 12 noon at the Town Hall. Found it was a toss-up between leaving girls without a dinner and going to service. Rushed some stew on. Anne still in bed at 10.50 a.m. Made her get up and told her about the dinner and then made Sheila accompany me to the Town Hall.

Crowds of people all with the same intention – but no service!

Thanks to bungling of notices and broadcasts everyone mixed up and standing about in dismay. Left Hall, didn't know what to do. Badly wanted Sheila to remember V-Day but nothing happened to make any impression on her. Decided to go to Odeon until 2.30 p.m. when we came out and once more in dismay – pouring down and couldn't wait to hear Churchill speak, with the crowd at Victoria Square. Miserably went home. Gave Sheila her stew as Churchill was speaking. Afterwards went to my sister's and met Anne there.

Sister wanted to go to the club but I didn't feel like drinking so persuaded her to go to the pictures. Twice in one day, brrr! Had to come out at 10 p.m. to get a train home. Arrived home to find husband stretched on settee reading. No word spoken. Has not spoken to me for three weeks – don't know why – but feel that if he won't speak on V-Day, he'll never speak! Simply couldn't bear it. Rushed round to Mrs M. with Anne. Had a cry and then a lump of her apple pie and sat and talked to her until 1 a.m. Made some tea when I went back home. No word from T. God! What a day. Wish I were back at work with my friends!

May 9th
Got up late. A., S. and I took our time over breakfast. Heavenly to feel that time is our own for another day! Felt rather guilty because I hadn't attended any services but the girls seem to come first and after all we did thank God at home on Monday night when we went to bed. Tried hard not to let T. worry me. All went to Mother's at about 3 p.m. Enormous queues in town for trams to R. Park. People looking considerably more cheery than they did on V-Day. I think we were all too stunned when peace did come and did not know what to do with ourselves. To me people looked like a lot of sheep just drifting around town (V-Day) all looking for someone else to stand on their heads and shout 'Whoopee' but no one did. Truly they were a subdued, happy mass, lost and off their bearings because all at once their best 'toy' had been taken from them – the war!

I know because I felt the same! I had a good yell in the Odeon when President Wilson's wife died but I think her death was only an excuse to let myself go. I heard someone on the tram say, 'They never ought to have announced it until Japan is licked.'

However, back to May 9th . . .

Arrived back at Mother's 4.20 p.m. Took ages to get there. Sat and listened to a friend of hers (Cambridge and University, BA and cap and gown musician) play the piano and sing. Played all the old waltzes while the girls did old-time dances, very sweetly. Felt very proud of them and vowed never to leave them to T.

Arrived back home at 10 p.m. Had tea and biscuits and eventually went to bed. Heard T. coming in so all stopped talking and pretended to be asleep. Precaution quite unnecessary – he did not come up. Can't understand why he won't speak to me. Evidently his neurosis has got him well and truly!

PS Started having piano lessons myself 7 weeks ago. Getting on fine. Love it and find it my sole interest in life, apart from G. [her manfriend].

> The second account of VE Day is taken from the diary of a 23-year-old clerk in the ATS. She was based in London but her family were from Norfolk.

May 7th

Noon: Leaving home this morning to return to my unit, I said goodbye to my mother and brother, and 'See you after the war!' At last I am beginning to feel fluttery inside. There is an atmosphere of exhilaration in the office, with everyone cracking feeble jokes and laughing enormously at each other's efforts. I have just bought a couple of yards of red, white and blue ribbon, a paper Union Jack and a tawdry Stars and Stripes on a stick – the latter price 3/9, from Harrods!

Very much later: What a day! It hardly seems possible that it was only this morning that I got up! There has been a steady crescendo of excitement, and the lack of any official announcement only added to the chaotic conditions. At the 3 p.m. news broadcast, there was a report from the German radio that they surrendered unconditionally this morning, but SHAEF has said nothing. Now this really is something; the office is buzzing with excited, facetious chatter. A woman clerk comes in and we tell her the news: 'Six years I've sat in this chair waiting to hear that, and *now*, when it comes, I have to be out of the room!'

At 4 and 5, we listen to news headlines, but still nothing official; in between times, we half-heartedly toy with the work on our desks. It is impossible to concentrate. At 5.15, the evening papers

come in, and are scanned for concrete news. The war is over –
that's obvious – but when is Churchill going to say so? Everyone
gives his opinion – 'At nine' – 'Not till tomorrow' – 'At midnight'.
Normally, the office is clear by 5.55, but tonight every single
member of the staff stays to hear the 6 p.m. news – and *still* it is
the same.

Feeling frustrated, we ATS trickle back to the billet; it is our
CB night – it would be! We are determined, however, that when
the balloon does go up, we will break out and see the fun.
Knightsbridge is beginning to blossom with flags and bunting,
and it is a lovely sunny afternoon. The conductress ignores our
outstretched bus fares, but collects it from civilian passengers.

We have an egg and boiled bacon for tea; in our rooms, we
grouse at the way the public has been built up to this point only to
be let down by lack of official news. Suddenly, one of the girls,
leaning out of the window, yells, 'Hey – something about 3 o'clock
tomorrow!' With one accord, we race round to the Rec. room,
where the radio is, but it is turned off. At this moment, the bell
rings for Parade. We troop into the Concert Hall, all talking at
once. I realise that I have my bedroom slippers on, and have to
dash back to put my shoes on! Then, the Company Commander
announces that tomorrow is VE-Day, Churchill will speak at
3 p.m., gives out a few other items, then, 'Any questions?' The
shout goes up – 'Can we go out?' Smiling broadly, she gives us
permission, but we must be in by midnight. Next night, we can
have an extension til 2 a.m., if not going home.

We rush back for our hats, and jump on a bus to Hyde Park
Corner. The western end of Piccadilly is no more crowded than
usual, just smiling people, mostly in uniform, strolling in either
direction. 'I thought there'd be *millions* of people out,' remarks K.
Nearer Piccadilly Circus, there are more, and we stop to buy red,
white and blue favours at exorbitant prices from hawkers, who
already line the pavements and are doing a roaring trade. By an
entrance to the Tube, a soldier is being helped along, a white cloth
round his forehead, his hand to his face, and blood pouring from it.
M. says, 'I don't think I'm going to like this,' but as it happened,
this was the only distressing sight we were to see all evening.

In Piccadilly Circus, the crowds are fairly dense, and also down
Coventry St. We exclaim at a neon sign in Leicester Sq. and at the
lighted revolving dome of the Coliseum – sights forgotten in these

six years. The crowds are hilarious in Trafalgar Sq. Students march by in bands. The chimes of Big Ben come through loud-speakers, and the 9 p.m. news, but no one listens. Down Whitehall – and more marching students. Not a pub seems to be open. ATS duty personnel wistfully watching the merrymakers from a War Office building. A little quiet area around the Cenotaph. Then Westminster – and the face of Big Ben clock lit up – another forgotten sight! Rosy floodlights are being tested on a Government building, but a policeman tells us that the Houses of Parliament floodlights are not going up till tomorrow night. Some of us want to go into Westminster Abbey for a few minutes' prayer, but it is closed. So into a YMCA for a lemonade (all we can get to toast Victory!) The canteen is gaily beflagged, but quiet, and half filled with serious-faced soldiers, some of them reading the evening papers.

But outside, London is really getting into the Victory mood, without waiting for Mr Churchill. The Embankment is quiet, but Trafalgar Sq. is gayer than ever, dancing and singing, the Marseillaise and 'Knees up Mother Brown'. The Palais Glide in the Haymarket, and little bonfires on the pavements, fed by newspapers. Then – Piccadilly Circus again. It is dark now, no street lights and few lighted windows. But it is one mass of yelling, laughing, singing, shrieking people; a small sports car is trying to wriggle through, and its folded roof is in shreds. A brilliantly lit bus is bogged down beside Eros, with people swarming all over it, inside and out. A man has climbed a lamp standard, and is beating his hands against the unlit lamp. Most of the men are in uniform – all services and nationalities. The Canadians are noisy, the sailors are merry, the airmen are drunk (or pretend to be), the Americans have a girl apiece, and are the quietest of all. Back along Piccadilly, the crowds are thinning; another bus rattles by, with figures clinging on all round. All the way to Knightsbridge, happy groups pass, and people still hope to get buses home. This is midnight, Victory Eve – and – Oh, my poor feet!

May 8th
VE-day – and a holiday. I called my room-mates at 8 a.m. K. opened her eyes, beamed, and said, 'It's *Victory* Day!' in a tone of delighted wonder. As we are dressing, she remarked, 'Well, the

Master Race has had it.' This was the first time I had heard the Germans mentioned since all this excitement began!

We all went home for VE-day. All through the East End the battered little streets are gay with bunting – recent V2 damage, barely tidied up, borders the bravest shows of all. My home town looks bright in the sunlight, the shabby paintwork masked by flags. Housewives are getting their rations in for the holiday, and in one queue I hear a woman say, 'Wouldn't I like a lorryload of Jerry prisoners to go by now.' Again, the gloating note is so unfamiliar that I have to record it, and it was the last of its kind I have heard throughout the celebrations.

VE-day was very quiet at home. My father came home from Liverpool, and we stayed in listening to the radio, and had a family party at teatime. In the centre of the table was a dish of canned pineapple, which Mother had saved through all the long years for this day. We went to the village church for a short service; it was full, and everyone sang 'Onward Christian Soldiers' with might and main. Back home to hear the King's speech and the news. The children have built a bonfire, and, unable to wait for darkness, have a lovely blaze at dusk, under the watchful eye of an NFS man. At intervals during the day, the ships and tugs in the river set up a lively chorus on their hooters and sirens – the traditional 'Cock-a-doodle-oo' and the 'Victory-V'. This usually signifies a BLA leave ship coming alongside.

Feeling rather flat, I was ready for bed by midnight; none of my friends is left locally, and others live too far away. I watched the signs of other festivities from an upper window; at midnight, when the Cease Fire came officially into force, searchlights went mad all over the sky, rockets and flares went up, the ships started off again, and a group of youngsters danced and sang in the road. Feeling rather out of it all, and wishing I were in London, I went to bed.

May 9th

VE 1, and a dull, close day. In spite of drizzling rain, we set out in the early evening for London, and the 'lights'. By the time we reached Victoria, the rain had stopped, the pavements were dry, and it was a lovely evening. We made for Buckingham Palace, where a large crowd was milling. As the sun set, the crowd grew larger and larger, singing, cheering and whistling at intervals.

Loudspeakers relayed popular music, and everyone stood patiently, occasionally chanting, 'We want the King.' A group of young people behind us sang, 'Come out, come out, wherever you are.' It grew darker, and a lamp lighter leisurely lit gas lamps in front of the Palace; a wan searchlight climbed into the warm air, and beyond Green Park a flag was floodlit.

In the room behind the red-draped balcony of the Palace, lights came on, showing through the blitz-shuttered windows. A roar went up from the crowd. Then, against the dark sky, the Palace sprang into light, like an immense wedding cake. The crowd burst into life, swaying and roaring, and on the crest of the cheers, the Royal Family came on to the balcony – the King in naval uniform, the Queen in white, with a tiara gleaming in her dark hair, Princess Elizabeth in grey, and Princess Margaret in blue – an attractive group. They stayed for a few minutes, smiling and waving, with the people happy and noisy below. As they left the balcony, the crowd dispersed, swarming in all directions.

I left my parents at Victoria, and made for Westminster alone. Victoria St. and Parliament Sq. were practically empty, but Westminster Bridge was packed with people admiring the lights on the river. As I stood there, a roar went up behind me. I turned around, and started back towards Whitehall; I was soon swept along by a hurrying crowd, and east up at the corner of Whitehall and Bridge St. As I expected, Churchill was on the floodlit balcony of the Ministry of Health, puffing at a huge cigar, and saluting the cheers through a cloud of smoke. After a few moments, he indicated that he was going to speak, and the crowd tried to hush itself. After a few attempts, he made himself heard over a microphone; it was a short, disconnected, but impressive speech, about London and the Londoners, and even I felt moved. Personally, I have no great admiration for the *man* Churchill, but as a war leader he has been unsurpassed, and his command of the language is wonderful. He recited the verse of 'Rule Britannia', then lifted his hand, and with a tuneless voice roared out the first notes of the chorus: 'R . . . Rule . . .' and the crowd took up the refrain. It was impossible not to be moved.

Amid the cheers, he left the balcony, and the lights went out. Excitedly, the crowd broke up and tried to get away. It was impossible to move for fully 10 minutes; trying to get away in all directions at once, the mob was bogged down. Finally, I broke through into the comparatively clear space around the Cenotaph, and proceeded up Whitehall. Trafalgar Sq. was surrounded by floodlit buildings, with searchlights playing on Nelson's column. Long queues were formed at the entrances of tube stations, the only means of transport available. I decided to walk, and proceeded by way of Pall Mall, ablaze with burning torches and coloured lights. Movie cameras, with people festooned all over the trolleys, moved through the gay streets.

Along Piccadilly and Knightsbridge, the crowds had thinned slightly. Instead of mafficking throngs, there were merry groups tramping steadily towards Hammersmith and heaven only knows what points west. Searchlights wagged all over the sky, and an exuberant pilot zoomed up and down, throwing out coloured flares with gay abandon. London is having a wonderful time.

May 11th
Well, the party is all over, and we are back at work again. This phlegmatic nation let itself go for a while, slightly self-consciously, but none the less whole-heartedly. It all seems slightly absurd now, but at the time the spontaneous celebrations were great fun. Now, it doesn't seem possible that only a week ago the war was in full tide, and it is really amazing how we have become adjusted to the change. I find that most people *are* thinking about the war against Japan; after all, a great proportion have, or will have, a personal interest in it. I am beginning to feel much more confident about it now. It is obvious that it is only a question of time – but that *is* the question! If only Russia would come in, that time could be reduced so much. Russia is the great query of the moment; I am wondering if she is going to use her participation in the Pacific war as a bargaining weapon – but for what? Not being a strategist or a diplomat, I feel rather bewildered by it all. We still have great events ahead of us.

May 14th
Normally, when an item is published on ATS daily orders, it is ignored as long as possible, and forgotten at the first opportunity. Just two days ago, however, an item appeared which everybody seems to know about. Presumably, no more girls than usual read that day's orders, but the news spread like wildfire, and every girl

affected has acted in accordance with instructions . . . The order concerned the application for release from the ATS of married girls! All weekend it has been the main topic of conversation, and the billet is buzzing with it. The married girls themselves have most to say, naturally. I have no access to statistics, but should estimate them to be 10–15% of the total, with a sharp increase in the near future, as the overseas men come home. I should say, too, that 95% of those girls want to take advantage of early demobilisation. They have submitted their applications, and are now counting the days until their release. Even those merely planning to be married are also planning to get out. As one girl, getting married next week, put it, 'I'm going to make out my application before the wedding, then dash up the aisle, out of the church, and drop it in the nearest letter-box!'

A small proportion of girls, by reason of their husbands' being overseas, or being themselves of sufficient rank to make it financially worthwhile, are staying in the ATS till their husbands come home. From a purely selfish point of view, I wish that more would do this. It seems rather unfair that girls who live at home should be released from the service while their husbands are away, thus making the rest of us wait even longer. It is pretty obvious that if all the married women are demobbed, none of the rest of us will come out for a long time, and the more that are released now, the longer that time will be.

I try to banish such selfish thoughts, however, and think of the necessity of girls trying to get homes together. I am wholeheartedly in agreement with wives being released to be with their husbands, however – and as soon as possible.

I find my whole attitude to the ATS changing recently. Up to two or three months ago, I was perfectly content, apart from a few legitimate grouses. Now, I find the petty restrictions irksome, even infuriating, and resent being treated as a schoolchild. Victory in Europe seems to have brought this on, and now I must make up my mind to get back in the groove until final victory comes. I think many of us are going to find this difficulty now.

May 17th
It is little more than a week since VE-day, but already the reaction is setting in. I find the news extremely depressing. Britain and the US seem to be at loggerheads with the USSR over

nearly every controversial point, and the US Isolationist Press, in its usual unhelpful way, is fomenting this state of affairs. Trying to look at it dispassionately, it seems to me that Russia is being very dogmatic and uncooperative, but on the other hand, the Allied diplomats do not seem to have the respect they should for the power of the USSR, and her right to have a say in the future of Europe. At the moment, however, the Russians are acting in a high-handed way, without consulting the other nations, and naturally, we are sore about it. Also, I simply cannot understand how Molotov, at the San Francisco conference, can demand bases in the Pacific when his country is not even at war with Japan. It is all a very big problem, and we are not tackling it in a sensible way. Surely, surely, it could never come to war between the Democrats and the Communists. And yet it is only a few years since the USSR was the subject of all kinds of abuse from this country, and Stalin linked with Hitler and Mussolini as objects of opprobrium.

There seems to be nothing but strife and confusion ahead when we should be seeing the bright skies of peace – and we are all feeling tired and hardly capable of coping with it.

May 22nd
I came back to the world of newspapers and radio today, after three days of blissful isolation in a Norfolk village. I found a state of political upheaval, Parliament in the act of being dissolved, and Churchill and Attlee being rude to each other in public letters. I find it all rather bewildering, and am hunting out the weekend newspapers to find out just what it is all about. I feel as if I am being rushed into something I know nothing about, and must try to catch up with myself.

May 24th
Well, the General Election is upon us, and we have to face up to the fact. Yesterday, for the first time, I heard one of our ATS girls bring up the subject voluntarily. She said, 'Well, I suppose I've got to vote for somebody now. I think I'll vote for somebody who'll bring the boys home.' (This was meant quite seriously.)

I admit myself that, politically, I feel very ignorant, but the notions that some of our girls hold are astounding. They have absolutely no idea what the parties stand for, and transcribe everything into terms of their own position in the Forces. This is a typical remark: 'Now that they've got the demob. plans all drawn up, they want to change the Government. If a new one gets in, they'll alter it all. We shall never get out.'

I expected apathy, but apparently most of the girls intend to use their votes; this is even more disturbing. Better not to vote at all than that their votes should be cast blindly. A few have expressed the wish to learn more about the parties, but time is so short. I am worried lest our political education is to come from our Unit officers, most of whom come from 'privileged' or comfortable classes, and have a Conservative bias.

Churchill still seems to have much personal popularity with our girls and among the civilians with whom I work. To summarise generally, it appears to me that people who profess to be Conservative do so because 'they always have been' or 'that's what my people are', whereas the Socialists have generally thought things out for themselves. Quite a number say that the present Government should see the war through, with Churchill at its head.

Personally, I think I should have preferred the Coalition to remain until the real end of the war. On the other hand, I do not want the Conservatives to be in power during the peace. My theory, crude and uninformed, is: As long as there is money to be made from munitions and war, there will be war. Conservatism is on the side of big business and the armament kings. I do not want any more war, therefore I will not vote Conservative. I am all for the levelling out of class distinctions and the improvement of the workers' conditions, so am attracted to Socialism. The Liberal policy I know little about, but it seems to have a progressive trend, so I would like to investigate it further.

I find it helps to put these half-formed theories on paper, but it convinces me more than ever that there is so much to learn.

> The third extract is taken from the diary of a 34-year-old teacher from Thornaby-on-Tees.

8 May 1945

Very quiet and ordinary early. The buses are running. Many men go to work and return having been told to work until Mr Churchill declares the European war ended. Rag and bone man comes round as usual, and the butcher's boy brings meat. I go out to buy bread and see other people doing likewise. Decoration of streets is proceeding at a leisurely rate, and street discussions are taking place about having teas. E.g. 'I can bring the sugar', 'We've got a lovely victory cake, all red, white and blue decorations'. Some groups mostly of older women are very thoughtful. 'It isn't as if the war was really over, when there's Japan.' 'I'm only doing it for the kids.' Most people are using their Coronation decorations – the little streets have done the best, some even painting lamp-posts, steps or window sills, but most of the larger houses are sporting a flag of some sort. Young girls are wearing their hair bands of red, white and blue, and older people rosettes. Many people have gone to great trouble to give enjoyment to their children – red, white and blue dresses (I see three beautifully made from bunting, the children being sisters), decorated tri-cycles, toy motor cars. Most dogs have bows and horses are gay too.

I walk towards the aerodrome. A group of RAF officers are having drinks outside the open windows of a pub opp. the drome. They secure a cart and horse. A woman brings bunting and they drape the cart and the horse. They wear bowler or top hats and one has a Britannia helmet. One has a trumpet and the other a mouth organ. They mount the cart and one gets astride the horse. Singing and playing they set off into town. Someone standing says, 'They only returned from Germany last week.'

It pours the whole of the afternoon and there is no out-of-doors activities. We listen to the celebrations on the wireless, including Mr C.'s speech, and jealously listen to the comments about beautiful spring weather. It is fair after tea and we visit a friend's house. Most people seem to be walking round looking at the decorations. Mrs P.'s corner of the street had been going to have their tea this afternoon but had postponed it until Saturday. She had made trifles which she had given away.

Boys are dragging down the road huge branches and bonfires are getting quite big. There are numbers of crude guys of Hitler appearing in back gardens. Many bonfires can be seen after dark. People are thronging the streets until about 4 a.m. when there is heavy rain, thunder and lightning.

9 May

Get up quite late and walk round different streets to see decorations. Go to fish shop which contrary to expectations is open. Very few there (most unusual) therefore get served quickly. Go by train to Darlington to see football match, Darlington v. Middlesborough. Train is comfortably full of local travellers. Kids let off a few fireworks in the goal mouths. Crowd very good humoured in lovely weather. Returning I see signs of parties at the parish halls and races on the recreation ground. Many people are out walking but it is very like a normal fine night. Mrs C. says all the parish halls are being lent free to parties.

10 May

We have holiday today for Ascension Day, and have been given Friday to make the week complete from Monday. Arise 7 a.m. Have breakfast and go to station. Get a return ticket to York. Miss E. is looking out for me. Few people travelling to Darlington. Train . . . is full and we have to stand. We talk about what we have been doing. Miss E. cleaned on VE Day but enjoyed a street party yesterday from 2–8 p.m. . . .

Arrive at York 9.30. Have tea and scones in refreshment room. Walk round town looking at shops: red, white and blue displays in the windows. Buy some Basildon Bond stationery and a Puffin book. Have lunch at Terry's – interesting but dear. Cold pork pie or spiced ham and salad, cream ices. We're not coffee drinkers. I say there are many people whom this war hasn't even touched.

Buy 4 2oz bars chocolate for Mr W. Go to New Earswick. Mrs W. is waiting at the front for us, her house and the neighbouring one being profusely decorated. Have cups of tea and biscuits. Mrs We. calls in. We talk about clothes, coupons and people. We all expect to be stringently rationed for a lot longer. The arch criminals – 'Is Hitler dead?' No one seems to think so. 'Will the war with Japan be a long one?' Three of us think 'No!' Miss E. says 'Yes' (she has a relation in Burma). Mrs W. had been talking to a man who had been working close to Monty. She said she supposed he would be very popular with the men. He said, 'No! They admire him greatly as a leader but he is too strict a disciplinarian to be popular. He drives them too hard.'

The village children had tea and sports yesterday. The W. family have toasted Victory in whiskey two nights.

We have tea, discuss books we have been reading and then return home on a slow train. People are sitting on steps in poorer streets at home as it is so warm. Mother has been playing bowls at the park.

Feelings and moods [on the 8th]: rather surfeited chiefly by the wireless and so much red, white and blue. Interested in *what* is happening but not *why*. Things are not different. Relaxation of the blackout came before, air raids ceased a long time ago for us. Other restrictions are likely to remain. No surprise. We have known about it and waited for it so long that it is all very tame. I feel envious of the crowds depicted by Howard Marshall, Richard Dimbleby, etc. Wish I were in London. It seems to be different there and the weather is fine. We had pouring rain all afternoon and I was terribly bored.

[On the 9th] Nothing at all. Ordinary night. No reactions. Feeling that tomorrow we return to normal and life will be much as it was before. [On the 10th] Rather depressed. So little is different although I did not expect it to be so and therefore should not be disappointed. I feel unsettled, cannot get on with anything . . . Cynical about the future when I think about the audiences at cinemas mocking the Germans and cheering anything belonging to the Allies. Hopeful when I think of the numbers taking an intelligent interest in the Housing Exhibition at the Town Hall. We *could* make the future different if only we widened our interests. Why can't we act together as we do in wartime? I wonder what people will do at the General Election, and how much it matters. Will there be more food and clothing soon? I am very bored and cannot do with any satisfaction now, the things which have been until recently pleasing me.

> The fourth and final account of VE Day is taken from the diary of Muriel Green. In 1945 Muriel and her sister Jenny are working in Somerset in a hostel for war factory workers. Muriel works in the hostel shop. During the war they have both acquired boyfriends. Jenny's boyfriend, K., works with them but Muriel's (John) is far away in Devon. E. is her best friend.

Fri May 4th
Mrs C. says Sunday is to be the great day and that seems to be the general opinion chiefly because it began on a Sunday. It all seems

wonderful to think we have really and truly whacked the Nazis. I thought it would be impossible for us to smash them in their own land. They deserve to have it at their heart after the way other countries have suffered. I wonder if the world has learned the lesson of war this time. Will my unborn children know the horrors that my generation has known in the same way that our parents knew before us?

Tonight, Jenny, A. and E. (my workmates) and myself discussed whether we should get drunk on V-Day. As none of us have ever done so before we thought it a suitable opportunity to 'try anything once'. We have decided we shan't worry a snap of the fingers as to what our bosses and the residents think then and we have as much right on that day to be [as] uncivilised as anyone else. We have always kept up appearances to 'keep the hostel running for the war workers' and living on the spot there has never been any absenteeism of hostel staff. I don't really think we shall get drunk but we have told the management not to rely on us to do anything that day or the following days as we have for once as much right to experience 'hangovers' as any of the residents.

Sat May 5th
There seems a general tenseness about the atmosphere. We are all on edge waiting for the end.

Sun May 6th
The hostel 3rd anniversary week and there are a number of events. V-Day is sure to come during it as it is all over bar the shouting. Tonight we had the film *Three Smart Girls*. Afterwards K., Jenny's gentleman friend, took J., E. and I (three smart girls) to the local to start celebrating with gin and orange. Churchill's statement thrilled everyone a lot.

May 7th (written at the end of the week. Pure elation prevented concentration to write during the time written about). This afternoon we were supposed to be putting [up] the decorations for the anniversary or whatever else came but hadn't done more than get them out and look at them and say how dusty they were when one of the residents came along and told us the 3 o'clock news said that the Germans had agreed on unconditional surrender to the 3 allies. We were very pleased and really began to hang up the decorations. J. came in and said the housemaids were racing round the blocks telling one another it was all over. She wanted to know if it was true and if this was *the* day we stopped working. Various other people said it was all over. We weren't sure whether we ought to shut the shop or not. I was thinking if *this* is V-Day I had a full-shift with double pay to my credit but thought it a bit mean to call from teatime onwards a public holiday.

After Churchill's speech saying that by Thursday we should have V-Day, there has been a lot of speculation about it. Most people thought Tuesday.

We all felt terribly excited from 3.10 p.m. onwards and I didn't feel I could concentrate on anything for long. It was staff pay day and the pay queue were all asking themselves if *this* was really V-Day or was it tomorrow and how did we decide? Mr F. said at tea that if it was announced at 6. p.m., which we expected, we would light the bonfire tonight. We listened to the 6 p.m. news and still weren't sure. Tuesday was my day off anyhow and tonight we had a ladies *versus* gents cricket match which J., E. and I were playing in. After dinner I had the radio on and heard the 7.45 p.m. announcement that it was really settled and Mr Churchill would speak at 3 p.m. tomorrow. We still weren't sure if we had to work up till 3 p.m. and felt sure some people would take the day off anyway. Everything seemed frightfully exciting and I felt I wanted to jump about and sing. I felt ten years younger!

We had the cricket match. The wireless had been put on out of doors and was going through the match. When Big Ben chimed at 9 p.m. everyone stopped playing and waited in tense silence for the news. A general cheer went up when Tuesday was announced a holiday. After the headlines and beginning of the news the game went on. It was drawn at 19 runs either side, the men having been handicapped into playing left handed and bowling underarm.

We had [a] snack and went in to dancing to records. There was more than the usual crowd there and lots of people were the worse for drink already. About 11.15 p.m. an American sailor who was being entertained by some of the Irish girls forced his way up to the platform where the mike was. He, as well as the girls, was obviously the worse for drink. He said he would do an impersonation of Bing Crosby (rousing cheers) and sang 'Irish Lullaby' and 'Lula-lula'. The girls who were sitting beneath the stage asked

him to sing 'If you ever go to Ireland' which he then followed up
with another Irish song at their request. The last was unknown to
the English people present who were by this time not so enthusiastic in their applause. In the corner where we were sitting
undertones were saying, 'The Irish haven't won the bloody war'
and 'It's time we had an English song'. A drunk boy beside us said,
'What English song can we sing?' and E. said 'There'll always be
an England'. In the next interlude the drunk boy led off in this
song and in no time everyone in the room was singing it. The
social director who was putting on the records on the stage then
saw the way clear to get the mike away from the Yank and
suggested that we should sing 'Land of Hope and Glory' which we
did. Then another man (also drunk) clambered up on to the stage
and said we mustn't forget the jolly old Eighth Army and started
the crowd singing another modern soldier song, 'Lily of the Island'.
This led to another after which the social director gave out
appropriate words for the occasion and told of arrangements for
the following day. She said she would now put on the last dance as
we had two late nights in front of us. I didn't think many of the
crowd felt like going to bed, especially the night shift who had
been sent back from the factory. We retired anyway and everything seemed too good to be true . . .

VE Day Tues May 8th
The weather was unsettled and showery when we came over to
breakfast at 9.30 a.m. There was a large crowd in between 9–10
a.m. and they were queuing for boiled eggs to be cooked. Breakfast is usually staggered from 5.45–10 a.m. so there was a rush
later when everyone was not at work. After breakfast we sat in
the foyer talking and looking at the closed shop with delight.
There was a sharp shower before the most glorious sunny day, as
though the heavens were weeping for the dead before rejoicing.
Two elderly women were saying, 'It was like this on the last
Armistice Day.' At 11 the staff had coffee, biscuits and cigarettes
given them in place of the usual tea. After this J., E. and I decided
to cycle into the town to see the decorations as the sun had come
out by then. The town is decorated well considering the five years
of shortages of flags, bunting etc. The streets were very narrow so
that the pendants across the street could easily be put up. Most of
the shops which were closed had red, white and blue window

dressings with a number of photographs of Churchill, Stalin, Roosevelt and the King and Queen. There was a lot of people walking the streets. We decided to take ourselves to the best hotel in town and have a drink. We had a glass of good old sherry which made us feel just too jolly. The hotel bar was crowded but we managed to get served with difficulty. We drank to 'Peace in the future'.

We returned to lunch at the hostel and spent the afternoon until 3 p.m. in the sun on deckchairs on the lawn. Churchill's speech was broadcast outdoors and in. A few drunken men were rather disturbing in the foyer where I was listening along with about 40 others. One interrupted frequently with such comments as 'Good old Churchill'. Immediately after the speech a thanksgiving service was held in the assembly hall with about fifty present including some of the drunks. The service opened with 'God save the King' and other hymns included 'Praise my soul the King of Heaven', 'How beautiful my country' 'Praise God from whom all blessings flow' and 'Onward Christian soldiers' . . .

. . . When the silence for the memory for the dead took place there was not a sound of an eyelid. I ran through in my mind all those I knew had been killed and realised how lucky I am for none very near or dear to me are gone. During the short sermon given by the leader of the service which was on past histories of 'glorious' victories of our country, one of the drunks shouted out, 'Talk about the Bible, man, not about wars!' Voice from the back of another drunk: 'Shut up! Let him alone.' The service seemed inclined to lose its seriousness after this interruption and was brought to a conclusion shortly after. I noticed the housekeeper was crying during the proceedings. She has lost her dearest son.

. . . After dinner Jenny and K. went for a walk to the favourite country inn two miles away. E. and I arranged to follow them. We talked about the future most of the way there. We found Jenny and K. already drinking. We each had a pommia, a refined bottled cider and the strongest drink I know. After one we were giggling and after two we had made ourselves weak, partly I suppose we imagined we were tight but we didn't have to imagine very hard. E. never stopped talking and each time I spoke I thought what a silly thing to have said as I found myself speaking without thinking! We were sitting in the sun in the back garden on a long grassy bank and when E. said she wanted to hear the King's speech I came down the bank on all fours. We stood in the bar to hear it and afterwards I couldn't have told anyone a word he said, as I felt in too much of a dream. The inn was crowded but shortly after 9 p.m. when we left there appeared to be no one drunk. We walked home by way of the woods, still very talkative but quite sober by the time we got back to the hostel for snacks and to see the bonfire lit at 10 p.m.

It was a roaring blaze and seemed to have a significance in saying 'Goodbye' to many wartime restrictions. The radio lively programme of music was on and dozens of village children appeared on the scene with fireworks and crackers (squibs). We stood watching it for a long time and about quarter to 11 went into the dance hall. Here I have never seen such signs of unrestricted merry-making. People who in the usual way never unbend were simply romping like healthy children in circles with joined hands. They were all young people with a larger proportion of women than men and they were simply letting themselves go in a way most joyful and unselfconscious to behold. Some had the necessary amount of alcohol to make them like this but most of them were drunk with the spirit of victory. Everyone in the room, which was packed, had a smile on their face. The romping continued till the end of the radio music and with exhaustion the circles were broken up. Dance records were put on and dancing began but 'Jitterbugging' and 'Conga' type of dancing was the rage, most of the crowd being at a pitch too high to concentrate on serious ballroom dancing. This went on until 12 o'clock when the ballroom was cleared. The next move was out to the bonfire. Until 3 a.m. dancing round in a circle of joined hands, one of the crowd, went on tirelessly. I went to bed after looking for a while at the others. I was very tired and had no male escort in the fun. All manner of songs were being sung, the old ones being popular.

Years of monotonous clocking-in to war factories had brought this feeling of supreme elation to the young workers, many of whom have turned yellow with their work. They have given vent to their suppressed feelings tonight as never before. They would not go to bed while the last ounce of energy could be summoned to carry on. The night nurse told me afterwards that at four she crossed the site in her duties and there were about ten couples round the dying embers of the fire.

Several people today have said that as they had relations in the Far East they could not celebrate properly. That has been in everyone's heart that more fighting, more dying and more atrocities are still to come. Also that all the flag waving and dancing will not bring alive the dead to their homes. Men that have lost their sight and limbs cannot be the same. Life will always be the sadder for those of us who think. If we knew this had been a war to end war we would feel more jubilant but when it may happen again without extreme care, it makes life seem a dilemma . . .

Sat 26th May
Jenny has gone home this weekend to take some of her things. Mother has written today begging her to come home as soon as possible. This last month I have not known what to do to decide my future. I am constantly changing my mind. Some days I want to marry John as soon as he can afford it, the next I think he is not the right one for me. Then comes the uncertainty of, if I reject him, shall I ever replace him by anyone as true. Then I think single life is all I want, the next day I feel crazy for love and sex. Sometimes I decide to leave here and go to Devon to him as he wishes, then I want to stay here. Then I want to go home. Home with its many attractions will be another two hundred miles from John and it will annoy John immensely if I go. I like my present job and [will] have difficulty in getting one with so many benefits. When Jenny goes it will be less attractive here and I shall be lonely. I think then I shall not mind leaving but I feel I could do with two months' rest before going to another job. This will annoy John who thinks I can go to him straight away from here. Lately my nerves have been very bad and if they do not improve after Jenny goes I intend to see a doctor. The slightest thing makes me jump lately. I feel a bundle of nerves. Lots of staff are on sick leave, I suppose the war and food has got most of us down.

Sun May 27th
I definitely feel I shall not stay here long when Jenny goes. I have missed her immensely this weekend. Also E. who is my real friend is away. I have been more than lonely, downright depressed. I am still worrying about the Future. Events have mostly determined the future of my life and I hope that again they will save me

making decisions. This seems weak but I feel very undecided as to what I want from life at present. Some might think I wanted a man and that I'm suffering from sex-starvation. I wonder . . . !

22

A weaver's diary for the General Election of 1945

Beryl Johns was employed as a weaver in a Huddersfield mill. She did not write for Mass-Observation very long (perhaps because of her prior commitments to her demanding job and her political activities). This diary for June to September represents almost everything she wrote. She is in her fifties. It is unclear whether she is married and has children. She only refers to taking care of dependants all her life.

June 15th
I asked about Ellen Wilkinson talk last night. General opinion 'very good' . . . A turner when asked if he'd heard it said, 'Some on it – but her'd ha bin better at home mending stockings.' Usual working class male attitude. I thought Ellen got her speech over very well; voice rather shrill, but she kept it down as well as she could. Style a little artificial at times, but argument sound and delivery varied.

One of our women weavers said this morning, 'Even t'little lads were amused at t'milk mentioned by Churchill.' I gather that the working class attitude is that Churchill will give us milk. Milk! Ugh! He doesn't keep going on milk! Though most of us are short of milk at the moment I doubt if a promise of more in the distant future impresses anyone, neither did his appeal to 'My friends'. Churchill's friends are all in the Govt., son-in-law, Private Secy. and so on. His chief friends are those who can get something out of him. When he has served their purpose he can go. I think he would have liked to be remembered as a great statesman more than anything, but he is too much of a politician ever to have been or become a statesman. A statesman puts the real needs of his country first. This means that the WORKERS must be considered. If the welfare of the workers is put first, international affairs fall into correct perspective. When all countries consider their workers in both national and international aspects, peace and goodwill will be assured.

Churchill had a real opportunity to do this during the war. He could have gathered round him men of goodwill from all parties. Instead he let the big industrialists run their businesses as usual with some curtailment of choice of production, but little curtailment of profits – income tax does not offset cost plus. True, he allowed a sprinkling of Labour men to prevent Labour interests being utterly crushed; but he has done all he could to make things easy for a return to the status quo after the war.

However Labour Ministers have had a chance of high office and shown their ability. The workers are tired of govt for benefit of the few, and a change of govt seems inevitable. If Churchill had been on the side of the people instead of kings, he would have gone down to history as he would have wished – a great statesman. Instead he will go down as a great war leader, an able writer, a character, a man of great ability – but not one of the world's greatest men.

His chief concern has been to keep England's greatness. A really great man recognises universal greatness and has universal aims. His fight against Fascism petered out when England ceased to be threatened – witness his kind words for Franco.

Britain is part of the world, and must fit into the mosaic with the rest. If one country tries to overtop another wars will continue. A peaceful world will only become a reality when countries emulate each other in seeing how quickly they can give the five freedoms mentioned by Beveridge both in their own countries and throughout the world. This means that women must be given full and complete status as citizens economically as well as politically. Russia is the only country to do this as yet. This means that the contribution of over half the population in this and other countries is both warped and incomplete. Here, women are alternately put on a pedestal by chivalry and on a lower level as drudges. If a woman cooks for a living, she gets a certain wage – not too big. If a man cooks, his status goes up, he becomes a chef, and cooking by the male becomes a profession and is paid accordingly. In textiles men weavers get from 10% to 20% more than women, merely because they are men. True they carry their pieces on their shoulders a few yards up the shed, while the women merely lift theirs off and place them beside the loom for collection later. But the woman weaver who works beside the door to which the men carry theirs, receives no more than the rest of the women. And all the pieces have to be taken across to the mending room by men employed for the job. So for carrying a piece of cloth on his shoulder a few yards once or twice a week, a man gets anything from 10/- to 30/- a week more than a woman weaver, doing exactly the same work. The idea that a weaver should not only weave the piece, but carry it away, dates back to the days when cloth was woven at home and carried to market, whether on the weaver's back or on pack horses. I doubt if any other industry expects the worker to make something and then take it on to the people responsible for the next process. There is one firm in the valley where the woman weaver has a penny docked from her wages for each completed piece – this penny is paid to a man weaver. Men weavers are allotted so many women's looms each and the pennies put on to their wages. This firm pays men and women the same rate – but they are a non-union firm and their rate is lower than the TU rate, so that in effect the equal pay boils down to paying both sexes low rates. Weavers should be paid for the cloth they weave and any additional jobs paid for as extras.

Sat 16th June
Shopping Sat morning at Holmfirth. Queued up 40 mins for 1 lb new potatoes, one tomato, and 2 small spring cabbages. Plenty of green vegs – potatoes and tomatoes scarce. Went up again Sat afternoon. Got ½lb strawberries, just arrived. No fish. Evening went to Huddersfield Theatre. Priestley's *They Came To A City*. Interesting play, well cast and put over. Good and receptive audience. *Hudd. Examiner* had given it lukewarm reception. Made point that Priestley did not show us the city. I should have thought the kind of city was obvious to those who believe in production for use and service and a world run to fulfil the real needs of humanity rather than a world run for private profit irrespective of the needs of humanity as a whole.

Sunday 17 June
Big political meeting at Palace Theatre Huddersfield. Stafford Cripps and Mallalieu, Labour candidate for Huddersfield. Went

down on 5–8 bus. Good number queuing when I got there at 5.30, though meeting did not start until 7. Full house and overflow meeting outside. £16.10.0 collected outside. £131.1.0 collected altogether. Many in outside queue said they had changed political views during war and veered to left. (Two good Labour candidates in Hall [for] Colne Valley – and Mall. for Hudd.) Hall sitting member last six years. Mall. young naval lieut., journalist and writer – three books to his credit: *Rats, Passed to You Please*, and *Ordinary Seaman*. Had read and enjoyed the latter which was on sale for party funds at the meeting along with *Passed To You* which I bought. Altogether that weekend – theatre ticket, bus fares, book, theatre programme, collection etc. – cost me 15/-. My wage was £2.10.0 less 2/- ins[urance], hosp[ital], Red Cross etc.

Monday 18 June
Went to election meeting at Holmfirth for our Candidate – Hall. Chairman prevented from coming, asked [me] to take chair. Two other meetings higher up valley. Our meeting called for 8.15. Councillor Whitehead, old-timer in the Labour movement, began. Good speech outlining birth of Labour movement, SDF, Fabians, Keir Hardie, etc. Said he was as enthusiastic for socialism today as he was when ILP first began. Councillor Jessie Smith arrived 8.15, held forth until Hall arrived 9.15. Carried on until after ten. Good meeting, useful propaganda for Labour Party, and £3.12.0 collection.

Wednesday 20 June
Went to Hall's meeting at Honley. Hall not full but good audience. Lecturer in economics for National Council of Labour colleges spoke. Grammar faulty, but figures and inferences correct and audience grasped and enjoyed them. Lord Winster spoke on finance etc. Hall came in later having attended meetings at the hill village of Thurstonland and at Brockholes village below. In good form . . . introduced *Daily Express* of that morning showing headline accusing Laski, and Labour's reply to it in *Daily Herald* of same day. Some printer in *D. Express* must have blown the gaff. Spoke of usual Tory method – Zinoviev, money scares, etc.

Thursday 21 June
Went down to Honley Labour Club and addressed 120 of Hall's
election letters to Farnley Tyas ward voters. His message is pithy,
sound and should help. About thirty men and women there. (I
would like to go again tonight but must do some housework. I
worked hard on Tuesday evening. Washed four windows and
mirrors, took down curtains from the living room windows,
washed, creamed, ironed, and put them up again; then washed
and lacquered my kitchen stove, ash tidy, and kerb, which are
now a beautiful shining black.)

I walked home from Honley, two miles over the fields and
through the wood, getting in about 10.30. It was very quiet and
still and rather heavy and close. Before me the moon rode high in
a clear blue sky, with masses of cumulus white cloud sweeping
around on either side. Behind me a mass of low heavy cloud, black
as night, surrounded the red ball of the setting sun – a ball of fiery
red. Red tinged the edges of the heavy black mass and pierced
across the centre of the cloud. There was clear daylight all round
me, though the hills were topped with cloud on either side, the
dark cloud was all behind me. It was most impressive. Let's hope
it was symbolic – angry war clouds and fire behind, prospects of
peace before. But what hope would there be if the PM's invective
was representative of the great mass of opinion. I did not hear him
last night, but can imagine the effect having read the account in
the paper. If these election speeches go down to posterity in the
BBC archives – and I suppose they will – what will posterity think
of them? Surely twenty years [of] Tory misrule will convince anyone with any intelligence at all. Nevertheless people who have
had only elementary education, hardly ever open a book and who
speak of the Govt as 'they', are easily stampeded. It happened
before and may happen again. I am one of the few persons in the
shed who openly belongs to a political party, but the majority will
vote Labour I know. Having served on TU and Labour Party
committees in the past my views are known, and I am labelled –
indeed in slumps I am victimised. The fact that I have had no
office for the last ten years owing to being away from the district a
good deal and owing to illness makes no difference, and it is not
part of my makeup to hide my views. If only the workers would
realise that they have remedies in their own hands we could have
stopped this sort of work, and victimisation would stop . . .

Monday 25 June
More election talk. There has been plenty each day yet . . . Letter in our local paper accusing Labour of being 'Red' and 'Naxis' (their spelling) and why don't Libs and Cons get together and put up one Candidate only etc. Some weavers mentioned Hannen Swaffer's article in *People*, others *Sunday Pictorial*. I mentioned various items in *Reynolds News* and *New Society*. I had left a chalked note on my piece as I had a wire heald come off just as I was going home Friday night. One of the men weavers put a new one on for me Sat. morning. Another chalked on my piece 'Vote Tory'. But the women made him rub it off, so then he wrote 'Three cheers for Bevin'. (I don't work Sats.)

Tuesday 26 June
When I got to work this morning there was a huge photo (*Daily Dispatch* supplement) of Churchill on the partition behind my loom. I only laughed and proceeded to read the useful list of Parl. Candidates which it illustrated. They kept coming to me and giving the V sign and I said I would certainly vote for him. However the man who put it up took it away and put it on the shuttle guard of a weaver who is a Churchill fan. (She is looked upon as being rather simple-minded.)

Wednesday 27 June
Churchill at Huddersfield. Two weavers, the one above and another nearly as bad, went to Hudd. to see him straight from work. Indeed the first one went off about 3–3.30. Had any of us walked out on business of our own what a to-do there would have been. But it was alright to go early to see a Tory PM. There was a large crowd. One of my neighbours went. She said she saw the top of his head and heard him speak. No one seemed to think much of his speech and no one has repeated any of it. This neighbour said a woman near her remarked, 'He hasn't had to queue for potatoes.'

Thursday 5 July
When I got to work on election day my loom was all trimmed up with blue yarn (Tory colours). Ropes of it on the frame shuttle guard and tied round the wheel so that I had to remove it before I could weave. But I only laughed and waved my red handkerchief, and showed my red belt and the red bow on my dress. I had put

those on specially for Hall's visit to the mill the day before. I know
our member personally and went to shake hands with him and
wish him luck and introduced him to one or two people.

It was very hot on voting day. When I went out to dinner I
wondered how I was going to work during the afternoon. However
when I went back a good number of weavers were sitting in the
main alley. As I passed somebody said, 'We're on strike!' I only
laughed, thinking it a joke – but discovered it was earnest. So
didn't set up. Gradually all the looms stopped, and eventually a
deputation went off to interview the manager and ask if two
windows which were sealed up could be opened and if the glass
roof of the shed could be whitewashed. This was always done to
keep the sun out in peacetime, but has not been done during the
war. We had asked for this to be done several times, but nothing
had been done about it.

The manager was in the adjoining mill. When he saw them
coming the silly ass set off and ran from the bottom room to the top
fourth storey. With them following on. When they had said their
say, he said, 'Oh yes, I could provide you with white flannels for
summer and red ones for winter and give you red flags to wave as
well.' They could get no sense out of him, and said if nothing was
done we were going home as it was impossible to work with the
sun blazing down and little air coming in. He said he didn't care if
we went home for a fortnight. After sitting in the yard for a time
to give him time to change his mind, we decided to go home for the
day, and come again in the morning, and if it was so hot the next
day ring up the TU. However, when I got to work at nine o'clock,
men were already whitewashing the roofs and the sealed windows were opened in the afternoon.

Why we should have to have all this fuss to get such things done
I don't know. However I was home by 3–3.30 on election day, too
exhausted to do anything much. So I made a cup of tea and got
something to eat, and then bathed and changed and went to
record my vote. I have a new red dress and thought this a suitable
time to give it an airing. It was quite warm enough to go with[out]
a coat so it got a real airing. I went to do a bit of shopping after
that, then sat in a deck chair until 7.30, when I went up to guide
the cars round for a few last-minute voters.

Now 'the shouting and the tumult dies' and the half million
spent by Tories on Churchill posters, the advert for man and wife

to garden and do housework for Mrs Churchill for £2.15*s* a week, the six tons of coal for the Churchill train, not to mention Laski and the Labour Gestapo, will fall into the limbo of the past, and we have to wait for the results with what patience we can.

There was a curious aftermath to our request for better conditions. It transpired that a woman weaver, working on one side of me as a matter of fact, is not in the Union. A few of us tackled her about it, and she said she would leave before joining. I asked her if she was willing to give up her two weeks' holiday money won by Trade Union Agreement, by Trade Union funds and officials she had done nothing to support. None of us have spoken to her since. She did a little weep on the Friday afternoon, but no one took any notice; finally she went home 'ill'. Previously one of the men had bumped into her quite accidentally when passing, and she and her sister (who is in the Union) tried to make out it was because of the Union difference and went to the manager and complained. The manager spoke to the man concerned, who stoutly denied any ill intent, maintaining that she came out of her loom gate just as he was passing and that it was a pure accident – as I believe it was. I have been told she is going to join, as it is Union day tomorrow; I am waiting to see. Non-unionists should work at non-union shops, then when they found their wages reduced they might come to their senses. Or would they? Anyhow these people are nuisances. They usually agree to anything asked of them by the employer, and if allowed to stay out it becomes impossible to get newcomers in. They have no more right to refuse to pay Union fees than they have to refuse Nat. Health Insurance etc.

Tuesday 10th July
We had a supper and election workers' social evening tonight. About forty to fifty of us ate meat and potato pie with green peas, plus apple pasty, biscuits, butter and cheese, and soft drinks – and beer, for those who wanted it.

Thursday 12th July
I got a cheque for £10 from the Co-operative Wholesale Society today, having won this sum in an essay competition. It has to be spent in attending the Co-operative Summer School at Bangor. I saw three lines about the essay comp. in *Reynolds News* in April. I

wrote for particulars and had a week to write the thing, which had to be in under a *nom de plume* by May 1st. I forget the title of the essay, but it asked for my opinion on Joint Industrial Councils. Did I think they were of use during the war and should they be continued, or something to that effect. I had already booked for a [WEA] summer school at St Andrews, Scotland (July 21st to 28th) this being the only school I could get in to – though our holiday week is Aug 18th to 25th. A mistake in advertising the dates of the Scots school gave it as ending Aug 28th, and by the time this was clear it was too late for me to book anywhere else. The Co-op asked me which week I could go, but when I asked for my own holiday week, said they had only vacancies for Bank Holiday week so I have booked for then.

That means I get a month's holiday. For I can't go to Scotland, come back and work a week and then take the next week off work, another week [on] and then have our usual week [off]. No straightforward request for time off is ever granted. Even in peace time, I have offered to get a weaver when wanting time off for summer schools, but the refusal was always emphatic. Anyway, at fifty, having worked since I was twelve, plus running a home since I was seventeen and supporting dependants in addition, I feel I have a right to a bit of time off. My health isn't too good, and I don't stand up to the winter very well without a decent break in the summer, so I shall see my doctor and arrange things that way. That will give me the opportunity to do a bit of cleaning in what should be holiday week.

3rd September

I was on holiday when the news of the General Election came through – being at the WEA Summer School at MacIntosh Hall, St Andrews, Scotland. There was much cheering as the election results came through and they were announced at meal times, some of us staying in during the afternoon to glean further details. Most of the students were Scots, and there were some surprises – but one of our members was a Labour election agent for a losing candidate, and he had to go away a day or two for the count. We had had a Scots Nationalist to speak to us one evening – and I was bold enough to say that all the schemes he outlined – better transport, better organised fishing industry, houses, electricity etc. – were bound up with Gt Britain as a whole and that a

Labour Govt would plan for the country not for sections of Gt Britain. Next day's election results when no Nationalists were returned showed that the majority of Scots voters agreed with me, as did many members of the school. Everyone seemed surprised, though pleased.

I was in North Wales at a co-operative Summer School at Bangor when the Japanese surrender news came through. There was much cheering – then when the news seemed doubtful some tears from those who had men imprisoned in the Far East. However it was eventually verified. I have a nephew who has been imprisoned since the fall of Singapore (ROAC) but I was not among the tear shedders. I felt sure that the advent of Russia in the Far East, plus the atomic bomb, would settle matters.

I haven't heard anyone say much about the atomic bomb. Many people do not realise its power. One finds people talking of reducing Germany's industrial power so as to prevent them making armaments, and one realises they are thinking of the kind of preparations which went on for this war; evidently not realising that, just as the aeroplane of the last war became the big bomber, transport plane, seaplane, gliders etc. of this war, so the atomic bomb which finishes this war will add new frightfulness and unseen dangers for any future war. My attitude to the atomic bomb of this war is the same as it was to the other new methods of destruction – that it is a sad waste of man's scientific ingenuity. If only that ingenuity could be used for the true benefit of man to enable all to live a good life instead of destroying life, then we might stand a chance of becoming really civilised.

As to Peace – it is good that the fighting is stopped, but it looks as though economic warfare is to continue. Bevin's speech smacked of appeasement. Surely a line-up with Russia would have made America come cap in hand to us, rather than our government going cap in hand to America. It may be that the new Government is feeling its way – and does not want to antagonise capital – but surely we do not wish to antagonise the progressive people of Europe who look to us for a lead. Whatever our relations with America may be, we have to live in Europe. Surely we should work with Continental progressives. *New Government.* A very well-educated government, representative of all types of workers, which has not yet sorted itself out, but shows a potential will to work together, to hear all points of view and to make use of all the talent and knowledge it possesses. They seem to be feeling their way carefully and trying to antagonise as few people as possible. This makes them seem slow to those of us who know where we want to go, and want to get there quickly.

But if this socialist government can deliver the goods – that is, if it can give the people food, work and houses; not only here but throughout the liberated countries, then socialism and democracy will go ahead. That is the testing point. If America continues to muddle through with her employment policy, if the GIs find only unemployment under private enterprise, then a real Labour movement may be born in [the] USA and things will be much easier for the democracies. But we are not spreading the democratic way of life as we might. We are not deposing the Nazis and fascists quickly enough in Germany, Italy, France, or Greece. France may be governing herself, but we are not doing what we might to stop her fantastic black market; neither are we encouraging the non-Nazis in Germany or Greece. America seems to be aiding De Gaulle – if he plays their game (Britain having gone socialist) America stops Lend-Lease. That, they think will 'larn us'. The idea of a Socialist Govt sending Halifax to Washington makes one wonder if Chamberlain and his umbrella are haunting Whitehall.

In regard to controls. Many should not be lifted. But income tax allowance should be returned to prewar level for single people – £120 instead of £80 – indirect taxes gradually removed, excess profits tax taken off necessities, some of the excess profits tax removed; but large incomes should continue to be taxed, and low wages and high profits discouraged.

No one should be allowed to make money by manipulating stocks and shares, and cartels and monopolies should be controlled in order to stop them creating artificial scarcities in order to put up prices. Patent laws to destroy them and render them useless, or to put them in cold storage. I would like to see Govt encouragement to all workers to join trade unions. I want our education overhauled, especially history, so that the history of the working-class movement is given as large or a larger place in school time than the history of kings and princes. I want the economic system controlled in such a way that the necessities of the many come before the luxuries of the few.

VJ celebrations not up to much in this district. I was not

working, having had five weeks on the panel in order to have a rest and get to Summer Schools. I have to earn my living at a job I didn't choose, run a house, and do the things I really want to do in the time which is left over from these two jobs; and I can only keep going by frequent rests.

The announcement was made at the wrong time. Those who did not hear the midnight news went to work as usual and had to come back. Having got up and made the journey to work they were rather peeved, and considered the first day spoilt. Some workers did not go back and worked Wednesday, and so were able to finish for the week then. At Bridge Mill where I work, they went home Weds., had Thursday in addition, and then had to go back to work Friday. The local holiday week started Saturday. One or two did not go Friday [and] so had nearly a fortnight's holiday. Huddersfield workers were having their holiday week during VJ week. Some went back to work on the Weds. of the week following, [having been] notified in the local press. Some are to have it later.

Most people said sudden holidays of this kind were a mistake. It wasn't possible to arrange anything, and housewives had to rush off to the shops, and altogether it was rather a nuisance – the holiday, not the peace!

Textile workers have arranged to take their third VE Day on Monday Sept 22nd. It is thought that the third VJ day will be tacked on to this, making a long weekend.

There was no celebration here much. A local committee had been elected, but did not do anything. The local band started at the top of the valley and gave a concert in the local park. Loudspeakers were sent round to announce this, but only those in the centre of the town would hear this – and not all of them. There were very few people at the concert. Some merrymakers from a local pub robbed a joiner's yard of combustible material and made a fire at the top of the main street and promenade and sang around it – until the police stopped them.

Huddersfield was having its holiday at home entertainments and there were fireworks etc., the park having illuminations etc. My young nephew wanted to go, and I set out to take him. But all the buses went through Thongsbridge without stopping and after waiting half an hour I gave it up. I was glad I didn't as there were twenty-five thousand people in the Park, and neighbours who went, and stayed long enough to see the fireworks, had to walk the five miles home as the last buses had gone, and got home at 12.30 p.m. My young nephew was disappointed, but as he had been to the Park the week before and seen the concerts, floodlighting etc., he had to be satisfied.

Please excuse the paper. I find paper hard to get, and expensive.

EPILOGUE

23

Mrs Last's New Year's resolutions

Mrs Last was one of the few diarists to keep up her writing for Mass-Observation after the war. She didn't stop until 1967, twenty-nine years after she first joined Mass-Observation. This extract, then, is simply a pause for reflection on her part. The war was over but her life went on and in many ways, as she herself expressed so poignantly, without the sense of meaning and purpose which war work had been able to offer her. Her sons are far away, Cliff still in the army (and soon to emigrate to Australia) and Arthur tied up with his own family commitments.

Sunday 30 December 1945
I felt really thankful it was Sunday. I could hardly bear to stand on my right leg. After I'd had tea my husband brought up, I knelt in very hot water in the bath and bathed it. Afterwards rubbing it well with wintergreen and it was a little better. I'd had a busy morning with letters and rose at 12 to make lunch – good mutton soup in which too were some goose bones. There was cold mutton, as tender as chicken – a nice 'chunky' bit of chilled mutton, so much better meat than I've had lately – chutney and wholemeal bread and butter, egg custard and bottled apples and then a cup of tea when I made some to put in a flask to take out.

All was white with frost. It never lifted all day – and we went to Sparkbridge to wish them a happy new year and take a jar of good dripping, a bit of marg., a glass of sherry each and a big slice of Xmas cake. We went on for a little run to Coniston Lake and I never saw my dear lake lovelier. The bracken-clad hills were mirrored on the silver surface till it was a fantasy of gold and grey, with patches of blue sky in the mosaic. My husband stopped the car to pump up the tyres as he thought the pressure too low and I sat with the windows wide open with the sun on my face.

Such utter peace and beauty. I felt it was enough for all the troubled world. No sound but the gentle murmur of a wee beck as it hurried to lose itself in the placid lake. I could have sat all afternoon and just 'listening to the silence' – caught up in the rhythm I always feel in that quiet spot, nearer to God than anywhere else I know. I sat so quiet and still, thinking of the New Year, longing for a job of some kind. There seems so little to do in Barrow and so many to do it. Women like myself who have been busy and useful, feeling they were 'helping' cannot find a way to help the 'peace' as we did in wartime. With 2,000 women at the Labour Exchange, it would not be right to do anything they could do, yet I know many who, like myself, long to do something. I felt I put my name down as I sat. My New Year's resolutions formless but willing.

Appendix 1

The Tom Harrisson Mass-Observation Archive

The papers generated by the work of Mass-Observation came to the University of Sussex in 1970 at the invitation of Professor Asa Briggs, now Lord Briggs, who was then the University's Vice Chancellor. The papers had lain mostly unused for two decades in the basement of the offices of M-O (UK) Ltd in London and might have been forgotten had it not been for the concern of Len England (who had been with the organisation since 1939) and for the interest of two social historians, Angus Calder and Paul Addison, both researching the Second World War and on the look out for new sources for the period.

The papers date from 1937, when the organisation began, to 1949 when it was registered as a company and began to turn more towards mainstream market research (some later material from the 1950s has been included and a few diaries go on to the 1960s). When the collection reached Sussex, it was in a poor physical condition – the papers were trussed up in dusty old folders with string and perished elastic bands. They had been ravaged by mice and different sorts of fungi and eroded by rusty paperclips. Considering their history, which included the London blitz and several moves on the backs of lorries, not to mention a flood or two, it is surprising that so much actually did survive.

The papers did not come alone. Asa Briggs also invited Tom Harrisson to organise the collection and establish it as a working archive. Harrisson had not been involved in a regular way with Mass-Observation since he left London to join the Army in 1942 but he had managed to retain impressive links with successive generations of M-O staff. These links were consolidated during several return visits to England, and at least once, in 1959, by a 'repeat' investigation in Bolton which resulted in the publication *Britain Revisited* (Gollancz, 1960). He had remained a director of the company, with ownership of the early papers, even while he was pursuing his other interests – animal conservation, palaeontology, ethnography – in South East Asia.

There were two tasks crying out for attention: the Archive badly needed physical care if anyone was ever going to be able to make anything of it; and it needed publicity and funds in order to establish its respectability (and survival) as a valuable historical resource. Harrisson was hopeless at the first task – indeed his very presence among the papers seemed to increase the degree of disarray – but he was excellent and much experienced at the second. Sussex had already provided premises, first in its main Library, later in a new building (and now in 1989, back in the main Library); the Leverhulme Trust was prevailed upon to provide funds. Harrisson employed a series of part-time but very dedicated clerical assistants between 1970 and 1974 who boxed up the papers and began to produce a semblance of order. Their work might have been faster had Harrisson himself not embarked on a number of new projects which required their help: he reworked the material collected during the blitz (which appeared as *Living Through the Blitz* in 1976). He also planned an autobiography, a book on the meaning of royalty in British culture and a book using the Worktown project papers. His energy was boundless. His sudden death in a road accident in January 1976 brought it all to an abrupt end.

His efforts on behalf of the Archive, however, had borne fruits. In 1975, according to his wishes, it had been established as a charitable trust in the care of the University. The four trustees were Professor Briggs, Harrisson's friend James Fulton, former wartime Observer Henry Novy (now succeeded by Professor Sandra Wallman) and David Pocock, Professor of Social Anthropology at Sussex, who, as the new Director, championed the Archive's cause within the University. I joined the Archive on a very part-time basis in 1974 in time to work with Harrisson and learn something of the original organisation. When he died in 1976, it seemed natural for me to take over the care and administration of the collection and I have shared in its vicissitudes ever since.

The Archive comprises several main groups of material arranged not in the first instance by subject matter but by form. About a fifth of the collection is personal writing contributed to Mass-Observation by volunteers: diaries and detailed replies to questionnaires or 'directives'. A set of 3,000 typed reports summarises M-O research from the beginning of the war until 1950. Topics range from wartime themes – attitudes to politicians, evacuation schemes, ARP, food and clothes rationing, conscription and war work, propaganda, air raids, demobilisation – to wider issues – health, education, the position of women, religion, hopes for the future. The greater part of the Archive is made up of the boxes of observations, interviews, questionnaires, surveys, descriptive accounts of people and places, as well as printed ephemera, leaflets posters etc. Papers resulting from the Worktown project fill some 64 boxes, mostly on the key themes of politics, religion and leisure.

These papers are complemented by 400 photographs taken by Humphrey Spender in Bolton and Blackpool just before the outbreak of war.

Since 1970, the Archive has grown partly as a result of accepting small donations of personal diaries and other private papers and partly because we have offered a home to other groups of papers which relate closely to the themes and years of Mass-Observation (further details can be found in the Archive's *Guide for Researchers*). The most significant growth, however, has resulted from a revival of Mass-Observation's volunteer panel idea. Since 1981, new diary writers and directive respondents have been sending in their writing to the Archive. At the time of writing, the panel is almost 1,000 strong with people from all over the country volunteering to take part. The project was the brainchild of David Pocock who personally acknowledges virtually every contribution received. Three times a year (or more often if they feel like it), the 1980s Observers send in their thoughts on contemporary themes suggested to them by us: the Falklands/Malvinas war, the NHS, the General Election of 1987, Royal Weddings, the Miners' Strike, panics about food, what clothes they wear, what food they eat, who does the housework in their homes, their holidays and leisure activities, their views on thrift, on pocket money for children, on moral questions and on national disasters, on television and on events in the news. This new project is funded by the Nuffield Foundation and will continue until 1991 to give a portrait of the decade.

The Archive is open to anyone with a serious interest in the collection. It isn't necessary to be engaged in academic-related research. Visitors must make an appointment in advance. The Archive's income is supplemented by royalties from publications and fees received for consultation and reproduction of extracts. Commercial researchers (TV and radio personnel, journalists and some professional writers), therefore, will be charged. If you are interested in becoming a new observer or you wish to carry out research on M-O papers, please write to: The Mass-Observation Archive, The Library, University of Sussex, Falmer, Brighton BN1 9QL, UK. Potential new observers should enclose a large stamped self-addressed envelope.

Dorothy Sheridan
Archivist
University of Sussex Library
1989

Appendix 2

References relating extracts to their locations in the Archive

Extract number	Location
1	Diarist 5296 and Day Survey writers 4, 13, 16, 18, 38 and 53
2	Munich Crisis boxes, Diarist 5390, Day Survey writers 153, 138, Diarists 5353, 5244 and 5336
3	Diarists 5419 and 5370
4	Diarist 5324
5	Evacuation box 1, file E
6	File report 26
7	Diarist 5324
8	Diarist 5420
9	Diarist 5427
10	File report 520
11	File report 615
12	Diarist 5284
13	Diarist 5423
14	File report 1151
15	File report 1496
16	Women and wartime box 3, file F
17	Diarist 5410
18	File report 1611
19	Family planning box 2, file A
20	Directive replies, January 1944
21	Diarists 5253, 5323, 5358, 5284
22	Directive respondent 3648
23	Diarist 5353